DICKENS:
LONDON INTO KENT

Dickens:
London into Kent

Peter Clark

Armchair Traveller
at the bookHaus

First published in Great Britain in 2013 by
The Armchair Traveller at the bookHaus
70 Cadogan Place
London SW1X 9AH
www.thearmchairtraveller.com

Copyright © Peter Clark, 2013

The moral right of the author has been asserted

Pages 21 to 137 were originally published in 2012 as *Dickens's London*

A CIP catalogue record for this book is available from the British Library

Print ISBN: 978-1-907973-80-2
ebook ISBN: 978-1-907973-83-3

Typeset in Garamond by MacGuru Ltd
info@macguru.org.uk

All cartography produced by ML Design
Maps contain Ordnance Survey data © Crown copyright and
database right 2011

Printed in China by 1010

Contents

Introduction

WEALTH AND BEGGARY, vice and virtue, guilt and innocence, repletion and the direst hunger, all treading on each other and crowding together, are gathered round [London]. Draw but a little circle above the clustering housetops, and you shall have within its space everything with its opposite extreme and contradiction, close beside.

I have many happy recollections connected with Kent and am scarcely less interested in it than if I had been a Kentish man bred and born, and had resided in the county all my life.

This book is a sequel and development of *Dickens's London*, published for the bicentenary of the birth of Charles Dickens in 2012. London and Kent were the two principal geographical inspirations for Dickens's creativity. By the time he was writing his first fiction in his early twenties, he had spent impressionable years in both places. His mind, eye and ear had absorbed everything – places, people, sights, sounds and smells. The two places were to provide an enormously rich harvest in Dickens's fiction.

In the course of researching the first part, on London, I found that a lot of the fabric of the places and buildings familiar to Dickens had not survived. We have to reconstruct in our minds a building that no longer exists, or a place that has changed beyond recognition, in order to understand how it was seen and used by Dickens. Moreover we have to remember that his novels are fiction, not reportage or documentation. But such is the power of Dickens's writing that we have difficulty in separating fiction from fact. Earlier commentators had the same problem – as did Dickens himself; he would take people around parts of London and tell them just where some incident in his novels took place.

Outside London, there is no part of Britain that has such intimate and sustained associations with Charles Dickens as Kent. His earliest clear memories were of a childhood in and around Chatham. They were made rosy in retrospect by grim years afterwards, when his father was imprisoned for debt and he worked in the blacking factory, undergoing humiliation, poverty and privation. Kent provided the background for some of his first ventures into fiction, in tales that became part of *Sketches by Boz*. Kent was also the inspiration for parts of his first novel *The Pickwick Papers*, written when he was in his early twenties. Some of this novel was written on his honeymoon at Chalk, between Gravesend and Rochester, when he revisited the places that appear so fresh in this early work. Kent provided the foreground of his last, uncompleted, novel, *The Mystery of Edwin Drood*. Indeed on his last day of consciousness he wrote a beautiful word-picture of the city of Rochester.

Dickens's boyhood was restless and nomadic. He accompanied his parents from house to house. His adulthood was not very different; three places in London were his main homes but Kent was always there as an escape from his life in the capital. In the year after his honeymoon he stayed for several weeks in Broadstairs, the first of many summer and autumn residences in that town. When Broadstairs became too noisy for him, he tried Dover and Folkestone – and also Bonchurch on the Isle of Wight – and, when those towns did not meet his needs, he sought a satisfactory alternative outside this country, and found it in the coastal French town of Boulogne.

Dickens's childhood in Chatham, where his father worked in the Navy Pay Office, fed his emotions and his imagination for the rest of his life. The river, the boats, the navy personnel, the garrison town as well as the buildings, old and new, gave him material that can be detected in most of his fiction. He always had sympathy for men in the services. They may be eccentric, even dotty, but there are no naval or military villains. The personal and geographical landscape of the Medway Towns and its surrounding countryside appear in his first stories, in his own favourite novel, *David Copperfield*, and in his mixture of fiction and journalism, brought together in *The Uncommercial Traveller* and *Reprinted Pieces* as well as in the obvious Kent novels – *Great Expectations* and *The Mystery of Edwin Drood*. We learn much about his life in Broadstairs from his letters, and from the memories of his friends.

Kent represented for Dickens the ideal of the English countryside. He had a townsman's view of the country – pretty cottages, wild flowers, rolling fields and a stable, harmonious community. The rich were kind to the poor, who knew their place and accepted it. He overlooked some of the darker aspects of contemporary rural poverty and distress from which Kent was not immune. The Captain Swing riots, with rick-burning and other rural outrages, were taking place in the 1830s. Kent even had the extraordinary event, the Battle of Bossenden Wood in 1838, when disaffected farm-labourers were swept up by a messianic charlatan demanding a redistribution of property. But none of this features in Dickens's work. By contrast, the city – and especially London – was made up of restless people on the move or on the make. Dickens was outstanding in documenting the urban or urbanised poor.

During the nineteenth century London expanded to meet the needs of a huge immigration from rural England. It is sometimes useful to see nineteenth-century London as analogous to a twentieth-century Third World city. In the generation between the 1820s and 1850s, the period of Dickens's maturing and of his most intensive creativity, the population of London rose from one and a half million to two and a half million people – 60 per cent. Unlike twentieth-century population increases it was not as a result of improved health services and a lower death rate; it was mostly the consequence of immigration. It meant that by the 1850s, a large proportion of Londoners were born outside the capital. Dickens himself, born in Portsmouth and brought up in Chatham, was such a migrant. He described the world and values of individuals who were from outside an inherited and prescribed social pattern, and who had to live off their wits and establish their own identity; much as Dickens himself did.

Kent was one of the areas from where the migrants arrived. During Dickens's lifetime there were few changes in the east of the county, but there was a marked transformation in the west, with the development of *suburbs* and the revolutionary impact of the railways. Instead of being five hours from London, the Medway towns were only one hour away. "Villadom", as HG Wells called it, was spreading into rural Kent. But the Kent of Dickens's imagination is more static than Dickens's London. The novels relating most to the county – *Great Expectations* and *The Mystery of Edwin Drood* – reproduce the Kent of Dickens's childhood, and so do the novels that have important Kent chapters – *The Pickwick Papers* and *David Copperfield*.

Before the impact of the railways, London in the 1840s was still relatively compact. It was possible to get to know the whole of built-up London on foot. In the 1690s King William III had built Kensington Palace as a rural retreat. A century and a half later it was still in a fairly rural location. To the east were Kensington Gardens and Hyde Park. To the west, the village of Kensington. To the north, Paddington was on the edge of the urban area. Warwick Avenue was being laid out for construction. There was ribbon development along Edgware Road as far as the village of Kilburn, but the Swiss

Cottage Tavern was surrounded by fields. Belsize Park was a park and Primrose Hill a hill. There were few buildings north of Regent's Park. Railway development in the previous decade – noted in *Dombey and Son* – was transforming Camden Town, where Dickens lived after coming to the capital at the age of 11. Camden Town was on the Regent's Canal, to the north of which were gardens and orchards. To the north of the present Euston Road was a smart newly planned suburb – Somers Town, but the Kings Cross/St Pancras railway complex had not yet been built; some squalid streets and a gas works occupied that site. The new suburb of Pentonville had recently extended the city to the north, linking London to the village of Islington. Open land separated the Regent's Canal from the village of Hackney. Victoria Park had already been designed and opened for the grimmer suburbs of Bethnal Green and Globe Town. Then to the south, Bromley New Town was being planned but otherwise amidst the ribbon development between Mile End Road and Commercial Road all, apart from a cemetery, was open and common land. South of Commercial Road, the Docks had seen huge development in the previous decade, parallel to the development of large steam-powered ships. The Isle of Dogs was marshy land below sea level. Greenwich had a separate identity, and Deptford had long been a well-established port and town. Away from the river, what is now Evelyn Street passed through open country from Rotherhithe to Deptford. Walworth, to the south-east of Southwark, was built up, as were the areas of Newington and Lambeth. North of the river, outer Westminster was marked by the penitentiary in Millbank and the Bridewell (another disciplinary detention centre) but uninterrupted, albeit modern, buildings were beginning to stretch to the village of Chelsea. Earl's Court was surrounded by open country but the area between the Fulham Road and Kensington was on the point of being urbanised.

In the 30 years after the 1840s London lost its eighteenth-century character. Public transport, the underground and the railways led to a drift to the suburbs. Central London became emptier. It was a city primarily for work. There was a social cantonisation; at the beginning of the century smart quarters were close to slums. Legal London was cheek-by-jowl with criminal London. But with affordable public transport people no longer walked up to 20 miles a day from their homes to their places of work and back. They were able to live further away. The London of 1870 – the year of Dickens's death – with its wider streets, neo-Gothic buildings and advertisement hoardings, is familiar to us today in a way that the narrow streets and close-packed communities of the eighteenth century are not.

The changes of the last century and a half have not only been physical. There have also been seismic social changes. The greatest of these have been in Southwark, Bermondsey and the East End of Wapping and Limehouse. Former slums have been replaced by properties that fetch the highest prices. Sometimes an old working man's pub has survived, looking like a man in overalls who has strayed into a smart reception. It is still possible, however, to read the social archaeology of a district.

One of the biggest social changes since Dickens's time has been the internationalisation of the city. Today it is reckoned that over 300 languages are spoken by the children at inner London schools. Dickens recorded foreigners' London – French, Spanish and Italian immigrants, and Jews, bad like Fagin in *Oliver Twist* and good, like Mr Riah in *Our Mutual Friend*. They were social outsiders. The social and racial mix in inner London today would have been inconceivable in Dickens's time. Dickens had racist views, regarding many people outside Europe as savages. Apart from Americans in *Martin Chuzzlewit* non-Europeans rarely appear in his novels. One exception is the **Native** servant of Major Bagstock in *Dombey and Son*. But he is a comic figure, with no inner life; indeed, he does not even have the dignity of a name. In *The Mystery of Edwin Drood* visits to an opium den are described. There we meet a sleeping Chinaman and Lascar, but there was not yet a Chinatown in London.

Some parts of London, however, have remained socially unaltered: the squares of Mayfair and Belgravia are still the homes of the very rich, albeit an international plutocracy. In Dickens's time these areas provided the homes of the rich and sometimes vulgar, people like Merdles in *Little Dorrit* and the Veneerings in *Our Mutual Friend*. Dickens was not assured in writing about the wealthier or more influential classes, especially in the earlier novels. Sir Mulberry Hawk and Lord Frederick Verisopht in *Nicholas Nickleby* are caricatures, as is Sir Leicester Dedlock in *Bleak House*. Lady Dedlock less so.

Dickens was most familiar with the areas from Camden Town to the river, with Southwark and the City. But his knowledge of the whole of London was phenomenal. As one friend observed, *I thought I knew something of the town, but after a little talk with Dickens I found I knew nothing. He knew it all from Bow to Brentford.* George Augustus Sala, son of an Italian immigrant, worked with Dickens on *Household Words* and *All the Year Round*. He was amazed at Dickens's range of contacts. *Everybody seemed to know him ... the omnibus conductors knew him, the street boys knew him ... he would turn up in the oddest places, and in the most inclement of weather ... he knew all about the backstreets behind Holborn, the courts and alleys of the Borough, the shabby sidling streets of the remoter suburbs, the crooked little alleys of the City, the dank and oozy wharfs of the river-side. He was at home in the lodging houses, station-houses, cottages, hovels, Cheap Jacks' caravans, workhouses, prisons, school-rooms, chandlers' shops, back attics, barbers' shops, areas, back yards, dark entries, public-houses, rag-shops, police-courts, and markets in poor neighbourhoods.* His powers of observation and memory – and his skill and speed at transforming observations into prose – have made his novels, journalism and correspondence a unique source of information on the social history of the capital.

Dickens described his methods to an American admirer,

GD Carrow, saying that he used to walk around the seedier parts of London, preserving an air of preoccupation, and **affecting as near as possible the ways of a collector of house rents or of a physician going his rounds. When any scene of especial interest attracted my notice I usually halted at a crossing as if waiting for a conveyance or as if undecided which way to go. Or else I would stop and purchase some trifle, chatting with the vendor and taking my time for making a selection, or would order a glass of half-and-half, wait for the froth to subside, and then consume an hour in sipping it to the bottom.**

As a boy, he walked the three miles from Camden Town to the Strand every morning, and back at night. This was not unusual. In his novels he had people coming to work in a similar way over comparable distances. In *A Christmas Carol* Bob Cratchit walks each day from Camden Town to the City. In *Great Expectations* Wemmick, John Jaggers's clerk, commutes on foot from Walworth to Smithfield. And in *Our Mutual Friend* Reginald Wilfer walks regularly from Holloway into central London.

During his meal breaks at the blacking factory where he worked – on the approximate site of which now stands Charing Cross station – he wandered along the riverbank or around the Strand, through districts that, during his lifetime, became completely transformed by improvements.

At the beginning of the nineteenth century London streets were often narrow and congested, and in many places there were horrendously squalid slums. Over the course of the century whole areas were cleaned up. New roads destroyed unhealthy blocks of overcrowded and insanitary flats, to provide more direct access across London: Queen Victoria Street, Victoria Street, Northumberland Avenue, Charing Cross Road, Southwark Street. Bridges across the Thames were widened or made more accessible with the removal of tolls. Above all, the railways revolutionised the urban geography. Railway termini provided new focal points.

Many of the physical changes are so taken for granted that it is hard to imagine London without them. Three of these improvements were in areas most familiar to the young Charles Dickens. Trafalgar Square was built in the late 1820s ostensibly to celebrate the victory of Nelson over the French. But it was also built with an eye to social control; broad roads led to the square, facilitating the movement of troops. It must be remembered that the years after the Napoleonic wars were years of social unrest. Comfortable classes felt threatened. Paradoxically, since the 1880s the square has become a focus of agitation, usually against policies supported by the comfortable classes.

Dickens wandered around the unimproved area as a child when it was a labyrinth of alleyways and courts. The stretches between the Strand and the river were also transformed during Dickens's lifetime. Until the nineteenth century the Strand was literally just that, a strand, a beach. Houses on the river side of the road, including palaces like the Savoy and Somerset House, had jetties and piers that brought river craft from the river to their back doors.

Between Camden Town and the Strand was Holborn. The suffix "born" is the same as *burn*, a Celtic word meaning river. The old parish of Holborn had been built on both sides of a valley along which flowed the River Fleet. Holborn Viaduct was built in 1865, together with the road to the west, New Oxford Street, in order to improve communications between the commercial centre of the City of London and Oxford Street, a smart residential and consumer servicing district. Before the building of the viaduct, travellers along the east-west axis had to go down a sharp and relatively steep gradient to the valley of the Fleet and then up again. The Fleet here in the early nineteenth century was a noisome ditch, with a notorious prison – home briefly to Mr Pickwick – to the south. Hovels and filthy streets flanked the stream. This was the Fagin country of Snow Hill and Field Lane in *Oliver Twist*. All these slums were swept away with the improvements of the 1860s. The name of Field Lane disappeared but Snow Hill has been retained.

Dickens was not nostalgic. He campaigned for and welcomed improvements in public health. But at the same time, the central London before these improvements had inspired him from the moment he arrived as a boy, when he gazed at the city from semi-rural Camden Town. From there he would look at London **over the dust heaps and dock-leaves and fields ... at the cupola of St Paul's looming through the smoke, ... a treat that served for hours of vague reflection afterwards.**

His powers of observation were not limited to the physical environment nor to the range of dialects overheard. He had an acute sense of place and social hierarchy. For example, in *Nicholas Nickleby*, he writes of Cadogan Place, the home of the pretentious Mrs Wititterly (and incidentally the location today of the publishers of this book): **It is in Sloane Street, but not of it. The people in Cadogan Place look down upon Sloane Street and think Brompton low. They affect fashion too ... Not that they claim to be on the same footing as the high folks of Belgrave Square and Grosvenor Place, but that they stand, with reference to them, rather in the light of those illegitimate children of the great who are content to boast of their connections, although their connections disavow them**.

That was written when Dickens was in his twenties. Thirty years later he was rubbing shoulders with people unquestionably at the top of the social tree. In March 1870, three months before he died, he had an audience with Queen Victoria. In spite of frailty, he complied with protocol by standing up throughout. He was already a friend of the aristocratic Bulwer Lytton and a regular visitor to his country house, Knebworth in Hertfordshire. One of Dickens's sons went to Eton. And in the last few weeks of his life he had breakfast with the Prime Minister, WE Gladstone, dined with the head of the United States Embassy with the former and future prime minister (and fellow-novelist), Benjamin Disraeli, and also dined with Monckton Milnes, Lord Houghton, in order to meet the Prince of Wales.

Much of his earlier fiction was located in the London of Dickens's childhood, drawing on those adolescent memories. London, in these novels, is a kind of drug. When, from the 1840s, he started living abroad for months at a time, he missed the variety and stimulus of the city. In 1846 he took a villa in Lausanne, Switzerland, where he wrote much of *Dombey and Son*. **For a week or a fortnight I can write prodigiously in a retired place,** he wrote expressing how he missed London. **But the toil and labour of writing, day after day, without that magic lantern is IMMENSE!!**

As he came to maturity, prosperity and celebrity, he expressed more mixed feelings, and even some detachment about the capital. **A city of Devils**, he called it. **London is a vile place**, he wrote to Bulwer Lytton in 1850, **I sincerely believe. I have never taken kindly to it since I lived abroad. Whenever I come back from the Country now, and see that great heavy canopy lowering over the housetops, I wonder what on earth I do here, except on obligation**. It was not only in private correspondence that he berated London. In an article, reprinted in *The Uncommercial Traveller*, he wrote that **the shabbiness of our English capital, as compared with Paris, Bordeaux, Frankfort, Milan, Geneva – almost any important town on the continent of Europe – I find very striking after an absence of any duration in foreign parts. London is shabby in contrast with Edinburgh, with Aberdeen, with Exeter, with Liverpool, with a bright little town like Bury St Edmunds. London is shabby in contrast with New York, with Boston, with Philadelphia.** Indeed it was his travel and residence abroad that gave him detachment. He was impressed by the efficiency and broad streets of Paris, by the readiness to oblige the visitor. He cruelly and sarcastically contrasts the quality of the food and the service at a French railway station with what is available at the British equivalent. In the 1850s he wrote to his not yet estranged wife, **the streets are hideous to behold, and the ugliness of London is quite astonishing**. And in his last novel, *The Mystery of Edwin Drood*, he saw London as full of melancholy streets in **a penitential garb of soot**. There were **deserts of gritty streets, where many people crowded at the corners of courts and bye-ways, to get some air. And where many other people walked with a miserably monotonous noise of shuffling feet on hot paving-stones, and where all the people and all their surroundings were so gritty and so shabby.**

In later years Dickens had a nervous restlessness when in London. Although he lived in three houses for substantial periods, each house more spacious than the previous, he was never attached to them as he became attached to Gad's Hill Place, near Rochester in Kent. He was in Doughty Street for only three years. The house in Devonshire Terrace, where he lived for 12 years, was the place of his greatest activity. Tavis-tock House, which he occupied for nine years, was perhaps too closely associated with the breakdown of his marriage. He had simultaneously bachelor quarters above the offices of the magazines he edited. After the collapse of his marriage he rented a different house almost every year for a few months, ostensibly for his family. He also took lodgings in Peckham for Ellen Ternan and her family. But in his last decade he was most at ease with himself, most at home, at Gad's Hill Place.

In 1855 Dickens purchased Gad's Hill Place, a building he had known, and perhaps coveted, from his childhood. For the rest of his life this would be his home, and he loved playing the part of benevolent squire and affable host. But that image was brittle. His personal life was in turmoil. He had left his wife, Catherine, and become besotted with Ellen Ternan (Nelly), 27 years his junior. He found homes for Nelly first in Slough and later in Peckham (with good train connections to Kent). This affair was known to close family and intimate friends, but was concealed – as was Nelly – from the general public. Dickens did all he could to control the narrative of his own private life, destroying personal correspondence and dominating his children. He had to maintain the public image of himself as a moral paragon, the personification of the happy family man. The older children married as soon as they could, escaping from the control-freakery of their father. Sons were educated in France and then dispatched to distant parts of the Empire. Only the eldest daughter, Mary (Mamie) was unquestioningly loyal and devoted to her father.

London and Kent were the two geographical poles of Dickens's exuberant creativity. In *Great Expectations* they are contrasted in the life of Pip; his expectations obliged him to move to London, which is presented as a city of dubious values, hypocrisy and pretence. You had to scheme and negotiate to survive. But Kent represented innocence, the innocence of Pip's childhood, the innocence of Joe Gargery and of Joe's second wife, Biddy. There is much of Dickens in Pip. In 1862 the Russian novelist, Dostoevsky, called on Dickens in London and later reported him as saying that all the good people in his novels were what he wanted to have been, and all the villains were what he saw in himself. Pip, perhaps like his creator, is morally ambiguous. He is vain, seduced by the glamour of becoming a "gentleman". His social position turns out to have been based on the wealth of the convict Abel Magwitch to whom he had, under duress, given comfort as a child. In the last part of the novel, with Magwitch's arrest, the wealth is forfeited to the state. Pip is penniless. The response is hard work, hard work, hard work. Meanwhile the object of his passion, Estella, is (in Dickens's final version) as unobtainable as ever. Life in the Kent village, however, escapes the seductive vanities and corruption of the city.

Dickens's last completed novel, *Our Mutual Friend*, implies the same message. In some ways it is his most ambitious novel. London is meretricious and materialistic at every level. In contrast, in *The Mystery of Edwin Drood*, the picture of Rochester is positive. There are absurd people like the mayor, Mr Sapsea, and possible rogues, like John Jasper, but Rochester is best represented by the modest and kindly innocence of the Crisparkles and the Topes.

In *The Pickwick Papers*, we have the story of "The Old Man's Tale about the Queer Client". In it, a family is incarcerated – as Dickens's father had been – in Marshalsea prison for debt. A child dies and then the wife. On her deathbed, she begs her husband, **"if ever you leave this dreadful place, and should grow rich, you will have us removed to some quiet country churchyard, a long, long way off – very far from here, where we can rest in peace."** In due course the widower thrives and fulfils the vow he pledged. And ... **Beneath a plain grave-stone, in one of the most peaceful and secluded church-yards in Kent, where wild flowers mingle with the grass, and the soft landscape around, forms the fairest spot in the garden of England, lie the bones of the young mother and her gentle child.** In actual fact Kent is physically not **a long, long way off** from Marshalsea, but, for Dickens's purpose it is the emotional and psychological distance that matters.

In the generation after Dickens's death, several writers traced the physical sites of the buildings and places that appear in his novels. Some of their books had "tramp" or "ramble" in their title, and referred to visits to places as "pilgrimages". In the first part of this book I have traced five walks around central London. They are based on walks described by one of the early Dickens topographers, Robert Allbut. His *London Rambles 'en Zigzag' with Charles Dickens* was published in 1886, 16 years after Dickens's death. It was a small brochure published by Chapman and Hall (Dickens's own publisher) and, expanded and updated, went through several editions. As the brochure became a book, so it changed its title to *Rambles in Dickensland*. Its author was born Robert Allbut Gollop in Poole, Dorset, in 1832. Professionally, he worked in a firm of travel agents. He was an avid reader of the works of Dickens from his youth and read many of them as they came out in monthly instalments. He became a frequent contributor to *The Dickensian* and died in 1915. The undated edition I have worked from was published in about 1903 and includes not just London, but places – Rochester, Chatham, Canterbury, Dover, Henley-on-Thames, Dorking and Portsmouth, that can be reached in a day's outing from the capital. The Midlands and Preston (now presumed to be Coketown in *Hard Times*) and northern Yorkshire (the site of Dotheboys Hall in *Nicholas Nickleby*) are excluded.

The early Dickens topographers often located sites with precision – Allbut particularly so. There is no doubt that many locations described in his novels were based on places familiar to or remembered by Dickens. But there was always a limit. His son, Charles Dickens Junior, wrote in 1896 that it was true that *many of the places described in Charles Dickens's book were suggested by real localities and buildings, but the more the question comes to be examined, the more clear it is that all that was done with the prototype was to use it as a painter or sculptor uses a sketch, and that, under the hand of the writer and in the natural process of evolution, it has grown, in almost every case, into a finished picture, with few, if any, salient points about it to render its origin unmistakeable.* He went on to quote approvingly of a review of *Bozland, Dickens' Places and People* by Percy Fitzgerald, published in 1893. The review said that Dickens *was not content simply to reproduce the places, persons, things that he had seen and known. He passed them through the crucible of his imagination, fused them, re-combined their elements, changed them into something richer and rarer, and gave them forth as products of his art.*

These observations could be further qualified. Sometimes Dickens used the names of real places and sites, and it is easy to locate them with precision, but he also slightly disguised the names of other places, or gave them names that are not difficult to decode – such as Cloisterham for Rochester in *The Mystery of Edwin Drood*. At other times he avoided giving place names at all. In *The Old Curiosity Shop* we are given few hints about the journey through the Midlands taken by Little Nell and her grandfather. It has been deduced that they passed through Buckinghamshire and that the walk, graphically described, through industrial England was from Birmingham to Wolverhampton, and that they ended up in the village of Tong in Shropshire, but this is only based on what Dickens himself revealed. Indeed Dickens was so prolific in his journalism and his correspondence that there are ample clues to infer what he had in mind. Even so there have been disputes about his locations. Today it is accepted that Eatanswill in *The Pickwick Papers* is Sudbury, Suffolk, and that Coketown in *Hard Times* is Preston, Lancashire. It was not always so. Early Dickens scholars argued that Eatanswill was Ipswich and that Coketown was Manchester. Today's consensus is based on a reading of Dickens's letters and tracing his movements in the years before the writing of these novels.

In London Dickens was usually quite specific about places. In Kent one can be reasonably sure, but not always. Some-times there is no doubt about locations – Cobham, Roches-ter's cathedral and High Street. At other times he disguised places – Great Winglebury or Dullborough, which are, from internal evidence clearly the Medway Towns. In *Great Expec-tations* he was often vague – **the market town ... our village**. It is, however, clear that Rochester and the marshlands were in his mind. And at other times he described one build-ing and switched it to another location; Eastgate House in Rochester becomes Westgate School in Bury St Edmunds in *The Pickwick Papers*. Betsey Trotwood's cottage is based on a house in Broadstairs but is transported to the Dover cliffs. He selects elements from three villages – each described in detail – for the village of Pip's childhood. Dickens was, after all, a creator of fiction. His novels are so persuasive that they read like journalistic reportage but he was under no obliga-tion to be consistent or authentic.

The year of Dickens's bicentenary saw the publication of

three books on Dickens's London and in the past there have been other books on the subject. But there has not been a book on Dickens's Kent for decades. Before the First World War there were several. I have benefited from the work of these pioneers. Robert Langton revised details about Dickens's childhood in the Medway towns that had appeared in the first major biography of Charles Dickens by his oldest friend, John Forster. One of the most useful and charming of the early books is *A Week's Tramp in Dickens-land* by the municipal treasurer of the city of Birmingham, William R Hughes, who, in 1887, travelled with Frederic Kitton, a great Dickens scholar who wrote a good early biography. They travelled around the Medway Towns, tracing people who had known Dickens as a child and as the squire of Gad's Hill. They packed a vast amount of fascinating information into their week. A generation later, one of the greatest Dickens scholars was Walter Dexter. Among his prolific output was a very good book on Dickens and Kent. Laurence Gadd wrote on the *Great Expectations* country. He had clearly walked over much of the lands of the marshes and of the Medway towns.

Thanet has received less detailed attention. Dickens wrote extensively about Broadstairs in his letters to family and friends, and in some journalism. Thanet appears in some of his very earliest fiction, but did not become the locus of any of his novels. It is as if his Kentish inspiration was based only on places that he had experienced in his childhood. Dickens knew and stayed in Dover and in Folkestone, but both towns appear only incidentally in the novels, as characters are in transit to the continent. This reflects the experience of the vast majority of visitors to those ports.

Finally, the other Kentish site that had a lasting impact on the remainder of Dickens's life was Staplehurst where he – and his mistress, Nelly Ternan – were involved in a railway accident. Dickens became a nervous railway passenger ever after.

Dickens died in Kent, at his home at Gad's Hill. There was the possibility of him being buried at the neighbouring village church of Shorne or in Rochester, but a national campaign made it impossible for him to be buried in any place but Westminster Abbey.

The core of the first part of this book consists of the five walks round central London. It is recommended that those who wish to follow one of the walks take their time – perhaps a day to each walk. It is also recommended that they take with them a good London road atlas as well as a waterproof. The walks all pass restaurants of every kind and cuisine, catering for all budgets. And there are also the taverns and public houses associated with Dickens and his work that provide food ranging from a sandwich to a slap-up meal.

These walks are supplemented by passages on six places in London outside the central area that have close associations with Dickens's life and work: Camden Town, Chelsea, Greenwich, Hampstead, Highgate and Limehouse. The net could have been cast wider: Chigwell with its public house celebrated in *Barnaby Rudge*; Shepherd's Bush, where Dickens and Baroness Burdett-Coutts set up a refuge for women who had fallen on hard times; Richmond, where Dickens loved to eat at the Star and Garter and where Mr Tupman in *The Pickwick Papers* retired to live in lodgings; Hounslow where at the Coach and Horses public house Bill Sikes and Oliver Twist paused on their way to the burglary at Chertsey.

There follows a central chapter linking London and Kent. I write about a walk Dickens made in October 1857 as his marriage was collapsing. The years before then were years of triumph, the years after were years of shade. He was walking out of London, where he had had his main residence, to Gad's Hill Place, the house that he had just bought and was to be his home for the rest of his life. It was in some ways as if he was trying to turn his back on the corruption of London and to recapture the tranquillity of his Kentish childhood.

The second half looks at the areas in Kent most closely associated with the life and work of Dickens – the Medway Towns and their surroundings, Thanet and East Kent, and finally Staplehurst, the scene of the railway accident that nearly killed him.

The Wellington Street offices of *All the Year Round*

From Trafalgar Square to Lincoln's Inn Fields

The first walk covers the area Dickens got to know when he worked at the blacking factory and is fictionalised in **David Copperfield.** *We pass by sites associated with his life and work around The Strand and Covent Garden.*

TRAFALGAR SQUARE with its soaring Nelson's Column is one of the most iconic sites of London. But when Dickens was a lad, the area was quite different. There was no Square, no Column. In those days three major roads converged – Cockspur Street from the west, The Strand from the east and Whitehall from the south. The London palace of the dukes of Northumberland, with extensive gardens, occupied the area to the south-east. Palace and gardens made way for Northumberland Avenue in the 1870s. There was no Charing Cross Road: that came in the 1880s. Tucked away on St Martin's Lane was the church of St Martin-in-the-Fields, the only building in the area that predates the design in the 1820s of Trafalgar Square, to commemorate Britain's greatest sailor and his battle of Trafalgar. The construction of Trafalgar Square brought out the church's spectacular position. The present church was designed by James Gibbs in the 1720s although a church has been on the site since early medieval

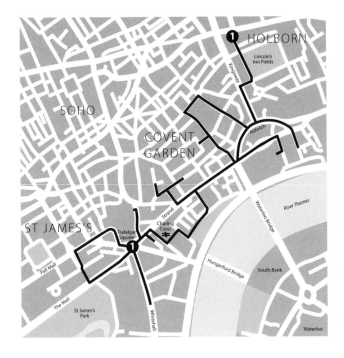

times, when it really was in the fields. In the time of Dickens's childhood, the area around St Martin's church was full of what a later generation would call fast food stalls and was known as "Porridge Island". It was opposite the church that David Copperfield met Mr Peggotty by chance before they both adjourned to the Golden Cross Hotel.

Dickens knew the area intimately before the changes and expressed regret for them. (**I particularly observed the singularity of His Majesty's calling *that* an improvement**, he wrote in 1851. And in a paper, published in *The Uncommercial Traveller* he wrote of **the abortive ugliness of Trafalgar Square set against the gallant beauty of the Place de la Concorde.**)

To the west of the Square is Admiralty Arch which leads into the Mall, the grand avenue leading to Buckingham Palace. King William IV, who was on the throne when

Dickens's first works were published, was the first monarch to turn what had been his mother's home, Buckingham House, into the home of the monarch and Buckingham Palace. Refurbishments were incomplete when he died in 1837 but his successor, his niece, Queen Victoria, established it as the London residence of the British monarch. She was a great admirer of Dickens's works and honoured him by granting him an audience at Buckingham Palace a few months before he died in the spring of 1870. It was to thank him for some photographs of American Civil War battlefields he had sent her at her request. Protocol required that he remain standing in the presence of Her Majesty, and he stood for an hour and a half, quite an ordeal for him on account of a swollen foot. He thought **she was strangely shy … and like a girl in manner … with a girlish sort of timidity which was very engaging**.

North of the Mall is Clubland. The Athenaeum is at the corner of Pall Mall and Waterloo Place. Dickens was elected to this club in 1838 at the same time as Charles Darwin. (Dickens was also a member of the Garrick Club.) He used to have his lunch at a table in the window, facing the United Services Club, now occupied by the Institute of Directors. The foyer of the Athenaeum witnessed the scene of a reconciliation of Dickens and his contemporary, WM Thackeray. Dickens was less than one year younger than Thackeray and achieved fame first. Both were admirers of the other's work and became friends, although they were very different. Thackeray came from a wealthy family that had made money in trade in India. He went to the major public school, Charterhouse, and on to Trinity College, Cambridge. There was always an assured social confidence about him. But when Dickens split with his wife and befriended the actress Ellen Ternan, there were rumours that Dickens was having an affair with his sister-in-law, Georgina. Thackeray is reported to have denied this, saying, *It's with an actress*. Dickens was acutely sensitive to such rumours and for several years

Dickens and Thackeray were not on speaking terms. But in 1863 both perchance bumped into each other at the Athenaeum. One story has it that Dickens made the first move. **"Thackeray, have you been ill?"** he asked. They both shook hands and felt better for it. *I am glad I have done this*, Thackeray is reported to have said. Within a month he was dead, and Dickens wrote a generous tribute to the other novelist.

The Golden Cross was the focal point of the junction of the three roads. This was one of the great coaching houses of the city. Just as London today has a number of terminal railway stations, each of which serves one part of the country so it was, to some extent, with the great coaching houses. The Angel at Islington was the coaching inn for Yorkshire. From The Bell at Whitechapel, passengers set off for East Anglia, as Mr Pickwick and his companions did, en route for Ipswich. For Bath and the west, one set off from the White Horse Cellar at the junction of Dover Street and Piccadilly. (The Bath coach was owned by a man called Moses Pickwick.) And for travellers to and from the south of England, the special inn was The White Hart, Southwark, where Mr Pickwick and Sam Weller first met. But the Golden Cross was the starting point for coaches to destinations all over England, though in the novels of Dickens it was the Kent destinations for which it was most celebrated, especially Rochester and Canterbury.

From the Golden Cross, on 13 May 1827, Mr Samuel Pickwick and his three fellow-members of the Pickwick Club – Alfred Snodgrass, Tracy Tupman and Nathaniel Winkle – set off on their Kentish travels in the company of Alfred Jingle. A dangerously low archway used to lead into a courtyard. Jingle told the story of how **other day – five children – mother – tall lady, eating sandwiches – forgot the arch – crash – knock – children look round – mother's head off – sandwich in her hand – no mouth to put it in – head of family off – shocking – shocking.**

The Golden Cross Hotel of Pickwick's time used to occupy

the area north of the present Trafalgar Square. The cross probably referred to the Eleanor Cross, erected in memory of the wife of King Edward I, who reigned from 1272 to 1307. The cross was originally located at the point currently occupied by the statue of King Charles I. It was known as Charing Cross and it has been romantically suggested that Charing was a corruption of the French, *chère reine*, dear queen, but the name of Charing is much older. The present cross outside Charing Cross Station was constructed in 1865.

Although there were inns of this name going back to the seventeenth century, the building that Dickens knew and referred to in *The Pickwick Papers* was built in 1811 in the Gothic style. It did not last long. It has been reckoned that the front gateway, immortalised by the words of Alfred Jingle, was roughly on the site of one of the lions below Nelson's Column, with the stable yard to the north. When Trafalgar Square was designed in 1829 the Gothic Golden Cross Inn was demolished and rebuilt in the area between Trafalgar Square and where Duncannon Street now is. That hotel lasted until 1931, when it made way for South Africa House.

At the Golden Cross Hotel, David Copperfield, after his education at Dr Strong's in Canterbury, met up with his old school friend, the dangerous and worldly James Steerforth.

Whitehall leads out of Trafalgar Square to the south, to Westminster. One of the first buildings on the left is the architecturally perfect Banqueting Hall, designed by Inigo Jones between 1619 and 1622, as part of the royal Whitehall Palace. From a room on the first floor King Charles I stepped out to his execution block. Or, as Mr Jingle in *The Pickwick Papers* said, **"Looking at Whitehall, Sir – fine place – little window – somebody else's head off there, eh, Sir? – he didn't keep a sharp look out either – eh, Sir, eh?"**

To the north of Trafalgar Square adjacent to the National Gallery is the National Portrait Gallery. In a room dedicated to Victorian writers is the 1839 painting of Dickens by his friend, Daniel Maclise, when Dickens was 27, at the height of his early fame. George Eliot described the portrait as *keepsakey*. Dickens is at a desk, his left hand awkwardly on a manuscript. His bright eyes look out, wide open and receptive to all he saw. His clothes are elegant and slightly flashy, his shoes highly polished. His studied neatness shines out. He always paid attention to his appearance, just as he was always tidy and punctual. His legs are crossed as if he was not entirely at ease.

If we turn into The Strand, before Charing Cross Station, some steps and a ramp between two shops take us down into Craven Street, which runs down to Northumberland Avenue. In the nineteenth century the street was full of boarding houses, providing a service for passengers who arrived by coach at the Golden Cross or, after the station was built in 1865, by train. Number 39, on the eastern side, was the home of Mr Brownlow in *Oliver Twist*, after he moved away from Pentonville. Four doors further down is the house that was the home of Benjamin Franklin when he lived in London. It is now a museum. If we go through the Arches underneath the station we come to Villiers Street. To the right is Hungerford Bridge for the railway with pedestrian crossings on either side.

Hungerford Bridge is all that is left of the name of an area called after a Somerset family that owned Farleigh Hungerford Castle south-east of Bath. Charing Cross Station was built on the site of Hungerford Market. Dickens worked at a factory that manufactured blacking (boot polish) here in 1824. The factory belonged to a relative, James Lamert, and Dickens was paid six or seven shillings a week – not a bad salary then for a boy of 12. (Grown men with families often had to manage on less.) His task was to put covers on to pots of paste-blacking and label them. It was humiliating work and though he rarely spoke openly about it he remembered the experience with bitterness for the rest of his life, **servitude**, he called it. Although the experience lasted under six months, nothing affected him so much. He had come to

London after five happy years in Chatham, where he had discovered reading, and enjoyed the city of Rochester and the countryside around. The family moved to London when Charles's father, John Dickens, was given a job at Somerset House. But soon after he started at the factory John was arrested for debt and incarcerated at the Marshalsea Prison in Southwark. The family needed the money. Some commentators suggest that the experience was central to much of his creativity. He empathised with neglected children, caught in what would later be called a cycle of deprivation. He had been lucky enough to escape because of his extraordinary talents – of which, without false modesty, he was fully aware. Thousands, millions of others were sucked down into humiliating poverty. At the age of 12 he was sensitive and observant and impressions remained with him with stark clarity for the rest of his life.

Though unwilling to talk about these experiences, he did open up to his friend and biographer, John Forster, and recorded his bitterness in an autobiographical manuscript he gave to Forster. He also used the memory in the account of David Copperfield doing similar work, thanks to his brutal stepfather, for the firm of Murdstone and Grinby. David's factory was further downstream, at Blackfriars. The site of Dickens's factory has been replaced by the railway. Dickens remembered the place as **a crazy, tumble-down old house, abutting, of course, on the river, and literally overrun with rats. Its wainscotted rooms and its rotten floors and staircase, and the old grey rats swarming down in the cellars, and the sound of their squeaking and scuffling coming up the stairs at all times, and the dirt and decay of the place, rise up vividly before me, as if I were there again.**

He was living at Camden Town when he started and would walk the three miles there and back each day. This was not unusual. Thirty years later it was reckoned that 400,000 people walked into the City every day. Dickens's youthful walks were a good preparation for his habit throughout his life of energetic urban walking. He worked here ten hours a day with breaks for lunch at 12:00 and an afternoon break for tea.

When Dickens was working here there was no Embankment. The Strand was so named because it was the upper limit of the strand, or beach, of the tidal River Thames. The Strand was the main road from the City of London to the royal and official establishments of Westminster and Whitehall. In late medieval and Tudor times the eastern side of the The Strand was flanked by mansions belonging to major aristocrats and leading churchmen. Their estates faced the river and used to have jetties for their craft. Travel by the river until the nineteenth century was preferable, more efficient and cleaner than travel on land. The Watergate, built in 1626, marked the access for people disembarking and entering the gardens of one of these estates, that belonging to John Villiers, Duke of Buckingham, a favourite of King Charles I. The property had earlier belonged to the archbishops of York. Hence the perpetuation of their names in the streets in the area.

The Victoria Embankment was built in the 1860s, although there had been proposals for such a project from as early as the seventeenth century. The huge increase in London's population in the first half of the nineteenth century led to acute problems of sewage: the basically medieval system could not cope. Most sewage went directly or indirectly into the River Thames – there were 60 outlets into the river. London, especially in the warm summer of 1858, suffered from what was known as *The Great Stink*. A Metropolitan Board of Works had been set up and its inspirational engineer, Joseph Bazalgette, had the idea of a huge sewage pipe parallel to the river, that would collect much of the sewage of the city north of the river and take it far away, towards the Thames Estuary. So the tidal area was reclaimed, the river became enclosed and a giant pipe was constructed under the road. At the same time the underground line – now the District and Circle Line – was built in another tunnel parallel to the sewer and the river. And above were built the attractive gardens of Victoria Embankment. These transformations took place during Dickens's lifetime. The gardens were opened by the Prince of Wales in July 1870, just one month after Dickens's death.

Dickens, got to know these quarters when he worked at the factory, with the wharves and squalid buildings, soon to be swept away. In later years the painful memories had made it impossible for him to return there until Hungerford Market was pulled down and the Hungerford Stairs destroyed. But he was able to reproduce aspects of the area in *David Copperfield*. In this novel Mr Peggotty spent a night over a chandler's shop in Hungerford Market, and when David Copperfield's aunt, Betsey Trotwood, came to London, her crazed companion, Mr Dick, occupied Peggotty's bedroom. It was very small and the landlady, Mrs Crupp, assured him that there was not enough room to swing a cat in it ... **but, as Mr Dick justly observed, "You know, Trotwood, I don't want to swing a cat. I never do swing a cat".** And the Micawber family had lodgings in this area just before they departed for Australia, **in a dirty, tumble-down public-house ... whose protruding wooden rooms overhung the river.** The darker aspects of the area have not entirely disappeared. Visitors to the outdoor seating of the bars by the gardens are reminded of pickpockets and are advised to thwart casual thieves by using "the bag hooks under the tables".

A little further downstream is what used to be the Adelphi. In the eighteenth century, the three Adam brothers, in Greek *adelphoi*, built a large grand riverside complex, with luxurious housing facing the river, and warehouses underneath. Access to them was by arches that were on the beach, as it were, of the river. Subsidiary streets running up to The Strand are all that are left of this ambitious project that could have rivalled Nash's Regent's Park or the Royal Crescent at Bath. It was never a success. Bureaucratic obstruction, aesthetic lack of interest, decay. The central block was ultimately demolished in 1936 and a graceless office block, the New

Adephi, constructed in its place. But when Dickens was a lad, he found it all alluring. His alter ego, David Copperfield, loved the area: **I was fond of wandering about the Adelphi, because it was a mysterious place, with those dark arches. I see myself emerging one evening from one of these arches, on a little public-house, close to the river, with an open space before it, where some coal-heavers were dancing.**

Away from the river, the building on the northern corner of John Adam Street and Adam Street is the site of Osborne's Hotel, where, in *The Pickwick Papers*, Mr Wardle, accompanied by his daughter, Emily, and the Fat Boy, Joe, stayed after Mr Pickwick was released from the Fleet Prison. Joe also discreetly observed Mr Snodgrass calling on his lady friend at this hotel.

Nearer the river – obviously before the building of the Embankment and the Victoria Embankment Gardens – there used to be a tavern, where Martin Chuzzlewit stayed on his arrival in London. Here he was visited by his faithful friend, Mark Tapley.

Another tavern, to the north-east of the Adelphi, was the Fox-under-the-Hill. It stood on the riverside and could be approached from Ivy Bridge Lane, now the entry to the service area of the Shell-Mex House, built (in 1931–32) on the site of the Hotel Cecil which, in its time – 1885 – was the largest hotel in Europe. The developer of the Hotel, Jabez Balfour, ended up in prison for fraud. Dickens used to visit the Fox-under-the-Hill after work at the blacking factory and, like David Copperfield, watch coal-heavers dancing and the half-penny boats setting off on the river. Steamers used to ply from here to London Bridge, fare one half penny.

In *Martin Chuzzlewit* he described what could be seen here. **Little steamboats dashed up and down the stream incessantly. Tiers upon tiers of vessels, scores of masts, labyrinths of tackle, idle sails, splashing oars, gliding row-boats, lumbering barges, sunken piles with ugly lodging for the water-rat within their mud-discoloured nooks;**

church steeples, warehouses, house roofs, arches, bridges, men and women, children, casks, cranes, boxes, horses, coaches, idlers and hard labourers – they were all jumbled up together.

And in *Little Dorrit*, published in 1857, Dickens reflected on the changes of the previous thirty years. **At that time the contrast was far greater; there being no small steam-boats on the river, no landing places but slippery wooden stairs and foot-causeways, no railroad on the opposite bank, no hanging bridge or fish market near at hand, no traffic on the nearest bridge of stone, nothing moving on the stream but watermen's wherries and coal-lighters. Long and black tiers of the latter moored fast in the mud as if they were never to move again, made the shore funereal and silent after dark; and kept what little water-movement there was, far out towards mid-stream.**

The next bridge downstream is Waterloo Bridge. The present bridge was built between 1937 and 1942, but its predecessor was built towards the end of the Napoleonic Wars. At first it was called the Strand Bridge but acquired its present name just one year after the Battle of Waterloo. In the middle of the nineteenth century it was a favourite bridge for suicides. In 1853 Dickens wrote an article for *Household Words* about a night he spent with the Thames River Police. **"If people jump off straight forward from the middle of the parapet of the bays of the bridge,"** explained one of Dickens's informants, **"they are seldom killed by drowning, but are smashed, poor things; that's what *they* are; they dash themselves on the buttress of the bridge. But you jump off from the side of the bay, and you'll tumble, true, into the stream under the arch. What you have got to do, is to mind how you jump in! There was poor Tom Steele from Dublin. Didn't dive! Bless you, didn't dive at all! Fell down so flat into the water, that he broke his breast-bone, and lived two days!"** People preferred to commit suicide from the southern side of the bridge, Dickens learnt.

A second blacking factory belonged to James Lamert in Chandos Place, parallel to and north of The Strand. The young Dickens and his fellow workers – including one called Bob Fagin – left the rat-infested warehouse by the river to work here. This can be reached by returning to The Strand, crossing over and walking up Bedford Street. This second factory is on the left at the junction with Chandos Place. The factory was pulled down in 1889, to be replaced by the curious red brick store, built in an Italian Renaissance revival style, looking like a parody of a Pall Mall Club. A plaque high up on the wall records that Charles Dickens worked here from 1824 to 1825. Dickens and his fellow-workers toiled by a window and Dickens was further humiliated by being the object of public curiosity as people stared in. Again, the humiliation of this work remained with Dickens all his life. There was a smell of cement coming from the warehouse and when in later years he passed this way he would cross the road to avoid the smell.

A happier Dickens association can be found round the corner in Maiden Lane: Rules Restaurant. Founded in 1798 it is London's oldest restaurant. Dickens, in his prosperity, was a regular guest and there is a Dickens Room with play-bills of his own productions and other memorabilia.

Doubling back westward along Chandos Place, Bedford-bury leads off to the north to New Row and, to the right, King Street. The Peabody Buildings on the right – the result of the work of George Peabody, the Baltimore-born philanthropist – were built in the 1870s, replacing a jungle of old tenement buildings. Robert Allbut locates Tom-All-Alone's, home of poor Jo, the crossing-sweeper in *Bleak House*, here. Its approach was grim: **Mr Snagsby passes along the middle of a villainous street, undrained, unventilated, deep in black mud and corrupt water – though the roads are dry elsewhere – and reeking with such smells and sights that he, who has lived in London all his life, can scarce believe his senses.** Others have sited Tom-All-Alone's at the burial ground attached to the church of St Mary-le-Grand in Russell Street. But it is more probable that Tom-All-Alone's existed only in his imagination, for Dickens was usually quite specific about locations in *Bleak House*. The site epitomised macabre grimness – a place crammed with **heaps of dishonoured graves and stones, hemmed in by filthy houses ... on whose walls a thick humidity broke out like a disease**. He may have got the term from a place with that name in the Chatham of his boyhood. This Tom-All-Alone's was named after an eccentric recluse called Thomas Clark.

Back on The Strand, somewhere around the present Savoy Hotel, lived Miss La Creevy of *Nicholas Nickleby*. Ralph Nickleby came here, stopping ... **at a private door, about halfway down that crowded thoroughfare** [The Strand]. Miss La Creevy was based, perhaps, on a sister of Dickens's mother. Further along The Strand on the right is Somerset House, where Dickens's father worked for a while in the Navy Pay Office.

The present palatial building is the most outstanding public building in the capital. The land here between The Strand and the river was in medieval times the property of the Bishop of Chester. King Henry VIII seized the estate and handed it over to one of his "new men", Edward Seymour. The King married Jane Seymour, Edward's sister. She was the mother of King Henry VIII's immediate successor, the boy, King Edward VI. Edward Seymour, as the King's uncle and with the title of Lord Protector, became the most powerful man in the land. The young King made his uncle Duke of Somerset. The Duke cleared the land of religious buildings for his new palace. Unfortunately he was impeached and died before it was finished. The property reverted to the Crown and it was a royal palace for two centuries.

When in the 1770s King George III moved to Buckingham House (later Buckingham Palace), which then belonged to his wife, the present building was erected to house learned societies that were also under royal patronage and some government offices, including the Navy Board. The offices were near the river, from where it was easy to travel to the dockyards of Greenwich and Deptford. The magnificence of the building – Sir William Chambers was the architect – reflected the importance and grandeur of the Navy. The Navy Board – where John Dickens worked – was located on the west side of the southern wing. This part was damaged in the Second World War.

In the twenty-first century the building has been transformed to become a centre of art, with galleries and a museum. It is now one of the capital's major cultural centres.

On the opposite side of The Strand in the 1830s were the offices of the newspaper, *Morning Chronicle*. Dickens himself worked for this paper when he was 20 and wrote his first reports for it. As a journalist he was sent on assignments around southern England, thereby acquiring a detailed knowledge of people and places. In the middle of the road is the church of St Mary-le-Strand. The church was designed in the early eighteenth century by James Gibbs, the architect of the church of St Martin-in-the-Fields. Thomas à Becket, the murdered twelfth-century Archbishop of Canterbury, was once rector here. This is also where Dickens's parents were married in 1809. This church was selected because John Dickens was working close by at Somerset House, but after the wedding the couple moved to Portsmouth, to the house in Mile End Terrace where Dickens was born three years later.

To the north of The Strand is Wellington Street North. At Number 16 is a huge block housing the Indigo restaurant, but in 1850 it was a building that was **exceedingly pretty with the bowed front, the bow reaching up for two stories, each giving a flood of light.** This used to be the office of *Household Words*, the monthly magazine founded in 1850 to absorb some of Dickens's superabundant energies. He used to arrive at the office at eight in the morning and dictate for three hours, striding up and down, often combing his hair at the same time, a public habit that offended the Americans on his first visit to the United States. A few years later the offices were moved to Number 26, which became the offices of *All the Year Round*, another of his magazines. This magazine developed young men of talent, who referred to Dickens as "The Chief". The Charles Dickens Coffee House now occupies the ground floor. Dickens maintained a bachelor flat in later years here, even though he had a home to go to. Years later the office boy recalled how Dickens used to send him to fetch ice-cream from a nearby restaurant. After Dickens's death, in 1872, some Chicago businessmen had the idea of purchasing the building and transporting it to the Chicago World Fair, as a memento of the novelist.

On one occasion in 1865 Dickens was eating out at a local coffee shop in this area and the young Thomas Hardy, then studying architecture in London, spied him. *I went up*, the future novelist recalled, *and stood at the vacant place beside the stool on which Dickens was sitting. I had eaten my lunch, but I was quite prepared to eat another if the occasion would make Dickens speak to me. I hoped he would look up, glance at this strange young man beside him and make a remark – if it was only about the weather. But he did nothing of the kind. He was fussing about the bill. So I never spoke to him.*

One block to the north-east is the covered Covent Garden. Dickens always loved this area. **We have never outgrown the whole region of Covent Garden**, he wrote in 1853. He recalled that to go there as a child was to inhale **the flavour of the faded cabbage-leaves as if it were the very breath of comic fiction**. He was nostalgic about the place. Covent Garden used to be the wholesale market in London for fruit and vegetables. In January – when there was no seasonable fruit – it was desolate, Dickens wrote in an article that was reprinted in *The Uncommercial Traveller*. A general description of Covent Garden appears in *Little Dorrit*. In *Oliver Twist* Bill Sikes observed that he could find fifty boy thieves at any time at **"Common Garden"**, as he used to call it. And Job Trotter in *The Pickwick Papers* spent a night here in a vegetable basket.

Dickens stayed at the Tavistock Hotel, north of the covered shopping area, in late 1844, when he broke his residence in Genoa in order to come to London to read *The Chimes* to his friends. Herbert Pocket and Mr Pip, in *Great Expectations*, used to hold fortnightly meetings of the club, **"The Finches of the Grove"** at the Hotel. The club's objective was **that the members should dine expensively once a fortnight, quarrel among themselves as much as possible after dinner, and get six waiters drunk on the stairs.**

To the north-west is the area of Seven Dials. Dickens used to walk through this area as a child, sometimes with his father. **What wild visions,** he recalled, **of prodigies of wickedness, want, and beggary arose in my mind out of that place!** He located **the little dark greasy shop** belonging to the taxidermist, Mr Venus, in *Our Mutual Friend*, at Seven Dials. Mr Venus talked about his shop to Silas Wegg: **"My working bench. My young man's bench. A Wice. Tools. Bones, warious. Skulls, warious. Preserved Indian baby. African ditto. Bottled preparations, warious. Everything within reach of your hand, in good preservation… ."**

North of Russell Street is Bow Street and on the right is a Palladian white stone building that was until 2005 Bow Street Magistrates' Court. There are plans to turn the site into a boutique hotel. The building of 1879 replaces an older Police Court where Barnaby Rudge was interrogated after his participation in the anti-Catholic riots of 1780 known as the Gordon Riots. It is also where the Artful Dodger, in *Oliver Twist*, stated his views of the justice of the procedures: **"This ain't the shop for justice; besides which my attorney is a-breakfasting this morning with the Vice-President of the House of Commons; but I shall have something to say elsevere, and so will he, and so will a wery numerous and respectable circle of acquaintance, as'll make them beaks wish they'd never been born."**

The Opera House is on the site of the Covent Garden Theatre, destroyed by fire in 1856. It is where David

Copperfield saw *Julius Caesar* on his first night as a young man in London – he had been staying at the Golden Cross Hotel. **To have all those noble Romans alive before me, and walking in and out for my entertainment, instead of being the stern taskmasters they had been at school, was a most novel and delightful effect.**

Opposite and to the north of the Opera House is Broad Court. Mr Snevellici, the actor in the troupe of Mr Vincent Crummles, said he could be found **in Broad Court, Bow Street, when I'm in town. If I'm not at home, let any man ask for me at the stage-door.**

Facing the north end of Bow Street is the site of St Martin's Hall, where Dickens gave the first of his paid readings in 1858. There was a large and expectant audience when Dickens arrived. He was greeted with a roar which, as an eye-witness observed, *might have been heard at Charing Cross.* Some years after that, the Hall was burnt down and replaced by a theatre. It is now part of a nondescript block of flats and offices.

If we turn right on to Long Acre we meet Drury Lane, just before Freemasons' Hall. This Hall was the venue for a banquet given by Dickens's friends before his second tour of the United States in 1867. There were 450 guests (all men) but with 100 women in the gallery above. The Union Jack and the Stars and Stripes were entwined and when Dickens appeared on the arm of Bulwer Lytton, *a cry rang through the room, handkerchiefs were waved on the floor and in the galleries ... and the band struck up a full march.* There were speeches from Anthony Trollope and Bulwer Lytton. When Dickens rose to reply there was almost pandemonium. Tears streamed down his face as he replied, **Your resounding cheers just now would have been but so many cruel reproaches to me if I could not here declare that, from the earliest days of my career down to this proud night, I have always tried to be true to my calling.**

Turning right into Drury Lane, we pass the back of the Theatre Royal, Drury Lane and pass the site – overtaken by developments in the 1890s of the burial ground, attached to the church of St Mary-le-Strand. On the same side there is another small burial site, turned into a minute garden, which used to be part of the parish burial ground of St Martin-in-the-Fields. The burial ground, now destroyed and lost, is described in *Bleak House* as **pestiferous and obscene, with houses looking in on every side, save where a reeking little tunnel of a court gives access to the iron gate.** Here Captain Hawdon, otherwise Nemo, was buried. As Joe described the burial to Lady Dedlock, **"Over yinder. Among them piles of bones, and close to that there kitchin winder! ... They put him wery nigh the top. They was obliged to stamp upon it to git it in. I could unkiver it for you with my broom, if the gate was open. That's why they locks it, I s'pose. It's always locked. Look at that rat! Hi! Look! There he goes! Ho! Into the ground."** And here Lady Dedlock was found dead.

A little further towards The Strand there used to be a court on the left – Clare Court. Dickens as a boy, with a few earnt pennies in his hand and a loaf of bread under his arm, called here, **magnificently ordering a small plate of *a la mode* beef to eat with it. What the waiter thought of such a small apparition, coming in all alone, I don't know, but I can see him now, staring at me as I ate my dinner, and bringing up the other waiter to look. I gave him a halfpenny, and I wish now that he hadn't taken it.**

On the other side of The Strand is Surrey Street. Fifty yards towards the river is an easily missed pedestrian path – Surrey Steps – that takes us to Strand Lane, from which access to The Strand itself is blocked. At Number 6 are the Roman Baths, administered by the National Trust. These are just outside the walls of Roman London. David Copperfield **had many a cold plunge** here. The baths are usually closed but can be opened by special arrangement. Mostly one has to be content with peering through the grubby windows to get an idea of the baths.

The next road to the east leading from The Strand towards the river is Arundel Street, formerly Norfolk Street. The street names indicate that this area of the The Strand was part of the London mansion of the Dukes of Norfolk. Their family name was – and still is – Howard; the Earl of Surrey was a courtesy title given to the Dukes, and Arundel was their Sussex seat. On the left, beyond Maltravers (formerly Howard) Street, was Mrs Lirriper's Lodgings, **Number Eighty-one Norfolk Street Strand – situated midway between the City and St James's and within five minutes' walk of the principal places of public amusement**. Norfolk Street was **a delightful street to lodge in**. Her lodgings were the location of stories in the Christmas numbers of *All the Year Round* in 1863 and 1864 and are available in the Penguin edition of *Selected Short Fiction*. Most of the nineteenth-century buildings have been replaced by boring concrete and glass blocks and it is not possible to locate where Mrs Lirriper queened it over her tenants.

Mrs Lirriper had been married in St Clement Danes Church which stands on the island just to the east of Aldwych. She still retained **a very pleasant pew with genteel company and my own hassock and being partial to evening service not too crowded.** The Church is the "parish church" of the Royal Air Force. It contains books of remembrance not only of RAF personnel killed during the Second World War, but also of 16,000 United States Air Force personnel who were killed in action while stationed in the United Kingdom. The church was bombed during the war and reconstructed afterwards. The organ over the western gallery was the gift in 1956 of the United States Air Force, their families and friends, to the rebuilt church.

If we go into Aldwych and walk up Kingsway, a street built only at the beginning of the twentieth century, and take the second on the right we go into Sardinia Street. Until 1910 there used to be a Roman Catholic chapel attached to the Italian Embassy. The chapel's history went back to the seventeenth century, when it was attached to the residence of the Sardinian Ambassador. In 1780 it had been a target of the anti-Catholic Gordon rioters and the attack on the chapel is discussed by characters in *Barnaby Rudge*. Dickens's musical sister, Fanny, was a professional singer and met her husband, Henry Burnett, here.

The first road on the right is Portsmouth Street. A few yards down this road on the left is a house, allegedly "The Old Curiosity Shop" in the novel of that name. This is unlikely, for at the end of the novel, the old house is alleged to have been **long ago pulled down.** Moreover this shop only received this name in 1868, 20 years after the publication of the novel. The owner, a dealer in old books, paintings and china, adopted the name to help his business. It is nonetheless an interesting house, a rare survival in this area from the seventeenth century.

The public house further down on the right, The George the Fourth, is more likely to have been the location of the Magpie and Stump, where Mr Lowten, Perker's clerk, in *The Pickwick Papers* used to meet up with friends. There is a Magpie and Stump in Fetter Lane nearby, but Dickens placed the pub near Clare Market, which is just a few yards away.

To the east runs Portugal Street. (The last stocks used for punishment were set up in this street, in 1820.) In *The Pickwick Papers* Tony Weller and fellow coach drivers used to meet in a public house in this road, probably on the southern side.

The gardens to the north are Lincoln's Inn Fields. On the left (western) side, number 58 was the home of Dickens's friend, agent and biographer, John Forster. It was here in 1844 that Dickens gave his first reading of *The Chimes* to a group of friends who included the historian Thomas Carlyle, the artist Daniel Maclise and the journalist Douglas Jerrold. The house was also where the lawyer, Mr Tulkinghorn, in *Bleak House* lived ... and died, murdered. **It is a large house, formerly a house of state ... It is let off in sets of chambers** now: and in those shrunken fragments of its greatness, lawyers lie, like maggots in nuts.

To the north-west of the Fields is the alleyway, Little Turnstile, that leads on to High Holborn.

Fountain Court Middle Temple

From Lincoln's Inn Fields to the Mansion House

This walk takes us through legal London; three of the four Inns of Court. There are many traces of **Bleak House.** *We pass by St Paul's Cathedral and end up with some of the sites in the City of London.*

CHANCERY LANE IS the spine of legal London. There are four Inns of Court, long established legal bodies that have the power to acknowledge lawyers who have qualified as Barristers-at-Law. Gray's Inn faces the northern end of Chancery Lane and Inner Temple and Middle Temple face the southern end. The Royal Courts of Justice are just to the west and the Old Bailey less than a mile to the east. When the courts are sitting, the area is full of busy bewigged people bustling around. And has been for centuries. When the courts are not sitting, the area is, said Dickens in *Bleak House*, like **tidal harbours at low water; where stranded proceedings, offices at anchor, idle clerks lounging on top-sided stools … lie high and dry upon some ooze of the long vacation.**

Lincoln's Inn is off Chancery Lane and at the heart of lawyers' London. It is a collegiate centre that provides accommodation, training and services for barristers. Membership is similar to membership of the colleges of the Universities of

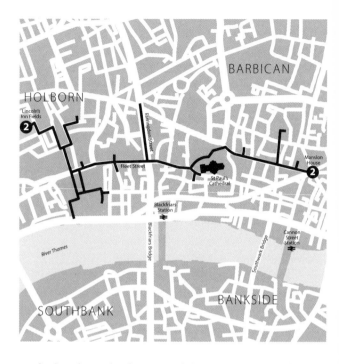

Oxford and Cambridge. Lincoln's Inn can trace its history back to the early fifteenth century. An "Inn" in those days was a term used for the London base of a grandee or bishop, and provided a home for all the potentate's hangers-on. The grandee after whom this Inn is named is either an Earl of Lincoln or a lawyer, Thomas de Lincoln – both individuals of the fourteenth century. Dickens contrasted the apparent rusticity of Lincoln's Inn Fields with the legal process. **In these pleasant fields the sheep are all made into parchment, the goats into wigs, and the pasture into chaff, the lawyer smoke-dried and faded, dwelling among mankind but not consorting with them, aged without experience of genial youth.**

For over a century and a half the main entrance to Lincoln's Inn has been from the eastern side of Lincoln's Inn Fields, from Serle Street, through a brick gatehouse. We pass the extensive New Square, dating back to the late seventeenth century, on the right and have the Old Hall, next to the chapel, ahead of us, overlooking Old Square to the left.

The Old Hall is a small construction of the late fifteenth century, just before Columbus "discovered" America. Over the years the Old Hall has served as a dining hall and a court of justice. It was here that the case of Jarndyce vs Jarndyce in *Bleak House* was held over the years, although the final verdict was given in Westminster Hall. **London. Michaelmas Term lately over, and the Lord Chancellor sitting in Lincoln's Inn Hall. Implacable November weather ... Fog everywhere. Fog up the river, where it flows among green aits and meadows; fog down the river, where it rolls defiled among the tiers of shipping, and the waterside pollutions of a great (and dirty) city ... And hard by Temple Bar, in Lincoln's Inn Hall, at the very heart of the fog, sits the Lord High Chancellor in his High Court of Chancery.** Thus the opening chapter of *Bleak House*. When Dickens was writing this the Old Hall was becoming obsolete. Moreover, membership of Lincoln's Inn was expanding, so a second central hall, the Great Hall, was constructed and opened in 1845, eight years before the publication of *Bleak House*. It was the Court of Chancery that specialised in issues of finance and property. Hence the Jarndyce case, which was originally a dispute over inheritance, with **bills, cross-bills, answers, rejoinders, injunctions, affidavits, issues, references to masters, masters' reports – mountains of costly nonsense.** Such a case was not untypical. The inheritance of a huge estate would be referred to the Court of Chancery. By the time it was resolved who was the legal beneficiary, there was no money left because the whole estate had been devoured by legal fees. **This is the Court of Chancery, which has its decaying and its blighted lands in every shire and which has its worn-out lunatics in every madhouse and its dead in every churchyard ... Suffer any wrong that can be done you, rather than come here.**

Lincoln's Inn chapel is above an undercroft. There are some tombstones among the pavings, and in earlier centuries mothers sometimes abandoned babies here. They were always looked after by the Honourable Society of Lincoln's Inn and usually given the name Lincoln. Access to the chapel is up stone steps. The chapel was built between 1619 and 1623. Inside is a memorial tablet to Spencer Perceval, the only British Prime Minister (so far) to have been assassinated – and that was in May 1812. A chapel bell chimes in the middle of the day when a senior member of the Inn has died. The poet John Donne was Divinity Reader at Lincoln's Inn when he wrote *Devotions*, which contain the lines, *Never send to know for whom the bell tolls; it tolls for thee*. He probably had this custom of the Lincoln's Inn chapel bell in mind. The words also provided the inspiration for the title of Ernest Hemingway's novel. Being a Reader of the chapel has often been a useful stepping stone to preferment in the Church of England. Several bishops and one archbishop (Tillotson in the seventeenth century) were formerly Divinity Readers at Lincoln's Inn.

We go past the Dining Hall and the Library on the left and New Square on the right.

In *Bleak House*, Miss Flite, a hopeful beneficiary of the outcome of the case, used to wait on one side of the Hall, day after day, **always expecting some incomprehensible judgment in her favour.** She herself lived **in a narrow back street, part of some courts and lanes immediately outside the wall of the inn.**

In the Old Square, Kenge and Carboy had their offices – in the north-west corner, at number 10. Esther Summerson describes her first visit there: **We passed into sudden quietude, under an old gateway, and down on through a silent square, until we came to an old nook in a corner, where there was an entrance up a steep broad flight of stairs, like an entrance to a church.** The steep broad flight of stairs can still be identified.

Mr Pickwick's counsel, Sergeant Snubbin, also had his chambers in this square.

An alleyway, Bishop's Court, goes from New Square by the left of the architecturally inappropriate Hardwicke Building, built in the late 1960s, to Star Lane. To the left was located Krook's Rag and Bottle Warehouse, described in *Bleak House*. **The shop was blinded by the wall of Lincoln's Inn intercepting the light within a couple of yards.** Above the shop lodged Miss Flite. **She lived at the top of the house, in a pretty large room, from which she had a glimpse of the roof of Lincoln's Inn Hall.** Above her a room was occupied by Captain Hawdon, alias Nemo. After he died it was taken over by Mr Tony Weevle.

Running off Bishop's Court to the south is Star Yard. At the junction with Chichester Rents there used to be a public house, The Old Ship Tavern, disguised as The Sol's Arms in *Bleak House* and the location for the inquest of Captain Hawdon. It was also a venue for popular singers. **The coroner is to sit in the first-floor room at the Sol's Arms, where the Harmonic Meetings take place twice a week, and where the chair is filled by a gentleman of professional celebrity, faced by Little Swills the comic vocalist.**

Chancery Lane is where Tom Jarndyce **in despair blew his brains out.** Off Chancery Lane opposite Lincoln's Inn is Cursitor Street. Immediately on the left was Harold Skimpole's sponging house, Coavinses' Castle.

Off Cursitor Street to the left is Took's Court, **a shady place**, which was Cook's Court in *Bleak House* and the location of Mr Snagsby's residence and law stationer's shop. **The little drawing-room upstairs commanded a view of Cook's Court at one end (not to mention a squint into Cursitor Street) and of Coavinses', the Sheriff's Officer's, backyard on the other.** Here Mrs Snagsby entertained her "Chaplain-in-Ordinary", the Reverend Mr Chadband. Mr Snagsby retreated in his imagination into dreams of a rural past. He would tell his assistants that **a brook once ran down**

Holborn, when Turnstile really was a turnstile leading slap away into the meadows.

Bream's Buildings, the road parallel to and to the south of Cursitor Street marked the northern boundary of Symond's Inn, another former inn of court. It was, in Dickens's words, **a little, pale, wall-eyed, woe-begone inn, like a large dust-bin of two compartments and a sifter. It looks as if Symond were a sparing man in his way, and constructed his inn of old building materials, which took kindly to the dry rot and the dirt, and perpetuated Symond's name with congenial shabbiness.** In *Bleak House* the lawyer of Richard Carstone, Mr Vholes, lived here. **Mr Vholes's chambers are on so small a scale, that one clerk can open the door without getting off his stool, while the other who elbows him at the same desk has equal facilities for poking the fire.** Richard lived next door with his new wife, Ada. Esther Summerson used to visit them in this **miserable corner which my dear girl brightened.** Symond's Inn was also of major importance in Dickens's own life. In 1827, at the age of 15, Dickens worked here with a solicitor, Charles Molloy. Here he developed his huge disdain for the profession, which was displayed most powerfully in *Bleak House*. Near Symond's Inn Mr Snagsby used **to lounge about of a Saturday afternoon, and to remark (if in good spirits) that there were old times once.**

If we double back on Chancery Lane, heading south, we can turn right into Carey Street and then take the first left into Bell Yard; the name of this road forms the title of chapter 15 of *Bleak House*. Here dwelt Gridley, **the man from Shropshire**, and Neckett, the servitor at Coavinses. Bell Yard leads to Fleet Street and Temple Bar, which used to be the western entrance to the City of London.

On the south side of Fleet Street is Child's Bank, now part of the Royal Bank of Scotland Group. It is the oldest bank in London, dating back to 1664. It has always had close relations with the legal profession, being the bank for the Honourable

Societies of Lincoln's Inn and of Middle Temple. The building is a heavy Italian Renaissance revival building and dates back only to 1879. Its predecessor was the model for Tellson's Bank in *A Tale of Two Cities.*

Tellson's Bank, by Temple Bar, was an old-fashioned place even in the year 1780. It was very small, very dark, very ugly, very incommodious. Any one of the partners would have disinherited his son on the question of rebuilding Tellson's. Thus it came to pass that Tellson's was the triumphant perfection of inconvenience. After bursting open a door of idiotic obstinacy with a weak rattle in its throat, you fell into Tellson's, down two steps, and came to your senses in a miserable little shop, with two little counters; where the oldest of men made your cheque shake as if the wind rustled it, while they examined the signature by the dingiest of windows, which were always under a shower-bath of mud from Fleet Street, and which were made the dingier by their own iron bars proper and the shadow of Temple Bar.

Just to the east is Middle Temple Lane. Further east, above Inner Temple Lane at 17 Fleet Street, is a building that was erected in 1610. Upstairs is Prince Henry's Room, perhaps named after a son of King James I. In the nineteenth century a Mrs Salmon had a display of waxworks here. David Copperfield brought his old nurse, Peggotty, **to see some perspiring waxworks in Fleet Street.** And here at Inner Temple Gate, Bradley Headstone in *Our Mutual Friend* jealously stalked Eugene Wrayburn, waiting for him to come out at the gate so he could follow him and find out if he was going to see Lizzie Hexam.

Dickens seems to have more positive impressions of the Temple than those stirred by Lincoln's Inn and the Court of Chancery. In 1839 he was at the height of his early success. Nonetheless, perhaps conscious of the bankruptcy of Sir Walter Scott and the vagaries of literary fame, he considered the fallback of a legal career and actually registered as a law student at the Middle Temple. Other members of the Inner Temple have included John Dickinson, who drafted the United States Declaration of Independence; five other signatories of the Declaration had been members of the Middle Temple.

The Middle Temple and the Inner Temple are two more of the Inns of Court. In medieval times it was the headquarters of the Templars, those monastic knights whose order was founded in the Holy Land to form a military profession to defend Crusader acquisitions. The Order was dissolved in the fourteenth century and their estates handed over to the Order of Knights Hospitallers who had had a similar history and connection with the Holy Land. Lawyers settled in this area and both the Inner Temple and the Middle Temple, like the other Inns of Court, became a centre for legal training and fellowship. Although each Inn has its own identity and rules of governance, it is not easy for the lay visitor to distinguish one from the other. The Middle Temple is larger and to the west. The Inner Temple is on the eastern side. Between the two is the Temple Church, built around 1185, with the Dome of the Rock on the Temple Mount in Jerusalem as the model. A round chancel is attached to a rectangular nave.

In *The Pickwick Papers* Dickens described how, **scattered about in various holes and crevices of the Temple, are certain dark and dirty chambers, in and out of which all the morning in vacation, and half the evening too, in term time, there may be seen constantly hurrying with bundles of papers under their arms and protruding from their pockets an almost uninterrupted succession of lawyers' clerks. There are several grades of lawyers' clerks – there is the articled clerk, who is a lawyer in perspective, who runs a tailor's bill, receives invitations to parties, knows a family in Gower Street, another in Tavistock Square, goes out of town every long vacation to see his father, and is, in short, the very aristocrat of clerks.** (Dickens had already lived in Gower Street and was to have a house in Tavistock Sqaure for ten years.) He came back to the Temple in *Barnaby Rudge*: **those who pace its lanes and squares may yet hear the echoes of their footsteps on the sounding stones, and read upon its gates, "Who enter here, leave none behind." There is yet in the Temple something – a clerkly, monkish atmosphere – which public officers of law have not disturbed, and even legal firms have failed to scare away.**

If we turn down Middle Temple Lane, beyond Brick Court and off to the right, we arrive, a hundred yards towards the river, at Fountain Court. There **was the splash of falling water in fair Fountain Court, and there are yet nooks and corners where dun-haunted students may look down from their dusty garrets, on a vagrant ray of sunlight patching the shade of the tall houses.** It was in Fountain Court that, in *Martin Chuzzlewit*, Ruth Pinch used to meet her brother, Tom, because **it would have been very awkward for her to have had to wait in any but a quiet spot; and that was as quiet a spot, everything considered, as they could choose.** She would also meet her future husband, John Westlock, by the fountain. When he turned up **merrily the fountain leaped and danced, and merrily the smiling dimples twinkled and expanded more and more.** It is still a favourite place for luncheon rendezvous. A plaque by the fountain records: **Brilliantly the Temple Fountain sparkled in the sun, and laughingly, its liquid music played and merrily the idle drops of water danced and danced, and peeping out in sport among the trees, plunged lightly down to hide themselves.** The mood is very different from the fog and despair of Lincoln's Inn. The present fountain was (re)constructed in 1975.

At the end of Fountain Court was Garden Court to the left, heading down towards the river. Here, in *Great Expectations*, was the shared chambers of Mr Pip and Herbert Pocket. **We lived at the top of the house.** And here, Pip's benefactor, Magwitch, turned up unexpectedly, and Pip had to find a temporary home for him **at a lodging-house in Essex-street,**

the back of which looked into the Temple, and was almost within hail of Pip's window. Essex Street is another street leading from Fleet Street to the river, immediately to the west of Garden Court.

There was once a jetty on the river, Temple Stairs, long since swept away by the building of the Embankment. But today there is an archway, built in 1868, with boys riding dolphins in bronze, and a tablet recording the name of this stretch of water as "The King's Reach", in commemoration of the Silver Jubilee of King George V in 1935. Mr Pip, in *Great Expectations*, kept a boat here and practised rowing up and down the river. From here he smuggled his patron, Magwitch, down the river to a steamer beyond Gravesend. In preparing for this section of the novel, Dickens made a note of tides and their times, and hired a Thames steamer to get the feel of a pursuit down the river.

Returning to Middle Temple Lane and going through a passage to the east opposite Brick Court, we can enter Pump Court where Tom Pinch may well have been installed as librarian. Dickens describes the neighbourhood as Mr Fips, the agent for an unknown patron, escorted Tom **through sundry lanes and courts, into one more quiet and gloomy than the rest; and singling out a certain house, ascended a common stairway.**

The grave of Oliver Goldsmith, one of Dickens's favourite writers, is outside the Temple Church. The present Goldsmith's Buildings have replaced the buildings where Mortimer Lightwood and Eugene Wrayburn in *Our Mutual Friend* had chambers.

Further to the east, we go past the southern wall of the Temple Church and through another archway to King's Bench Walk. On the eastern side is Tudor gate, which, as Whitefriars Gate, was where Mr Pip in *Great Expectations* received the message from Wemmick: **"Don't go home."** Facing the Walk is Paper Buildings, on the west side. The present buildings date from the 1830s and 1840s, replacing buildings where the odious Sir Edward Chester, in *Barnaby Rudge*, had chambers. Nearby were also the chambers of Mr Stryver, who was served by Sydney Carton in *A Tale of Two Cities*.

In 1869 Dickens was delighted to show his American friends, James T and Annie Adam Fields, round the Temple area. He showed them the sites associated with the events of *Great Expectations*, almost as if there was no difference between fact and his fiction.

If we return to Fleet Street, just to the east of Chancery Lane on the north is Clifford's Inn Passage, where Mr Rokesmith, in *Our Mutual Friend*, withdrew from the bustle of Fleet Street with Mr Boffin, to offer his services as secretary. Mr Boffin **glanced into the mouldy little plantation, or cat preserve, of Clifford's Inn as it was that day ... Sparrows were there, dry-rot and wet-rot were there; but it was not otherwise a suggestive place.**

St Dunstan's-in-the-West Church used to have a fountain where Hugh, in *Barnaby Rudge*, drenched himself in order to sober up, before calling on Sir John Chester at Paper Buildings. The fountain by the entrance, however, dates only from 1860. The church clock dates from 1671; the chiming of this church clock woke Scrooge in *A Christmas Carol*. David Copperfield came here with Betsey Trotwood to watch the giants strike the bells at noon one day. And Dickens dedicated his Christmas story, *The Chimes*, to this church.

Fleet Street used to be the centre of the British newspaper industry. There are a few traces of that activity – a bust of Lord Northcliffe, the founder of *The Daily Mail* in 1894, the first modern popular newspaper

If we continue east along Fleet Street, we come to Johnson's Court on the left. The *Monthly Magazine* had its offices here. They published Dickens's first story – "A Dinner in Poplar Walk" – in 1833. The address was number 166 Fleet Street, but the letter-box, through which Dickens posted his story, was in the archway that gives access to the Court; **it**

was dropped stealthily one evening at twilight, with fear and trembling, into a dark letter-box in a dark office up a dark court in Fleet Street. White concrete buildings have replaced newspaper offices. We pass, on the right, Bouverie Street, where Dickens's publishers, Bradbury and Evans, had their offices.

The next street on the right is Whitefriars Street. At the junction of that street and Fleet Street was the home of *The Daily News,* of which Charles Dickens was editor for a few days in 1846. Brief though his time as editor was, he managed nonetheless to employ his father as manager of the parliamentary reporting staff and his father-in-law as music and drama critic. The building was demolished at the end of the nineteenth century. Some instalments of *Pictures from Italy* were published in the newspaper. *The Daily News* was a Liberal paper that merged with another Liberal paper, *The Daily Chronicle*, in 1930 to form the *News Chronicle*, which, in turn, folded up in 1960. Jerry Cruncher, in *A Tale of Two Cities*, had rooms in Hanging Sword Alley, to the left off Whitefriars Street at the Fleet Street end. **They were not in a savoury neighbourhood, and were but two in number, even if a closet with a single pane of glass in it may be counted as one.** No buildings from the nineteenth century have survived. Indeed most of the corporate buildings date from after the Second World War.

Back on Fleet Street, if we cross the road to the northern side and turn left into Wine Office Court, we find Ye Olde Cheshire Cheese on the right, rebuilt in 1667 after the Fire of London. Here Charles Darnay, in *A Tale of Two Cities*, having been acquitted of high treason, dined with Sidney Carton. They had left the Old Bailey and, arm in arm, went **down Ludgate Hill to Fleet Street, and so up a covered way into a tavern.** The public house has other classic literary associations. It was a favourite of Dr Samuel Johnson and of Oliver Goldsmith, as well as Thackeray and Dickens himself. Dickens is reckoned to have had his favourite seat here – at a table to the right of the fireplace on the ground floor in what is today called the Chop Room, to the left of the entrance.

On the floor of Wine Office Court is a plaque in a paving stone with the totally incorrect suggestion that this marked the site of Mrs Lirriper's Lodgings, in the story published in *All the Year Round* in 1863. They were in fact half a mile to the south-west in Arundel Street.

On to Ludgate Circus. To the left is Farringdon Street, which follows the course of the now submerged River Fleet. If we go up Farringdon Street as far as the bridge over the road, Holborn Viaduct, we reach the site of Fleet Market, described in *Barnaby Rudge* as **a long irregular row of wooden sheds and pent-houses occupying the centre of what is now called Farringdon Street.** Until the 1950s there survived a second-hand book market on stalls in Farringdon Street, the last survival of the market.

On the east side of Farringdon Street, nearer Ludgate Circus, just to the south of Old Fleet Lane is the site of the Fleet Prison, where Mr Pickwick, attended by Sam Weller, was incarcerated until the costs of the shady lawyers, Dodson and Fogg, had been settled. The prison went back to the Middle Ages and used to occupy an island among the creeks and canals of the Fleet River that rose on Hampstead Heath and flowed into the Thames. It has long since been driven underground, but it is possible, in places, to follow its course. The River Fleet became a noisome sewer. The prison was burnt down during the Gordon Riots, as narrated in *Barnaby Rudge*, and rebuilt in the 1780s. Dickens described the prison when Mr Pickwick was there, with **a long narrow gallery, dirty and low, paved with stone, and very dimly lighted by a window at each remote end.** The prison was closed in 1842 and the building pulled down in 1844. It has been replaced on the southern side by a succession of buildings, the latest being another plate glass and concrete construction, put up at the beginning of the twenty-first century and already heading for stylistic obsolescence. It replaced a building of

1972, which itself replaced a building, the Congregational Memorial Hall of 1872 that was built after the demolition of the Fleet Prison. In this hall the British Labour Party was founded in February 1900.

Between Ludgate Circus and St Paul's Cathedral, shortly on the left is where the Belle Sauvage Inn stood until the 1830s. It was an old coaching inn. Originally called The Bell, it had a landlord called Mr Savage: whence the name. Sam Weller told the story of his father's interrogation at the time of his marriage.

"'What is your name, sir?' says the lawyer. 'Tony Weller,' says my father. 'Parish?' says the lawyer. 'Belle Savage,' says my father; for he stopped there when he drove up, and he know'd nothing about parishes, *he* didn't."

There is no trace of this inn, not even a name. Nor is there any mention of the London Coffee House, where the All Bar One now is. Arthur Clennam, in *Little Dorrit*, first stayed here when he arrived in London from overseas. He sat contemplatively looking out of the window, **in the same place as the day died, looking at the dull houses opposite, and thinking, if the disembodied spirits of former inhabitants were ever conscious of them, how they must pity themselves for their old places of imprisonment ... Presently the rain began to fall in slanting lines between him and those houses, and people began to collect under cover of the public passage opposite, and to look hopelessly at the sky as the rain dropped thicker and thicker.** The coffee house, which was founded in 1731, was a favourite resort of Americans. Benjamin Franklin was a member of a club that met to discuss philosophical issues there, and George Peabody, the philanthropist from Baltimore, hosted a dinner for Americans connected with the Great Exhibition of 1851.

Then St Paul's Cathedral, which so impressed the Yorkshireman, John Browdie, in *Nicholas Nickleby*: **"See there, lass, there be Paul's Church. Ecod, he be a soizable one, he be."** In 1856, at London's celebration of the conclusion of the Crimean War, Dickens obtained special permission to go to the gallery on the outside of the dome to watch the illuminations and display of fireworks. It was by the clock of the cathedral that Ralph Nickleby adjusted his own watch. Mr Pip, in *Great Expectations*, used the **great black dome** of the cathedral to work out where he was in the city. Jo, the crossing-sweeper in *Bleak House*, is puzzled by the cross on the top of the dome. And Peggotty in *David Copperfield*, brought here by David, is disappointed because it is not like the picture she has of it on her work-box.

To the right of the cathedral is Dean's Court, leading to Carter Lane Youth Hostel. Further south towards the river was Doctors' Commons where Dickens worked for a while in his early twenties. In *David Copperfield* he described it as **a little out-of-the-way place where they administer what is called ecclesiastical law, and play all kinds of tricks with obsolete monsters of Acts of Parliament, which three-fourths of the world know nothing about.** A plaque on the Faraday Building in Queen Victoria Street commemorates Doctors' Commons, which Mr Boffin in *Our Mutual Friend* personalised as **Doctor Scommons.** The offices of the lawyers, Spenlow and Jorkins, in *David Copperfield*, were in the vicinity. On the south side of Carter Lane, to the east of Dean's Court, there used to be a public house, the Bell Tavern, frequented by Dickens as he prepared *David Copperfield*. The New Bell Yard is the sole reminder of this association.

In the crypt of St Paul's Cathedral lies the body of George Cruikshank (1792–1878), the illustrator of *Sketches by Boz* and *Oliver Twist*.

The area to the north of St Paul's Cathedral used to be full of booksellers and small publishers. There is a story that Dickens was walking there and gazed at a picture of himself in a bookshop window. A boy by him was looking at the same image and then looked up at Dickens with awesome surprise. Dickens laughed and gave a nod acknowledging his identity before walking off briskly along Cheapside. For much of his life he became a distinctively public figure. His son, Henry, wrote that *to walk with him in the streets of London was a revelation ... people of all degrees and classes taking off their hats and greeting him as he passed.*

Cheapside is to the north-east of the Cathedral and leads to the financial heart of the city. When Dickens was 11 and before he worked at the blacking factory, he lost himself in the Strand and wandered into the City, **like a child in a dream, staring at the British merchants, and inspired by a mighty faith in the marvellousness of everything. Up courts and down courts – in and out of yards and little squares – peeping into counting house passages and running away.**

The third street on the left is Wood Street, which used to have the inn, The Cross Keys. This was one of 25 coaching inns in the City. By the end of the nineteenth century all but one had disappeared, such was the impact of railway transport. It was where Mr Pip arrived in London in *Great Expectations* on his first visit to the city. In the same inn, he anxiously awaited the arrival of Estelle. Dickens himself arrived here at the age of 10, an "unaccompanied minor", on the coach from Chatham. His parents had already settled in London, Camden Town, and the young Dickens stayed on at a school. **Through all the years that have since passed have I ever lost the smell of the damp straw in which I was packed – like game – and forwarded, carriage paid, to the Cross Keys, Wood Street, Cheapside, London?** (David Copperfield, on his arrival in London from Suffolk, was, **by invitation of the clerk on duty, passed behind the counter, and sat down on the scale at which they weighed the luggage.** Mr Mell met him and took him to Salem House, Blackheath. The clerk **slanted me off the scale, and pushed me over to him, as if I were weighed, bought, delivered, and paid for.** But this was at the Blue Boar, Whitechapel.)

The "cross keys" is a symbol of St Peter, who held the keys of Heaven. Before the Fire of London in 1666, St Peter's Church stood nearby. It was destroyed in the Fire and never replaced. The inn was demolished in the 1860s; a small court on the left has a few gravestones and is all that is left of the connection with St Peter's Church.

St Mary-le-Bow church is on the right hand side of the road. The firm, Dombey and Son, had its principal offices within earshot of the bells of this church.

King Street on the left leads to The Guildhall, or **Gold, or Golden Hall**, as the child Dickens heard it said. The building represents the headquarters of the City of London and was built in the fifteenth century and survived the Fire of London and the Blitz of the Second World War. In the City Court here, Mr Pickwick was the defendant in the trial of Bardell vs Pickwick. The Court of Common Pleas from 1822 to 1883 was located in the Gallery, the building to the southeast of the Guildhall itself.

Cheapside morphs into Poultry. Along Grocers' Hall Court to the left there used to be a restaurant in the last building. Here, Sam Weller brought Mr Pickwick for a quiet brandy and water. Here also Mr Pickwick met Sam Weller's father, Tony. There are no restaurants or even separate buildings here today. All is one white impersonal building, part of the Midland Bank complex.

At the end of Poultry on the right is the Mansion House, the residence of the Lord Mayor of London, who, in *A Christmas Carol*, **in the stronghold of the mighty Mansion House, gave orders to his fifty cooks and butlers to keep Christmas as a Lord Mayor's household should.**

And when Mark Tapley, serving Martin Chuzzlewit in the United States, spoke to members of the Watertoast Association about Queen Victoria, he said she **has lodgings, in virtue of her office, with the Lord Mayor at the Mansion House, but don't often occupy them, in consequence of the parlour chimney smoking.**

Raymond's Buildings, Gray's Inn

From Holborn Circus to Soho Square

This walk, which includes an optional two-stop journey on the Underground, takes us to the three major London houses that Dickens lived in. We follow in the steps of Barnaby Rudge *and* Martin Chuzzlewit *and the grim smart streets of the West End, unloved by Dickens.*

WALKING WEST FROM HOLBORN CIRCUS, we pass Fetter Lane on the left and then a branch of the HSBC Bank. This is on the site of Langdale's Distillery which was trashed during the anti-Catholic Gordon Riots in 1780. The proprietor was a Roman Catholic. Dickens describes the scene in *Barnaby Rudge*. **At this place a large detachment of soldiery were posted, who fired, now up Fleet Market, now up Holborn, now up Snow Hill – constantly raking the streets in each direction ... Full twenty times, the rioters, headed by one man who wielded an axe in his right hand, and bestrode a brewer's horse of great size and strength, caparisoned with fetters taken out of Newgate, which clanked and jingled as he went, made an attempt to force a passage at this point, and fire the vintner's house ... The vintner's house, with half-a-dozen others near at hand, was one great, glowing blaze ... The gutters of the street, and every crack and fissure in the stones, ran with scorching**

spirit, which being dammed up by busy hands, overflowed the road and pavement, and formed a great pool, into which the people dropped down dead by dozens. They lay in heaps all round this fearful pond, husbands and wives, fathers and sons, mothers and daughters, women with children in their arms and babies at their breasts, and drank until they died.

Mr Langdale and another Catholic, Mr Harewood, were rescued from the house by a back doorway that led on to the **narrow lane in the rear** [which was] **quite free of people. So, when they had crawled through the passage indicated by the vintner (which was a mere shelving-trap for the admission of casks), and had managed with some difficulty to unchain and raise the door at the upper end, they emerged into the street without being observed or interrupted.** This let them on to Fetter Lane – at a building now replaced by the southern end of the branch of the HSBC Bank.

Next door on the south side is Barnard's Inn, another former lawyers' Inn. Today it consists of a hotchpotch of mostly eighteenth- and nineteenth-century buildings with a series of courtyards, grouped around a sixteenth-century hall. Barnard's Inn used to provide residential accommodation for law students, but today fulfils a variety of functions, commercial and educational. It was occupied until 1959 by Mercers' School, attached to the Mercers' Company who own the building. The Company restored it sympathetically in the 1930s and again the 1990s. It serves as the home of the independent Gresham's College. Its attractive refurbishments contrast with the state of the place in Dickens's time. He made Mr Pip in *Great Expectations* describe Barnard's Inn as the **dingiest collection of shabby buildings ever squeezed together in a rank corner as a club for tom-cats**. Pip stayed here with Herbert Pocket for a short while on his first trip to London. Pip was not initially impressed.

We entered this haven through a wicket-gate, and were disgorged by an introductory passage into a melancholy little square that looked to me like a flat burying ground. I thought it had the most dismal trees in it, and the most dismal sparrows, and the most dismal cats, and the most dismal houses (in number half-a-dozen or so), that I had ever seen.

The confident brick Gothic building on the north side of the road, the headquarters of Prudential Assurance, was designed by Waterhouse in the last part of the nineteenth century and is on the site of Furnival's Inn, a block of flats for the then upwardly mobile. Furnival's Inn was another residential block for lawyers studying at Lincoln's Inn. It severed its connection with law in 1817 and Charles Dickens, escaping from his feckless parents, took an apartment here with his brother Frederick, from 1834 to 1837. The rent was £35 a year. In *Martin Chuzzlewit* he described the Inn as **a shady, quiet place, echoing to the footsteps of the stragglers who have business there, and rather monotonous and gloomy**

on Sunday evenings. In the first courtyard up on the right a plaque celebrates Dickens's time living here and writing *Sketches by Boz* and much of *The Pickwick Papers*.

In 1836 WM Thackeray, seven months older than Dickens, called here on the young successful author. Thackeray knew that Dickens wanted an artist to illustrate his writings, and brought along a portfolio of work. But Dickens did not find them suitable.

After his marriage in 1836, Dickens stayed on in Furnival's Inn, though in another, larger apartment. Here his eldest son was born. At the back of the Inn, accessible to it through a square, was Wood's Hotel, where Mr Grewgious in *The Mystery of Edwin Drood* used to go for dinner **three hundred days in the year at least.** He found rooms for Rosa Bud, when she fled from Cloisterham (Rochester). She was provided with a chambermaid and a bedroom and a sitting-room. It was safe, for, as Mr Grewgious said, reassuring her, **"Furnival's is fire-proof, and specially watched and lighted, and *I* live over the way."** Today Furnival's Inn houses the headquarters of English Heritage, as well as banks and the offices of hi-tech companies.

Further west, on the south side of the street is Staple Inn, with a half-timbered facade facing the street. **Behind the most ancient part of Holborn, London, where certain gabled houses some centuries of age still stand looking at the public way … is a little nook called Staple Inn. It presents the sensation of having put cotton in his** [the visitor's] **ears and velvet soles on his feet.** These half-timbers, the most impressive surviving timber building in London, go back to the sixteenth century. For over a century the half-timbers were plastered over but in 1884 the Inn was acquired by the Prudential Assurance Company who stripped the plaster and restored the timbers. There was more heavy restoration, even reconstruction, in the twentieth century. The Tudor exterior is in sharp contrast to the elegant eighteenth-century inner buildings around a quadrangle. Mr Grewgious, in *The Mystery of Edwin Drood*, had chambers here – at number 10 – as did Neville Landless in the same novel. The chambers overlooked a little garden at the back, **where a few smoky sparrows twitter in the smoky trees, as though they had called to each other, "let us play at country"**. Another resident of Staple Inn was Mr Tartar, also in *The Mystery of Edwin Drood*, who occupied **the neatest, the cleanest, and the best-ordered chambers ever seen under the sun, moon, and stars.** And Mr Snagsby, the law stationer in *Bleak House*, **being in his way rather a meditative and poetical man** used to wander around here **to observe how countrified the sparrows and the leaves are.** Nathaniel Hawthorne came here in 1852. *It was strange to have drifted into it so suddenly out of the bustle and rumble of Holborn.* The same is true 160 years later.

Another Inn, that provided a base for lawyers, is Gray's Inn, a few yards along Gray's Inn Road that leads north from High Holborn. It is one of the four surviving Inns of Court. The Inn is on the left, and can trace its history back to the fourteenth century. It is like the other Inns of Court, with common architectural features, and with family resemblances to colleges at Oxford and Cambridge. Residential and communal buildings are grouped around courts (or squares). In contrast to the rest of London the visitor enjoys a sense of spaciousness. (Be warned, however, that the Inns may be closed to visitors at weekends.) All of Gray's Inn suffered severe war damage in the Second World War and many of the present buildings date from after 1945. There are two squares and extensive gardens.

Charles Dickens was employed as a clerk to Edward Blackmore, an Attorney, between May 1827 – he was just fifteen – and November 1828; his wage ranged between 13s 6d and 15s (67p to 75p) a week. The office where he worked was at number 1, Holborn Court. The Court was renamed South Square in 1829. His office was at the back, overlooking a space between the Inn and the back of Holborn shops, on to which he used to drop cherry-stones. This passage, **a squalid little trench, with rank grass and a pump in it, lying between the coffee-house and South-square**, is now a smart access street for service vehicles and called The Paddock. In the 1820s, it was a grassy area given over to cats and rats.

Tommy Traddles, David Copperfield's chum, had chambers here – at number 2 South Square. He used to ascend by a rickety staircase, **feebly lighted on each landing by a club-headed little oil wick dying away in a little dungeon of dirty glass**. The ever cheerful Traddles claimed it was "**a very nice little room when you're up here**". Mr Perker, Mr Pickwick's legal adviser, also had chambers in Gray's Inn. We do not know exactly where his rooms were, beyond the fact that you reached them **after climbing two pairs of steep and dirty stairs**. In *Little Dorrit* Flora Finching, with whom Arthur Clennam had been in love two decades earlier, meets up with Arthur in the gardens of Gray's Inn. For Arthur the reunion is a disaster. When he was writing *Little Dorrit* Dickens had recently met up with his old flame of 20 years earlier, Maria Beadnell, with equal disillusion. The account of the reunion in the novel shows Dickens at his cruellest. Maria always read the novels of her old lover and would have been mortified to have seen herself portrayed so savagely.

The legal partnership of Ellis and Blackmore, solicitors, moved – taking Dickens – to number 1, and later number 6, Raymond Buildings. These Buildings can be found to the north-west of the Inn on the road leading to Theobalds Road. They were newly built when Dickens worked there. Flora Finching, in *Little Dorrit*, reminds Arthur Clennam of their old romance when they walked in the gardens at the back of Raymond's Buildings **at exactly four o' clock in the afternoon**.

Dickens derived his early impressions of the legal system and the legal profession during these years, and saw Gray's Inn in 1860, as **that stronghold of Melancholy ... one of the most depressing institutions in brick and mortar, known** to the children of men. **Can anything be more dreary than its arid Square, Sahara Desert of the law, with the ugly old tiled-topped tenements, the dirty windows, the bills To Let, To Let, the door-posts inscribed like gravestones, the crazy gateway giving upon the filthy Lane, the scowling iron-barred prison-like passage into Verulam-buildings, the mouldy red-nosed ticket-porters with little coffin plates … the dry hard atomy-like appearance of the whole dust-heap.** Dirt and filth. These were strong words for a man like Dickens who was clean in his habits, and almost dandy-ish in his dress.

If we leave Gray's Inn by the Holborn Gate that leads on to High Holborn and head west, we pass on the right much twentieth-century development. One street has been lost – Kingsgate Street where in *Martin Chuzzlewit* Poll Sweedle-pipe, barber and bird-fancier, had his premises, **next door but one to the celebrated mutton-pie shop, and directly opposite the cat's meat warehouse**. On the first floor dwelt Mrs Gamp, who was often summoned to her duties as night nurse, layer-out of the dead and midwife **by pebbles, walking-sticks, and fragments of tobacco-pipes, all much more efficacious than the street-door knocker, which was so constructed to wake the street with ease, and even spread alarms of fire in Holborn, without making the smallest impression on the premises to which it was addressed.**

New Oxford Street, which runs 150 yards to the west of Holborn underground station, was built in 1847 to by-pass St Giles High Street. In later years some appalling slum dwellings were destroyed with little consideration given to rehousing the 5,000 people who lived there. (**… never heeding, never asking, where the wretches whom we clear out, crowd.**) The whole area of St Giles was notorious for its "rookeries", huge blocks of buildings that were let and sublet. One man would rent a flat, then let each room to a family or families. (St Giles is, appropriately, the patron saint of out-casts.) Dickens used to wander around here, having what his friend and biographer, John Forster, called *a profound attrac-tion of repulsion to St Giles's*. In the 1840s famine forced many Irish to migrate to mainland Britain and the United States. Certain parts of London became the homes of exploited Irish families. St Giles was one such and became known as "Little Ireland". In 1850 Dickens toured the area in the company of his police detective friend, Inspector Field, on whom Inspec-tor Bucket in *Bleak House* is based. Tenants settled in **this compound of sickening smells, these heaps of filth, these tumbling houses, with all their vile contents, animate and inanimate, slimily overflowing into the black road ... Men, women, children, for the most part naked, heaped upon the floor like maggots in a cheese! Ho! In that dark corner yonder! Does anybody lie there? Me sir, Irish me, a widder with six children. And yonder? Me sir, Irish me, with me wife and eight poor babes. And to the left there? Me sir, Irish me, along with two more Irish boys as is me friends. And to the right there? Me sir and the Murphy fam'ly, numbering five blessed souls. And what's this, coiling, now, about my foot? Another Irish me, pitifully in want of shaving, whom I have awakened from sleep – and across my other foot lies his wife – and by the shoes of Inspector Field lie their three eldest – and their three youngest are at present squeezed between the open door and the wall. And why is there no one on that little mat before the sullen fire? Because O'Donovan, with his wife and daughter, is not come in from selling Lucifers!**

Doubling back we have Southampton Place to the north. This used to be called Southampton Street. It was here – at number 18 – where Mr Grewgious in *The Mystery of Edwin Drood*, found accommodation for Rosa Bud and Miss Twin-kleton at the house (or **'ouse**) of querulous Mrs Billickin who refused to sign documents using her Christian name for reasons of prudence and security. Two doors away is an archway. "**The arching**," Mrs Billickin observed, "**leads to a mews; mewses must exist.**"

Southampton Place leads to Bloomsbury Square. To the west of the square is the British Museum. Both Charles Dickens and Mr Pickwick were readers at the library at the British Museum. The former Reading Room was redesigned as the Great Court in the 1990s by Norman Foster. The books, documents and manuscripts were moved to the new British Library by St Pancras Station.

At 29 Bloomsbury Square, on the east side, lived Lord Mansfield, the great eighteenth-century liberal-minded lawyer. His house was destroyed in the Gordon Riots, as described in *Barnaby Rudge*. The trashing of his residence here – he had a country home at Ken (or Caen) Wood, Highgate – led to a **common ruin of the whole of the costly furniture, the plate and jewels, a beautiful gallery of pictures, the rarest collection of manuscripts ever possessed by any one private person in the world, and, worst of all, because nothing could replace the loss, the great Law Library, on almost every page of which were notes, in the judge's own hand, of inestimable value; being the results of the study and experience of his whole life.** (Dickens's hostility to the legal profession seems to have been suspended in the case of Lord Mansfield.) In the Square two of the rioters were hanged, facing Lord Mansfield's looted residence. The gardens of the square were originally designed by the landscape gardener Humphry Repton in the first years of the nineteenth century. There is no trace of Mansfield's home, the site of which is now occupied by Victoria House, built in 1928 as the then headquarters of the Liverpool and Victoria Friendly Society.

Leaving Bloomsbury Square at the north eastern corner we come after a few yards to Southampton Row. Turning left and then through the passageway, Cosmo Place, on the right, we come to Queen Square. Richard Carstone, in *Bleak House*, had an apartment in this area. It is believed to have been 28 Old Gloucester Street, which exits the square from the south-west angle.

If we head from the south-east along Great Ormond Street we arrive, on the left, at the Great Ormond Street Hospital for Children, founded as a small pediatric hospital in 1852. Charles Dickens presided over a dinner in 1858 held to raise funds for developing its work. He arranged for the proceeds of a public reading of *A Christmas Carol* to be dedicated to the Hospital. In *Our Mutual Friend*, the sick child, Johnny, made his will. **From bed to bed, a light womanly tread and a pleasant fresh face passed in the silence of the night. A little head would lift itself into the softened light here and there, to be kissed as the face went by – for these little patients are very loving – and would then submit itself to be composed to rest again.**

If we turn left, beyond the hospital, into Lamb's Conduit Street we come to face Coram's Fields, on the northern side of Guilford Street. This is on the site of an eighteenth-century charitable refuge for foundling children – the Foundling Hospital. For a while, when Dickens lived at Doughty Street nearby, he regularly attended the Hospital chapel. The servant of the Meagleses in *Little Dorrit*, Harriet Beadle, is called Tattycoram. The first part of the name is a corruption of Harriet, the second in deference to the founder of the Hospital from where she was recruited.

In the eighteenth century this area was the northern limit of built-up London. In *Barnaby Rudge* Sim Tappertit and his friends met at the Boot Tavern: a **lone place of public entertainment, situated in the fields at the back of the Foundling Hospital; a very solitary spot at that period, and quite deserted after dark. The Tavern stood at some distance from any high road, and was only approachable by a dark and narrow lane.** In Cromer Street, just off Judd Street, a quarter of a mile to the north of the Foundling Museum, the Boot public house still exists, the successor of the one Dickens knew. It is by Speedy Place, an alley to the west, filled with potted plants and providing a delightful and unexpected touch of greenery to an otherwise drab neighbourhood. Some of the turrets of St Pancras railway station can be seen to the north. The Speedy family, after whom the alley is named, were for several generations the licensees of the Boot Inn.

Walking east along Guilford Street we reach Doughty Street on the right. After a few houses on the left we come to no 48, now the Dickens Museum. Charles Dickens lived here for less than three years, from 1837, when he was aged 25 and newly married, to late 1839. He had moved out of Furnival's Inn and moving here was a confident acknowledgement that he had arrived. The rent was £80 a year and Mr and Mrs Dickens employed three servants. In the 1830s Doughty Street was a private road, gated at each end. There were twelve rooms over four floors. The study where Dickens wrote the last parts of *Pickwick Papers*, *Oliver Twist* and *Nicholas Nickleby* was at the back of the first floor. Mrs Dickens's sister, Mary Hogarth, was living with them. She died suddenly at the house at the age of 17. The three of them had gone to the theatre, Mary went up to bed and was heard uttering a choking cry. She died the following afternoon in Dickens's arms. He was so affected that he was unable to complete his allotted serial parts of *The Pickwick Papers* and *Oliver Twist* – he was writing both simultaneously. It was a death that scarred Dickens for the rest of his life, and many of his virginal heroines seem to be based on Mary. However within three years Dickens and his family moved out. His wife was usually pregnant and he is reported to have said unsympathetically that **the house in Doughty Street was nothing but a hospital ward**. After Dickens's time the house was divided into flats and served as a boarding house. It was purchased by the Dickens Fellowship in the 1920s and has been a museum ever since.

Let us double back along Guilford Street to Russell Square. Turning right along Woburn Place we come after one block to Tavistock Square. This square was designed in 1824. On the north-east side is the headquarters of the British Medical Association. It occupies the site of Tavistock

House, which Dickens purchased on a 45-year lease and which became his London home from 1851 to 1860. It was **decidedly cheap – most commodious – and might be made very handsome**. It was certainly commodious, with 18 rooms including a drawing-room that could hold over 300 people. There was also a garden, large even then for central London. The kitchen was underground and the bedrooms at the top of the house. Hans Christian Andersen stayed here in 1857. He had *a snug room looking out on the garden, and over the tree-tops I saw the London towers and spires appear and disappear as the weather cleared or thickened*. The original building was pulled down in 1901 and today a blue plaque marks the site of his residence here.

The house witnessed highs and lows in Dickens's life. It was where Dickens hosted parties with generous exuberance. Here he would entertain his friends and regiment his family in the performance of amateur dramatics at what became known as the Theatre Royal, Tavistock House. Here he wrote *Bleak House*, *Hard Times* and *Little Dorrit*. His study was next to the drawing room and was separated from it by sliding doors. When he was thinking hard, he used to open up these doors and stride up and down the length of the two rooms. Tavistock House was also the scene of the progressive disintegration of his marriage. In 1856 his wife's family stayed at the house; Dickens stayed away. Their bohemian untidiness distressed him. When they moved out he returned and at once threw himself into manically spring-cleaning the place. He **opened the windows, aired the carpets, and purified every room from the roof to the hall**. On one notable occasion he had a row with his wife, got up at two in the morning and walked to his newly-acquired house at Gad's Hill Place near Rochester – 30 miles, arriving there at nine in the morning.

After Dickens gave up his tenancy a later resident was the French composer, Charles Gounod (1818–93). For a while it was also a Jewish College before being demolished.

Twenty yards to the south of Dickens's plaque, on the railings, is another plaque, often accompanied by flowers, marking the site of the terrorist outrage of 7 July 2005, ("7/7"). A bomb was detonated on a number 30 double-decker bus, killing thirteen people and wounding many others. The names are recorded on the plaque – Muslim, Jewish, Indian, English – reflecting the diversity that is London.

If we leave the square at the south-west corner, pass Gordon Square and negotiate a dog-leg bend we reach Gower Street. On the western side of the street to the north is the site of number 145, just beyond Grafton Way. The former house has been replaced by a vast glass-plated building, part of the Elizabeth Garrett Anderson wing of University College Hospital. Charles Dickens's mother lived at number 145 and made a valiant though pathetic attempt to set up a school for young ladies while her husband was in the Marshalsea Prison. Charles lived here briefly – he was ten years old at the time. The endeavour was a total failure. As Dickens himself recalled, **I left at a great many other doors a great many circulars, calling attention to the merits of the establishment. Yet nobody ever came to school, nor do I recollect that anybody ever proposed to come, or that the least preparation was made to receive anybody. But, I know that we got on very badly with the butcher and baker.** The row of houses was demolished in 1895. Next door there had been a dancing "academy", which may have served as a model for that of Mr Turveydrop in *Bleak House.*

A journey of two stops to the west on the underground from Euston Square station close-by brings us to Baker Street. (The underground railway goes under Euston Road, off which to the south is Cleveland Street. In 1814 it was known as Norfolk Street and Dickens and his family lived there briefly between residences in Portsmouth and Chatham. In 1831 Dickens also had lodgings in the same street for a short time. It is the address he gave in his application to consult books at the British Museum.)

To the east and on the south side of Marylebone Road, opposite the Royal Academy of Music, is St Marylebone parish church. It was probably in the church that Paul Dombey was christened, and later buried alongside his mother, and where his father married Edith Grainger. **The tall shrouded pulpit and reading desk; the dreary perspective of empty pews stretching away under the galleries and empty benches mounting to the roof and lost in the shadow of the great grim organ; the dusty matting and the cold stone slabs; the grisly free-seats in the aisles; and the damp corner by the bell-rope, where the black tressels used for funerals were stowed away, along with some shovels and baskets, and a coil or two of rope; the strange, unusual, uncomfortable smell, and the cadaverous light; were all in unison. It was a cold and dismal scene.** Outside the realms of fiction it is also the church where Lord Byron was christened and where Robert Browning married Elizabeth Barrett.

The church is next door to the site of Dickens's second of three main London residences: 1 Devonshire Terrace. At the corner of Marylebone High Street is a frieze and a plaque on a modern building.

The frieze of 1962 by Estcourt J Clack illustrates characters that Dickens wrote about while he was based here, between 1839 and 1851, the years of *The Old Curiosity Shop*, *Barnaby Rudge*, *A Christmas Carol* and *David Copperfield*. The house had 13 rooms and was at the end of a terrace. It had a garden, at the end of which was a coach-house. Dickens kept a small pair of ponies, and hired a groom. He rented it all for £160 a year, and paid £800 for the last 12 years of the lease. In the 1841 census five servants are recorded as living here. Dickens described himself as *Gentleman*. Mrs Gaskell visited him at this house and described his study: *There are books all round, up to the ceiling, and down to the floor.*

When Dickens was at work he insisted on absolute

silence whereas when he was at leisure, in the words of his daughter, Mamie, *the bustle and noise of the great city became necessary to him.* His study at Devonshire Terrace opened on to the garden but there was an extra baize door to enable him to keep out the noise as he worked. The house became famous for the parties. **Such dinings**, he wrote to an American friend, Cornelius Felton, **such dancings, such conjurings, such blind-man's-buffings, such theatre-goings, such kissings out of old years and kissings-in of new ones, never took place in these parts before.** And to William Macready, his actor friend, then on tour in the United States, he wrote how he and his future biographer, John Forster, conjured a plum-pudding from an empty saucepan, **held over a blazing fire kindled in Stanfield's hat without damage to the lining; that a box of bran was changed into a live guinea-pig, which ran between my godchild's feet, and was the cause of such a shrill uproar and clapping of hands.**

In the garden Dickens used to keep ravens. One died and Dickens suspected that it had been poisoned. He arranged for an autopsy on the dead bird. Dickens's suspicions were unfounded and the cause of the raven's death was given as influenza. **He has left considerable property, chiefly in cheese and halfpence, buried in different parts of the garden.** The new raven (**I have a new one, but he is comparatively of weak intellect**) administered to his effects, and turns up something every day. The last piece of *bijouterie* was a hammer of considerable size, supposed to have been stolen from a vindictive carpenter, who had been heard to speak darkly of vengeance ... A later pet raven died unexpectedly by the kitchen fire. He kept his eye to the last upon the meat as it roasted, and suddenly turned over on his back with a sepulchral cry of "Cuckoo!" Dickens's ravens were the original models for Barnaby Rudge's pet, Grip.

Henry Wadsworth Longfellow visited him here in 1841.

The raven croaks in the garden, he wrote home from his host's study, *and the ceaseless roar of London fills my ears*.

Dickens was happy here. **I seem as if I had plucked myself out of my proper soil when I left Devonshire Terrace**, he wrote in 1844 from Genoa where he lived for 12 months, **and would take root no more until I return to it.** When he lived at Devonshire Terrace Dickens was an occasional worshipper – or "took sittings" – at a nearby Unitarian Church in Little Portland Street.

The second on the right after Marylebone High Street brings us to Harley Street. Dickens did not like this street. **The expressionless uniform twenty houses**, Dickens wrote in *Little Dorrit*, **all to be knocked at and rung at in the same form, all approachable by the same dull steps, all fended off by the same pattern of railings, all with the same impracticable fire-escapes, the same inconvenient fixtures in their heads, and everything, without exception, to be taken at a high valuation ...**

His villains lived in streets in and around here. The swindling financier Mr Merdle in *Little Dorrit* lived in Harley Street. And four blocks to the south and parallel with Harley Street is Mansfield Street, where Mr Dombey had his house.

Mr Dombey's house was a large one, on a shady side of a tall, dark, dreadfully genteel street in the region between Portland Place and Bryanston Square. (It is much nearer Portland Place than Bryanston Square; and one might add that the literal shadiness depends on the time of day and position of the sun.) **It was a corner house, with wide areas containing cellars, frowned upon by barred windows, and leered at by crooked-eyed doors leading to dust-bins. It was a house of dismal state, with a circular back to it, containing a whole suit of drawing rooms looking upon a gravelled yard, where two gaunt trees, with blackened trunks and branches, rattled rather than rustled, their leaves were so smoke-dried.** The house to the west on the corner of Mansfield Mews has a yard that could be dismal – a high wall separates it from the road. The house opposite on the corner of Duchess Street has a semi-circular bay window.

To the south is Cavendish Square. From here westward runs Wigmore Street where Madame Mantalini's dress-making establishment in *Nicholas Nickleby* was probably sited – number 11 has been suggested, though today Wigmore Place is where number 11 would be.

Along Wigmore Street we come to Wimpole Street on the right. Number 43 is believed to have been the residence of Mr and Mrs Boffin in *Our Mutual Friend* – **a corner house not far from Cavendish Square.** The house was later the property of Mr and Mrs John Harmon. Near here Silas Wegg had his stall.

Parallel to Wimpole Street further west is Welbeck Street. The building on the left, formerly number 64 and now Welbeck House, was the London residence of Lord George Gordon, the leader of the riots described in *Barnaby Rudge*.

Oxford Street is parallel to Wimpole Street to the south. If we walk along Oxford Street in a westerly direction, and turn left just at Bond Street Station, we head down Davies Street to Brook Street where, in *Dombey and Son*, the Fenix family had their town house. The Honorable Mrs Shrewton borrowed the house for her daughter's wedding to Mr Dombey.

Davies Street continues, passing (rich) Americans' favourite hotel, Claridge's. The hotel was founded in 1855 by an enterprising and resourceful former butler who bought an older hotel, Milvart's Hotel, on this site. It was probably Milvart's Hotel where Nicholas Nickleby paused for a pint of wine and a biscuit. **It was very handsomely furnished, the walls were ornamented with the choicest specimens of French paper enriched with a gilded cornice of elegant design. The floor was covered with a rich carpet, and two superb mirrors, one over the chimney-piece, the other reaching from floor to ceiling, multiplied the other beauties and added new ones of their own to enhance the general effect.** As Nicholas sipped the wine he overheard his sister being discussed in offensive terms by Sir Mulberry Hawk and a friend.

If we continue south to Berkeley Square and Berkeley Street, we reach Piccadilly. In the 1860s there used to be a hotel, St James's Hotel, at this corner. In 1869, the year before he died, Dickens came up from his Kent country house at Gad's Hill and stayed here for a few weeks in order to meet American friends and to be near a London doctor. In *Little Dorrit* Dickens described the area unsympathetically. **They rode to the top of Oxford Street, and, there alighting, dived in among the great streets of melancholy stateliness, and the little streets that try to be as stately and succeed in being more melancholy, of which there is a labyrinth near Park Lane. Wildernesses of corner-houses with barbarous old porticoes and appurtenances; horrors that came into existence under some wrong-headed person in some wrong-headed time, still demanding the blind admiration of all ensuing generations and determined to do so until they tumbled down.** He really did not care for this area, Mayfair.

Devonshire House, one of the greatest of aristocratic houses – the London base of the Dukes of Devonshire – was located on the right, facing Piccadilly and the western edge of Green Park. It had been built in 1749 for the third Duke of Devonshire but was demolished in 1924. Here in May 1851 Dickens directed a play written by Bulwer Lytton, "Not so Bad as We Seem", in the presence of Queen Victoria and the Prince Consort. The Queen was amused.

Let us turn left along Piccadilly. On the eastern corner of Dover Street is the site of the coaching inn, the White Horse, the starting point for coaches to the west of England. Being in the fashionable and leisured West End of London, people would come to watch the departure of the evening coach. Itinerant peddlers used to gather to sell fruit and sponges for the passengers. The inn had a travellers' waiting room, **divided into boxes for the solitary confinement of** travellers ...[It] is furnished with a clock, a looking-glass, and a live waiter, which latter article is kept in a small kennel for washing glasses in a corner of the apartment. From here Mr Pickwick and company set off for Bath. Sam Weller observed that the proprietor of the coach was another Pickwick. Sam thought this outrageous – **"An't nobody to be whopped for takin' this here liberty?"** It was also the destination of coaches from Reading, and here Esther Summerson in *Bleak House* first arrived in London, according to instructions. She was met at the Booking Office known as the White Horse Cellars, on the other side of the road, by Mr Guppy, who proposed disastrously to her, later referring to the place of that first meeting as **Whytorseller.**

If we walk up Piccadilly towards Piccadilly Circus we pass Albany (or The Albany – a very English controversy revolves around which is the correct form), which for 200 years was a favoured home for well-connected bachelors. It is located opposite Fortnum and Mason's 50 yards up a gated road, the Albany Court Yard. Part of the lease is held by Peterhouse, one of the colleges of the University of Cambridge. Dickens's older literary and lordly contemporaries, Byron and Macaulay, had sets of chambers in (the) Albany. Dickens housed "Fascination" Fledgeby, in *Our Mutual Friend*, here.

Mr and Mrs Lammles, also of *Our Mutual Friend*, used, in their days of prosperity, to live in Sackville Street to the left.

Beyond Sackville Street and before Air Street on the left is the place where St James's Hall used to stand. The site is now occupied by le Meridien Hotel. It was here that Dickens used to give most of his London readings. He was always an actor manqué and he threw himself into dramatic readings. They both invigorated and exhausted him. He was always punctiliously dressed and was meticulous about all the arrangements – position of the lectern, lighting, the manner and style and timing of his entry on to the stage. He also made plenty of money to meet the commitments of his later years, providing for his separated wife, for wayward and feckless offspring, as well as two of his own households, quite apart from a household for Ellen Ternan, his actress friend, and her family. His rendering of the death of Little Nell from *The Old Curiosity Shop* and the murder of Nancy from *Oliver Twist* made enormous physical and emotional demands on Dickens himself, but no less on his audience. After giving his readings he rarely appeared for an encore. But in March 1870, frail and prematurely aged, he gave a farewell speech: **For some fifteen years, in this hall and many kindred places, I have had the honour of presenting my own cherished ideas before you for your recognition; and in closely observing your reception of them, have enjoyed an amount of artistic delight and enjoyment, which perhaps it is given to few men to know … . Ladies and gentlemen, in but two short weeks from this time, I hope that you may enter, in your own homes, on a new series of Readings, at which my assistance will be indispensable; but from these garish lights I vanish now for ever, with one heartfelt, grateful, respectful, and affectionate farewell.** (Dickens was alluding to the forthcoming serialisation of *The Mystery of Edwin Drood*.) After these words there was a dead silence as he turned away, deeply affected. Then, his daughter, Mamie, recalled, *such a burst and tumult of cheers and applause as were almost too much to bear*. Within three months he was dead.

On the south side of Piccadilly, between the pedestrian Eagle Place and Piccadilly Circus, at no 193, were the premises of the publishers, Chapman and Hall, who brought out Dickens's earlier books, from *The Pickwick Papers* to *Martin Chuzzlewit*.

If we cross to the north of Piccadilly Circus and go up Sherwood Street, cross Brewer Street and continue on Lower James Street, we reach Golden Square. At number 6, on the east side, is the presumed house of Ralph Nickleby. The site has probably been rebuilt more than once since the 1840s. There is no trace of a numbered building. Today the site is occupied by a construction of brick, stone and glass, the offices of a public relations agency. Dickens described Golden Square as **one of the squares that have been; a quarter of the town that has gone down in the world, and taken to letting lodgings. Many of its first and second floors are let, furnished, to single gentlemen, and it takes boarders besides. It is a great resort of foreigners.**

Carnaby Street that runs from south to north, one block to the north of Golden Square, was – at number 48 – the home of the Kenwigs family in *Nicholas Nickleby*. Number 48 is in an eighteenth-century terrace house, now hosting a smart clothes shop. Another Nickleby connection is The Crown Inn, at the junction of Upper James Street and Beak Street. This was Newman Noggs's favourite watering hole. In his first letter to Nicholas, Newman Noggs wrote that **"they know where I live at the sign of the Crown, Golden Square"**. There is no Crown Inn today but an Old Coffee House with bars faces Upper James Street.

The prostitute in *David Copperfield*, Martha, also lived in this area, in **one of the sombre streets of which there are several in that part, where the houses were once fair dwellings, in the occupation of single families, but have, and had, long degenerated into poor lodgings let off in rooms.**

If we thread our way north, we reach Oxford Street. Dickens's maternal grandmother, former housekeeper of the Marquess of Crewe and possible model of Mrs Rouncewell, housekeeper at Chesney Wold in *Bleak House*, lived in Oxford Street, where Charles as a boy was brought to see her. Newman Street goes to the north. In this street, perhaps at number 26, Mr Turveydrop in *Bleak House* had his Dancing Academy – **in a sufficiently dingy house, at the corner of an archway**. Part of number 26 overhangs an arch that leads into Newman Passage. Here Mr Turveydrop occupied the best part of the house, and his son and daughter-in-law, formerly Caddy Jellaby, were quartered in upper rooms, normally occupied by domestic staff.

A little further to the east, off Oxford Street on the south side, is Dean Street. Carlisle Street goes off on the left to join Soho Square. If we head south from the Square into Greek Street we reach Manette Street on the left, passing under an archway that is part of the Pillars of Hercules public house. Manette Street leads on to Charing Cross Road by Foyle's Bookshop. Having previously been Rose Street, the street was given this name in 1895 in honour of Dr Manette, the French refugee in *A Tale of Two Cities*. He had lived, not in this street, but perhaps in Carlisle Street. **A quieter corner than the corner where the Doctor lived was not to be found in London. There was no way through it, and the front window of the Doctor's lodgings commanded a pleasant little vista of street that had a congenial air of retirement on it. There were few buildings then, north of the Oxford Road, and forest-trees flourished, and wild flowers grew, and the hawthorn blossomed, in the now vanished fields.**

From Bermondsey to Holborn Circus

The walk starts in Bermondsey and takes us to the City of London. Then, after another optional underground journey we move to Smithfield and Clerkenwell and to parts of London particularly associated with Oliver Twist.

Bermondsey has undergone several transformations since the 1830s. Slum clearances in the nineteenth century, extensive improvements during the twentieth century, and severe bomb damage during the Second World War have made it hard to trace the location of Jacob's Island where Bill Sikes in *Oliver Twist* made his last stand. He tried to lower himself from a building known as Metcalf Yard into a ditch with a rope attached to a chimney. But he lost his grip and hanged himself by the rope.

Near to that part of the Thames ... where the buildings on the banks are dirtiest, and the vessels on the river blackest, with the dust of colliers and the smoke of close-built, low-roofed houses. In such a neighbourhood, beyond Dockhead, in the borough of Southwark, stands Jacob's Island, surrounded by a muddy ditch, six or eight feet deep, and fifty or twenty wide when the tide is in, once called Mill Pond, but known in the days of this story as Folly Ditch.

St Sepulchre's Church Holborn

A street called Dockhead is still there and Jacob Street perpetuates the memory of the Island. Folly Ditch flowed into the Thames through what is now Mill Street, a narrow road that resembles a canyon between high buildings. The oldest building here is the Neo Concordia Wharf, fronting on to St Saviour's Dock, created out of one of the lost rivers of London, the Neckinger. Jacob's Island was to the north of Wolseley Street, formerly London Street. Wooden bridges over the sewage-filled canals led to the island and **crazy wooden galleries, common to the backs of half-a-dozen houses used to ornament the banks of Folly Ditch.** Dickens in the 1830s got to know the area when it was at its worst: **the filthiest, the strangest, the most extraordinary of the many localities that are hidden in London, wholly unknown, even by name, to the great mass of the inhabitants.** Cholera broke out here between 1849 and 1852 and there was a major fire in 1861. After that the area was demolished and the Victorian buildings replacing the slums have themselves been replaced. In the last 20 years there has been a further metamorphosis. Today the only water inland, away from the dock and the river is an ornamental pool, with fountain, in the gardens of Providence Square. The gardens are accessible only to the residents of the smart high-rise flats surrounding the gardens. A two-bedroom flat here goes for £525,000.

Dickens is commemorated in the blocks of flats in the area around, between Jamaica Road and the river. The blocks are named Brownlow, Tapley, Dombey, Copperfield, Nickleby, Bardell, Oliver, Pickwick, Weller, Tupman, Rudge, Micawber, Spenlow, Wickfield, Trotwood, Maylie, Wrayburn, Havisham. All have been built in the 1950s.

We can walk westwards near the river. A footbridge crosses the St Saviour's Dock and a wide path, an esplanade, follows the river up to Tower Bridge. A string of smart wine bars and restaurants occupy the former wharves. One, with extraordinary pretentiousness, calls itself Le Pont de la Tour. ("Le Pont de la Tour combines traditional yet innovative French cuisine, knowledgeable and friendly staff, thoughtful design that evokes the Parisian chic of the 1930s, and glamorous views of the City and Tower Bridge.") The small smart pier opposite is Butler's Wharf Pier. It was around here that Quilp, in *The Old Curiosity Shop*, had *his* wharf, a **small, rat-infested, dreary yard, in which were a little wooden counting-house, burrowing all awry in the dust as if it had fallen from the clouds, and ploughed into the ground; a few fragments of rusty anchors, several large iron rings, some piles of rotten wood, and two or three heaps of old sheet copper – crumpled, cracked, and battered.**

Today it is possible to take Riverboat Disco Cruises from the pier.

Let us now cross the Thames by Tower Bridge – built in the 1890s – and pass the Tower of London on the left, built in the eleventh century by King William I (the Conqueror). We come to Tower Hill. Lord George Gordon, in *Barnaby Rudge*, was imprisoned in **a dreary room** in the Tower of London. And David Copperfield took his aunt, Betsey Trotwood, to see it. On the north-west side of Tower Hill, Mr Quilp in *The Old Curiosity Shop* is believed to have had his home, living there with his wife and his mother-in-law, Mrs Jiniwin.

A mile to the west of Tower Hill – two stops on the Underground from Tower Hill to Mansion House, from where there is a walk of 200 yards – is Southwark Bridge. In *Little Dorrit*, this was Amy Dorrit's favourite walk. In that book it was known as the Iron Bridge. The present steel bridge was constructed in the 1920s, replacing an iron structure designed by John Rennie in 1814–19, who also designed the stone London Bridge. On Southwark Bridge Amy turned down the persistent proposal of John Chivery.

If we return to Mansion House station, and head westward along Cheapside, passing St Paul's Cathedral on the left, we see on the right the British Telecom Centre. Most of the constructions around here today replace buildings bombed during the Second World War. The British Telecom Centre appropriately replaces the Post Office. The bombed building had been built to a design of Robert Smirke in 1828, replacing a notorious slum. Smirke's building greatly impressed John Browdie, Nicholas Nickleby's Yorkshire friend. (Dickens took great efforts to reproduce authentically the Yorkshire dialect.)

"Wa-at dost thee ta' yon place to be, noo, that 'un ower the wa'? Ye'd never coom near it, gin ye thried for twelve months. It's na but a Poast-office. Ho, ho! they need to charge for double lathers. A Poast-office! What dost thee think of that? Ecod, if that's on'y a Poast-office, I'd loike to see where the Lord Mayor o' London lives!"

A plaque on the western side of the building records the fact that, in 1896, Gugleilmo Marconi made the first transmission of radio signals here under the patronage of the chief engineer of the General Post Office.

To the north is the Barbican complex that includes the Museum of London. A network of overground walkways includes one called Falcon Highwalk. This is the only echo of Falcon Square where the Falcon Hotel was sited. This hotel was the base of John Jasper in *The Mystery of Edwin Drood* when he came to London from Cloisterham (Rochester).

It is hotel, boarding-house, or lodging-house at its visitor's option … It bashfully, almost apologetically, gives the traveller to understand that it does not expect him, on the good old constitutional plan, to order a pint of sweet blacking for his drinking, and throw it away; but insinuates that he may have his boots blacked instead of his stomach, and may also have bed, breakfast, attendance, and a porter up all night, for a certain fixed charge.

The road going north from Barbican Underground station, heading for the Angel, Islington, is Goswell Street. This was Goswell Road in *The Pickwick Papers* where Mr Pickwick rented rooms with Mrs Bardell. When he looked out of the window, **Goswell-street was at his feet, Goswell-street was on the right hand – as far as the eye could reach, Goswell-street extended on his left, and the opposite side of Goswell-street was over the way.** Today Goswell Road is an undistinguished minor artery. A few houses on the eastern side of the road have survived from the time of Mr Pickwick. Neither then nor now was Goswell Street a particularly fashionable place to live. When at the beginning of the novel Mr Pickwick set off for Rochester, he walked the first mile to St Martin's-le-Grand from where he took a cab to the Golden Cross.

On the western side of Aldersgate, the road called Little Britain leads to Bartholomew Close. Mr Jaggers, in *Great Expectations*, had his offices here, assisted by Mr Wemmick. When Pip arrived here from Kent, he went for a turn in Smithfield, at that time the major meat market of the capital.

... I came into Smithfield; and the shameful place, being all asmear with filth, and fat, and blood, and foam, seemed to stick to me. So, I rubbed it off with all possible speed by turning into a street where I saw the great black dome of Saint Paul's bulging at me from behind a grim stone building which a bystander said was Newgate Prison.

Elsewhere in his journalism Dickens described Smithfield: The ground was covered, nearly ankle-deep, with filth and mire; a thick steam, perpetually rising from the reeking bodies of the cattle, and mingling with the fog, which seemed to rest upon the chimney-pots, hung heavily above. All the pens in the centre of the large area, and as many of the temporary pens as could be crowded into the vacant space, were filled with sheep; tied up to posts by the gutter-side were long lines of beasts and oxen, three or four deep. Countrymen, butchers, drovers, hawkers, boys, thieves, idlers, and vagabonds of every low grade, were mingled together in a dense mass. The whistling of drovers, the barking of dogs, the bellowing and plunging of oxen, the bleating of sheep, the grunting and squeaking of pigs; the cries of hawkers, the shouts, oaths, and quarrelling on all sides; the ringing of bells and the roaring of voices that issued from every public-house; the crowding, pushing, driving, beating, whooping, and yelling; the hideous and discordant din that resounded from every corner of the market; and the unwashed, unshaven, squalid, and dirty figures constantly running to and fro, and bursting in and out of the throng, rendered it a stunning and bewildering scene, which quite confounded the senses.

If we follow the pedestrianised part of Little Britain to the north we come to an open square – actually a circle – West Smithfield. From there we turn left, passing memorial tablets in the wall that commemorate first the Protestant martyrs who died in the reign of Queen Mary I in the 1550s, and then William Wallace, the Scottish leader executed here in 1305. (Film buffs will remember Mel Gibson playing the part of Wallace in the 1995 film, *Braveheart*, and his desperate cry of "Freedom" as he died.) Following Giltspur Street we reach Newgate Street and face the Old Bailey, the Central Criminal Court, which took over the site of Newgate Prison. Newgate marked the western limits of the City of London. In Roman times there had actually been a gateway here.

Dickens wrote about this prison in four novels, *Barnaby Rudge*, *A Tale of Two Cities, Oliver Twist* and *Great Expectations*. A medieval prison was replaced in the 1770s with one designed by the architect, George Dance the Younger (who also designed both the southern front of the Guildhall and the Mansion House). This new prison was, within a few years of its construction, burnt to the ground in the Gordon riots of 1780, as described in *Barnaby Rudge*.

The prison was rebuilt and lasted until 1902, when it was pulled down and replaced by the present building.

From when it was rebuilt in 1783 until 1869 Newgate was the principal prison for serious criminals and was the scene of public executions. Before 1783 prisoners sentenced to death were placed in a cart and transported along Oxford Street to Tyburn, now occupied by Marble Arch, for a public hanging.

In *A Tale of Two Cities* the Old Bailey, which then included Newgate Prison, was the scene of the trial of Charles Darnay. The year is 1775 and Dickens described how the building was **a kind of deadly Inn yard, from which pale travellers set off continually, in carts and coaches, on a violent passage to the other world ... It was famous, too, for the pillory, a wise old institution that inflicted a punishment of which no one could foresee the extent; also for the whipping-post, another dear old institution, very humanising and softening to behold in action.**

Dickens was fascinated by prisons and was a frequent voyeuristic visitor here. He also included visits to prisons and penitentiaries (and morgues) whenever he travelled abroad, in mainland Europe and the United States. He was not a liberal prison reformer and in public presented a "tough" approach to the treatment of criminals. Above all, he argued in an article, "Lying Awake", in *Household Words* in 1852, let us have **no PET PRISONING, vain glorying, strong soup, and roasted meats, but hard work, and one unchanging and uncompromising dietary of bread and water, well or ill.** On the other hand he was able to empathise with prisoners. We remember Fagin in the condemned cell. On the morning of his execution, neighbouring windows **were filled with people, smoking and playing cards to beguile the time; the crowd were pushing, quarrelling and joking.** Meanwhile **the black stage, the cross-beam, the rope, and all the hideous apparatus of death** were ready for the public hanging.

In *Great Expectations*, Pip visits the prison. **We passed through the Lodge, where some fetters were hanging up … It was visiting-time when Wemmick took me in, and a potman was going his rounds with beer, and the prisoners behind bars in yards were buying beer and talking to friends; and a frowsy, ugly, disorderly, depressing scene it was.**

On the northern side of the road is the church of St Sepulchre, just to the west of Giltspur Street. In the southern aisle are the remains of Captain John Smith, an early seventeenth-century Governor of Virginia. There is also a Newgate Bell by a pillar in the southern aisle. This has a grim history. It was a legacy of 1605 that stipulated that whenever there was an execution, the bellman should give the bell twelve solemn double-strokes, outside the cell of the condemned. A poem was to be recited for the condemned man:

> *All you that in the condemned hole do lie,*
> *Prepare you, for tomorrow you shall die.*
> *Watch all, and pray: the hour is drawing near*
> *That you before the Almighty must appear.*
> *Examine well yourselves, in time repent,*
> *That you may not to eternal flames be sent,*

And when St Sepulchre's Bell in the morning tolls,
The Lord may have mercy on your souls.

To the west of St Sepulchre's Church the road used to descend sharply into the valley of the Fleet River. The old road went down to the right along Snow Hill. In the first paragraph of *Bleak House* Dickens imagines that, in the November mud, **it would not be wonderful to meet a Megalosaurus, forty feet long or so, waddling like an elephantine lizard up Holborn Hill**. The improvements of the 1860s when the Holborn Viaduct was built cleared away much slum property and also an old coaching inn, the Saracen's Head. In *Nicholas Nickleby*, this was the London base of Wackford Squeers for conducting business. He was too mean to stay there overnight. **What a vast number of random ideas there must perpetually be floating about regarding the name Snow Hill. The name is such a good one. Snow Hill, Snow – Hill, too, coupled with a Saracen's Head.** On entering the inn yard, **you will see the booking-office on your left, and the tower of St Sepulchre's Church, darting abruptly up into the sky, on your right, and a gallery of bedrooms on both sides.** It was from here that Nicholas Nickleby set off with Squeers and some pupils for Greta Bridge by the Yorkshire coach. And here, in the same novel, John Browdie and his wife, with their bridesmaid, Fanny Squeers, arrived in London. He called it **Sarah's Son's Head.** (Mrs Nickleby called it, inconsequentially, **the Saracen with two necks.**) A police station is on the site of the old inn and a plaque records the memory of its predecessor, and fifty yards further north is an otherwise unmemorable construction with "Saracen's Head Buildings" carved in elegant nineteenth-century relief script.

Snow Hill leads down to Farringdon Road. If we head north for a third of a mile we reach the intersection with Clerkenwell Road. To the right is Clerkenwell Green (and the Marx Memorial Library). It is described in *Oliver Twist* as **an open square in Clerkenwell which is yet called by some strange perversion of terms The Green.**

A quarter of a mile to the north, Pear Tree Court, between Clerkenwell Close and Farringdon Lane, was a narrow court off the Green. Here Dickens located the bookshop where Mr Brownlow was absorbed in browsing through books on a stall outside. Oliver Twist was inveigled by the Artful Dodger and Charlie Bates into picking his pocket.

Pear Tree Court leads into Farringdon Road at the Betsey Trotwood public house, a watering hole that used to be popular with *Guardian* journalists – the offices of that paper were for twenty years across the road. The pub goes back to the 1860s and was built above the first underground railway line in London and was known as The Butcher's Arms until 1983 when it received its present name. Neither the pub nor the area has any connection with the great aunt of David Copperfield.

To the north is Exmouth Market, now a largely pedestrianised area. This used to be on the edge of London's Italian quarter, "Little Italy", and at number 56 a plaque marks the home between 1818 and 1828 of Joseph Grimaldi (1778–1837), the son of an Italian father (one of the first Italian immigrants) and a British mother. Grimaldi developed the art of the clown and introduced the Dame into pantomime. Dickens was a huge fan of Grimaldi and, after his death, edited a rambling manuscript that was the memoirs of "the prince of clowns". Dickens's work was creatively done. The original manuscript is lost but there are unmistakable Dickens touches. Dickens had happy memories of having seen Grimaldi in his prime and cheerfully undertook the work, at the same time as he was editing *Bentley's Miscellany* and writing *Oliver Twist*. But it was a labour of love, and Dickens (aged 25) got his father to help out in the task. Dickens acknowledged Grimaldi's professionalism, **his attention to his duties, and invariable punctuality ... perseverance and exertion.** These were qualities that marked Dickens himself. Grimaldi suffered financially and ended his life as a sad, poverty-stricken alcoholic one mile to the north of Exmouth Market. At Rodney Street in Pentonville the former churchyard of St James's Church is now the Joseph Grimaldi Park.

Dickens was acutely conscious of the need to be careful with money. His father's immurement in a debtor's prison was just one example to avoid. But two of his heroes, Grimaldi and Sir Walter Scott, in spite of their creative genius, also suffered severely from financial problems. Their fate probably encouraged Dickens's own prudence and concern for due rewards for his work. It also explains his passionate support for copyright laws to ensure that writers, not printers and publishers, receive the financial rewards of creative work. On his first visit to the United States in 1842, Dickens loudly complained that America did not recognise international copyright conventions.

On the left of Farringdon Road, just beyond Exmouth Market is Mount Pleasant (Post) Sorting Office. This occupies the site of the House of Correction, formerly Cold Bath Prison, which Dickens also liked to visit.

We cross the route that Oliver Twist traversed on his first visit to London, as described in the novel. Escorted by John Dawkins, they **crossed from the "Angel" Inn into St John's-road; struck down the small street which terminates at Sadler's Wells Theatre; through Exmouth-street and Coppice Row; down the little court by the side of the workhouse; across the classic ground which once bore the name of Hockley-in-the-Hole; thence into Little Saffron-hill, and so into Saffron-hill the Great ... A dirtier or more wretched place he had never seen. The street was narrow and muddy; and the air was impregnated with filthy odours ... Covered ways and yards, which here and there diverged from the main street, disclosed little knots of houses, where drunken men and women were positively wallowing in the filth; and from several of the doorways, great ill-looking fellows were cautiously emerging: bound, to all appearance, on no very well-disposed or harmless errands.**

From Exmouth Street (as Exmouth Market used to be called) they would have turned left, south, crossed Farringdon Road and then right into Baker's Row and then south. Some of the names of streets have changed. The Workhouse has gone, but Little Saffron Hill is Crawford Passage, leading to Herbal Hill that leads to Clerkenwell Road, on the other side of which is Saffron Hill (no longer Great, not very hilly, and no longer growing the saffron that flourished there in the eighteenth century).

Just to the south of Clerkenwell Road and to the right of Saffron Hill is Hatton Wall. On the south of Hatton Wall stood the Metropolitan Police Court where Oliver Twist was taken to face charges of picking the pocket of Mr Brownlow in Pear Tree Court. Oliver **was led beneath a low archway and up a dirty court into this dispensary of summary justice, by the back way. It was a small paved yard into which they turned.** Mr Fang was the presiding magistrate of the court charging Oliver for theft. Fang was based on an Allan Stewart Laing whose notoriously brutal methods of administering justice had been observed by Dickens.

In Saffron Hill nothing survives from the early nineteenth century but the name. We need to overwork our imaginations to understand what it was like in the 1830s, when Fagin had his den in this locality. Acres of slums were demolished with the building of the viaduct in the 1860s – described by Professor Andrew Sanders as London's first flyover. Field Lane, even the name, has been wiped off the face of the earth. It used to link Saffron Hill with Snow Hill. But Dickens caught its character: **In its filthy shops are exposed for sale, huge bunches of second-hand silk handkerchiefs of all sizes and patterns, for here reside the traders who purchase them from the pickpockets.**

The One Tun public house on the corner of Greville Street and Saffron Hill claims to be the original of The Three Cripples, described in *Oliver Twist* as **a low public-house situated in the filthiest part of Little Saffron Hill;**

a dark and gloomy den, where a flaring gas-light burnt all day. Inside the **ceiling was blackened, to prevent its colour from being injured by the flaring lamps; and the place was so full of dense tobacco smoke that at first it was scarcely possible to discern anything more.** The public house was frequented by Sikes, Fagin and Monks. It was where Noah Claypole (alias Mr Morris Bolter), on his arrival in London, met Fagin. Today the One Tun, built in 1875, provides Thai food but disallows customers who might have "dirty boots or soiled clothing".

The Saffron Hill district, the headquarters of Fagin's organised crime in the 1830s, was a century later the area of operations for another organised criminal gang, "the Italian mob", the leaders of whom were the Sabini brothers. Their gang leader, Charles, was known as "Darby" and was possibly the model for Colleoni in *Brighton Rock* by Graham Greene.

Saffron Hill at the southern end emerges on to High Holborn, to the west of the viaduct. The viaduct overshadows St Andrew's Church, built by Sir Christopher Wren, gutted in the Second World War and rebuilt since. When Bill Sikes took Oliver Twist to force an entry into the house at Chertsey, they passed the church **hard upon seven.** Its bells told David Copperfield he was a quarter of an hour late when he was due to call on Agnes Wickfield at the house of Mr Waterbrook in Ely Place.

Bleeding Heart Yard (the name alludes to a deer, a hart, that was wounded) lies parallel to Charterhouse Street and is tucked away behind St Etheldreda's Church. In *Little Dorrit* the Yard was the location of Arthur Clennam's family factory, Messrs Doyce and Clennam, and also the home of Mr and Mrs Plornish in the same novel. Today it is occupied by bistro restaurants and a repair shop for jewellery and watches. The craft of watch repairing was a speciality of the early Italian immigrants and of Clerkenwell to the east. Immediately to the west is Hatton Garden, centre of London's diamond trade.

If we walk down Hatton Garden to Holborn Circus and turn left and left again we find ourselves in Ely Place, a surviving gated street. In Dickens's time there were many such streets, including Doughty Street, his home in the late 1830s. David Copperfield met up with his old school chum, Tommy Traddles, here at a dinner party attended also by Agnes Wickfield and Uriah Heep.

An equestrian statue of a hat-raising Albert, Prince Consort (the husband of Queen Victoria and an admirer of Charles Dickens) is in the centre of Holborn Circus. On the south side, between St Andrew Street and New Fetter Lane, is Thavies Inn House, the residence – at number 13 – of Mrs Jellyby and her disorderly and dysfunctional family, mercilessly portrayed in *Bleak House*. Dickens described the street as a **narrow street of high houses like an oblong cistern to hold the fog.** Esther Summerson and Ada stayed here on their first night in London, and it was in the railings outside the house where the infant Peepy Jellyby caught her head in the railings, perhaps at a site now occupied by Pizza Express.

Remains of Marshalsea prison

From the Bank of England to Trafalgar Square via Southwark and Westminster

The last walk takes us from the City of London through parts of London south of the river, by the prisons associated with Dickens. We are in areas particularly associated with **Little Dorrit.** *We pass by the grave of Dickens in Westminster Abbey.*

THE HEADQUARTERS of the firm of Dombey and Son was close to the Bank of England: a **magnificent neighbour; with its vaults of gold and silver.**

If we walk from the Bank of England south-east along Lombard Street, past Hawksmoor's early eighteenth-century church of St Mary Wolnoth, we come to the church of Edmund King and Martyr on the left. Just past that is George Yard, which opens to a square. On the north-east corner is the George and Vulture Inn. This pub, today an eating and drinking centre for bankers and yuppies, is nearly always crowded. It can trace its history back to the twelfth century, when it was just called The George. Vulture was added later, certainly by the fifteenth century when the poet, John Skelton, wrote about it. The present building dates to the eighteenth century. It provided a base and residence – **good, old-fashioned and comfortable quarters** – for Mr

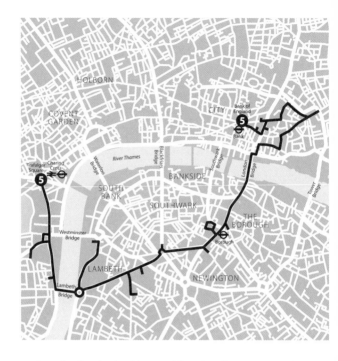

Pickwick after he had been obliged to leave Goswell Street, following the case of Bardell vs Pickwick. The walls of the downstairs rooms are covered with old prints of Dickens novels, and a copy of Maclise's 1839 portrait of Dickens. An upper room is called Mr Pickwick's Room, where descendants of Charles Dickens meet each Christmas. On one of my visits, Fernando, the Colombian-born waiter, pointed out where Prince William, Timothy Dalton and Chris Eubank sat on their visits to the restaurant. But not at the same time.

Dickens's first love, Maria Beadnell, lived with her family at number 2, Lombard Street. Her father was manager of Smith, Payne and Smith's Bank at number 1. And in Lombard Street, the **golden street of the Lombards**, William Dorrit, newly released from the Marshalsea prison, met the speculator, Mr Merdle.

Lombard Street leads to Gracechurch Street. If we turn

left we find on the right Bull's Head Passage which takes us to the site of the Green Dragon Tavern, which, it is believed, was The Blue Boar in *The Pickwick Papers*. Here it was that Sam Weller wrote his Valentine (or **"Walentine"**) to his future wife, the pretty housemaid, Mary.

If we continue north along Gracechurch Street and turn left into Cornhill we come to Newman's Court on the right. In *The Pickwick Papers* Dickens located the offices of the scheming lawyers, Dodson and Fogg, in Freeman's Court, Cornhill. There is a Freeman's Court off Cheapside but not in Cornhill, and it is believed that Dickens had Newman's Court here in mind. There are no entries to offices and most of the building is post-Pickwick, but there is an atmosphere of seedy shabbiness that would be appropriate to the world of Dodson and Fogg.

In *A Christmas Carol* Scrooge's counting house was around Cornhill and on the hill of Cornhill Bob Cratchit went **down into a slide in honour of its being Christmas Eve.**

Doubling back and crossing Gracechurch Street we come into Leadenhall Street. Number 157 was the House of Sol Gills in *Dombey and Son*, where Captain Cuttle was in charge – in Sol Gills's absence – of the ships' instrument makers. Over the door there had been an image of the **Wooden Midshipman; eternally taking observations of the hackney coaches.** A ships' instruments maker occupied these premises almost until the end of the nineteenth century. Today the plate glass offices of Tokio Marine Europe occupy the site.

We reach St Mary Axe Street, named after a church that was pulled down in the sixteenth century. In this street the good Jew, Riah, in *Our Mutual Friend* (created to offset the unfavourable impression left by Oliver Twist's bad Jew, Fagin) had his home and office, **a yellow overhanging plaster-fronted house.** Nothing survives from the nineteenth century. On the right we find one of twenty-first century London's most iconic structures, number 30, the Swiss Re

Building, but known from its shape as the Gherkin, designed by Norman Foster and Arup.

St Mary Axe leads on to Bevis Marks where, at No 10, was the house of Sampson Brass and his sister Sally, who was the more effective, if unofficial, partner in the legal business in *The Old Curiosity Shop*. Here lived their assistant, Dick Swiveller, and also the maid of all work, the Marchioness. Dickens wrote to his biographer, John Forster, describing how he **went to look for a house for Sampson Brass. But I got mingled up in a kind of social paste with the Jews of Houndsditch, and roamed about among them till I came out in Moorfields quite unexpectedly.** The office was **so close upon the footway, that the passenger who rakes the wall brushes the dim glass with his coat sleeve – much to its improvement, for it is very dirty**. Mr Richard, in the same novel, used to frequent the Red Lion inn on the northern side, long since gone.

If we continue south and then swing to the east, we pass Aldgate underground railway station. Just beyond the station on the left we are at the site of Bull Inn Yard, from where coaches set off for East Anglia. Mr Pickwick set off from here for Ipswich, the coachman in charge being Sam Weller's father, Tony. They set off and rattled along the Whitechapel Road **to the admiration of the whole population of that pretty densely-populated quarter.** There is no trace of this inn – no plaque, no surviving name – but, appropriately, on the other side of the road is a bus station with the successors of the coach and horses taking people not to East Anglia but to all parts of London.

Back at the road junction we turn left into Aldgate which leads on to Fenchurch Street. At the junction of that street and Leadenhall Street is the Aldgate Pump, to which Mr Toots in *Dombey and Son* made regular excursions to get away from the happiness of Sol Gills.

Mincing Lane is the fifth road on the left. A building on the left, by Dunster Court, is claimed to be where Messrs Chicksey, Veneering and Stobbles had their druggist stores in *Our Mutual Friend*. R Wilfer, in the same novel, had his office next door.

In 1860, Dickens wrote a piece, later published in *The Uncommercial Traveller*, about churches in the City of London. He wrote about distinctive smells in the churches in this area ... **about Mark-lane, for example, there was a dry whiff of wheat; and I accidentally struck an airy sample of barley out of an aged hassock in one of them. From Rood-lane to Tower-street, and thereabouts, there was often a subtle flavour of wine; sometimes, of tea. One church near Mincing-lane smelt like a druggist's drawer. Behind the Monument the service had a flavour of damaged oranges, which, a little further down towards the river, tempered into herrings, and gradually toned into a cosmopolitan blast of fish.**

Turning right into Great Tower Street we reach its continuation, Eastcheap, off the left of which is Fish Street Hill. Just past the Monument, (which Mrs F's crazy aunt, in *Little Dorrit*, says, quite correctly, **"was put up arter the Great Fire of London"**) we come to the site of King's Head Court, **a small paved yard**, on the south side of which was Mrs Todgers's Commercial Boarding-House, celebrated as the Pecksniff's London base in *Martin Chuzzlewit*.

Right and then left, we are now at London Bridge. On the south-west side of the bridge there used to be a wide flight of steps leading down to the river. These were Nancy's Steps, commemorated in *Oliver Twist*. **The steps ... are on the Surrey bank and on the same side of the bridge as St Saviour's Church. [They] form a landing-stair from the river ... These steps are a part of the bridge; they consist of three flights. Just below the end of the second, going down, the stone wall on the left terminates in an ornamental pilaster facing towards the Thames.** Nancy met Rose Maylie here, betraying Sikes and Fagin. Noah Claypole eavesdropped on the conversation and passed on what he heard to Fagin and Sikes, a betrayal that led to Bill Sikes murdering Nancy.

The bridge at the time *Oliver Twist* was written had only recently been built, replacing others that went back to the early Middle Ages. The then bridge had been designed by Sir John Rennie, and opened by King William IV in August 1831. It was replaced in the 1960s by the present construction. Rennie's bridge was dismantled and re-erected at Lake Havasu City, Arizona. The bridge included what used to be known as Nancy's Steps. Today there is a flight of steps on the west side of the bridge leading down to Tooley Street. These are erroneously known as Nancy's Steps. Indeed until a year ago there was a plaque on the wall stating this, and that Nancy was murdered here. In the 1960 musical, *Oliver!* by Lionel Bart, Nancy is killed here but this is a deviation from *Oliver Twist*.

The first chapter of *Our Mutual Friend* opens with Lizzie Hexam and her father on a boat, floating **on the Thames, between Southwark Bridge, which is of iron, and London Bridge, which is of stone, as an autumn evening was closing in**. Both bridges were designed by John Rennie, but Southwark Bridge was replaced in the early twentieth century. Amy Dorrit was fond of walking over Southwark Bridge, which was then a toll bridge. **"If you go by the Iron Bridge,"** she said, **"there is an escape from the noise of the street."**

We are now on what was known, in Dickens's time, as the Surrey side of the river. The borough of Southwark, at the beginning of the nineteenth century housed no fewer than seven of London's prisons. The borough also had some of the worst slums in all of London.

In this neighbourhood, **in a by-street in Southwark, not far from London Bridge**, but today impossible to identify further because of comprehensive developments, was the home of the mother of Barnaby Rudge. Southwark Cathedral, formerly the parish church of St Saviour's, to the southwest of London Bridge, used to have some almshouses next to its Lady Chapel. In *David Copperfield*, Mell, the usher at Salem House School, used to go and visit his mother in almshouses, described in the novel as by London Bridge. The almshouses were probably demolished with the construction of the railway bridge leading to London Bridge Station in 1849. Dickens used this station on his frequent trips to France. In 1850 the journey took 12 hours. In the early seventeenth century the name of one of the prosperous families of Southwark was Harvard. John Harvard was baptised in this parish church. He later migrated to America and was the founder of Harvard University.

If we walk on along under the railway bridge and past St Thomas's Street and King's Head Yard on the left we come to White Hart Yard. This marks the site of one of several old taverns that lined the eastern side of the road. The inn could trace its history back to 1400. The white hart was the emblem of King Richard II who died in 1399. The inn flourished in the early nineteenth century and the building Dickens knew had been built after a fire in the 1670s. A balustrade of the inn has been preserved and is housed in the Dickens Museum in Doughty Street. Otherwise only the name is left of the inn, described in *The Pickwick Papers* as one of half a dozen old inns having **preserved its external features unchanged, and which has escaped alike the rage for public improvement and the encroachments of private speculation. Great, rambling, queer old places they are, with galleries and passages and staircases, wide enough and antiquated enough to furnish materials for a hundred ghost stories.** It was at the White Hart that Sam Weller was working cleaning the boots of guests when Mr Pickwick recruited him as his personal servant. The sales of the serially produced *The Pickwick Papers* shot up phenomenally, from 400 an issue to 40,000 an issue, once Sam Weller was introduced into the story. That encounter and its literary consequences established Dickens as a best-selling author for the rest of his life. And it was at the White Hart Inn that Mr Alfred Jingle, having eloped with Rachel Wardle, ended up.

The White Hart Inn was demolished in 1889. But there are

traces of other old taverns. The King's Head was destroyed late in the nineteenth century, but a King's Head Yard leads to the New King's Head. The names of the Queen's Head, the Talbot, the Three Tuns and the Tabard can be identified by Yard or plaque. It was from the Tabard that Chaucer's pilgrims set off for Canterbury in 1386. Three taverns are still in operation. The George is still flourishing and, with its balconies overlooking a yard, gives some idea of what the White Hart must have looked like. The others, a little further south, are St Christopher's and the Blue-Eyed Maiden.

Further along the Borough, we come to one of Southwark's public libraries, named after John Harvard. A plaque celebrates the Harvard connection with Southwark. The alley just past the library is Angel Place, a name that recalls another old inn. On the right is an information board and some artwork indicating that this was the site of Marshalsea Prison. (Marshalsea Road opposite is a later misleading denomination; the road was not built until the 1880s.) Here Dickens's father was imprisoned for debt for three months in 1824, when Dickens was 12 years old. A few yards up Angel Place the brick wall on the right is all that is left of the prison. **Whoever goes into Marshalsea Place, turning out of Angel Court, leading to Bermondsey, will find his feet on the very paving-stones of the extinct Marshalsea jail; will see its narrow yard to the right, and to the left, very little altered if at all, except that the walls were lowered when the place got free; will look upon the rooms in which the debtors lived; and will stand among the crowding ghosts of many miserable years.**

While he was in the prison, John Dickens continued to receive his Navy Board salary, and was joined by his family who were free, during the day, to come in and out to see him. There was even a maid who came to look after him. John, a gregarious and social character, was chairman of a committee of prisoners, arranging social events.

When Dickens wrote *David Copperfield* his father was still alive. Wilkins Micawber, it is generally accepted, is partly

based on John Dickens. The high spirits, the financial irre-
sponsibility, the formal way he spoke and wrote, are all traits
copied from his father. But it would have been too painful
for Dickens to have described the humiliating years when his
father was in Marshalsea prison, so Micawber, when he is in
prison, is at the King's Bench prison a quarter of a mile away.
The description of the King's Bench prison is perfunctory.
By the time Dickens wrote *Little Dorrit* his father was dead
and he expanded his descriptions of the Marshalsea prison.

Indeed Little Dorrit is remembered in the area. She was
born in the Marshalsea prison and baptised in St George's
Church, built in the 1730s, just beyond Angel Place. A turnkey
was her godfather. As a little girl, one night Little Dorrit was
too late to get back into the Marshalsea Prison and found
shelter in the church vestry. Later on she was married here to
Arthur Clennam. The east window has a small stained glass
representation of Little Dorrit. Across the road can be found
a Little Dorrit Court leading to a Little Dorrit playground. It
has considerably improved since Dickens described the area:

**... all the busy sounds of traffic resound in it from morn
to midnight, but the streets around are mean and close;
poverty and debauchery lie festering in the crowded alleys,
want and misfortune are pent up in the narrow prison; an
air of gloom and dreariness seems, in my eyes at least, to
hang about the scene, and to impart to it a squalid and
sickly hue.**

If we head off to the south-west of the Borough, the first
road on the right is Lant Street, which used to be one of the
mean and close streets, **a ganglion of roads**, as Dickens
described them. **The majority of the inhabitants** [of Lant
Street] **either direct their energies to the letting of furnished apartments, or devote themselves to the healthful
and invigorating pursuit of mangling.** Half way along on the
left is the Charles Dickens Primary School; it has also taken
over the street, turning it into part of the school playground.
The school is around the site of a house that Dickens occupied

as a boy, while he worked at the blacking factory near Charing Cross and his father was in Marshalsea Prison. Rather than walk back to Camden Town each evening he preferred to find accommodation near his father. **An attic was found for me at the house of an insolvent-court agent, who lived in Lant Street, in the borough ... A bed and bedding were sent over for me, and made up on the floor. The little window had the pleasant prospect of a timber-yard; and when I took possession of my new abode, I thought it was a Paradise.** Just over ten years later, in *The Pickwick Papers*, he has the medical student, Bob Sawyer, living there. It was appropriately near Guy's Hospital. **There is an air of repose about Lant Street, in the borough, which sheds a gentle melancholy upon the soul. A house in Lant Street would not come within the denomination of a first-rate residence, in the strict acceptation of the term; but it is a most desirable spot, nevertheless.** The residents, Dickens said, were **migratory, mostly disappearing on the verge of quarter-day, and generally by night. His Majesty's revenues are seldom collected in this happy valley; the rents are dubious; and the water communication is very frequently cut off.** There are today only two residential houses in the street, but next to the school stands a salubrious block of flats. The other buildings are warehouses or office premises, though there is a pub, the Gladstone Arms, named after that other iconic Victorian figure, the Prime Minister, Mr Gladstone.

The streets in the area were, in Dickens's time, among the poorest and most depressed in the capital. Such districts were where penurious migrants to the rapidly expanding capital settled in vile lodging-houses. Mint Street, parallel to Lant Street, had the reputation of being one of the very worst streets in the 1840s. In the words of John Hollingshead, writing in 1861, *We seem to have left civilisation behind us.* Dickens had a curious fascination with slums and used to take friends to look at them. Peter Ackroyd has suggested it was *something very close to a spectator sport.* In 1842 he brought his American house-guest, Henry Wadsworth Longfellow, to Mint Street. They went with Dickens's friends, the artist Daniel Maclise and his future biographer, John Forster, and had the precaution of a police escort. Maclise found the experience too horrific and was unable to cope with the stench and filth. In 1851 Dickens accompanied one of the early London police detectives, Inspector Field, here. He wrote the experiences up for *Household Words*. The street is **full of low lodging-houses, as you see by the transparent canvas-lamps and blinds, announcing beds for travellers.**

Later in the nineteenth century, these slums were replaced by the Peabody buildings that exist to this day. George Peabody, a wealthy American from Baltimore who settled in London, was appalled by the grim housing and set up the Peabody Trust to provide *improved model dwellings for the respectable working class*. Some of the streets have been named after Dickens's characters – we now have a Weller Street, a Pickwick Street, a Copperfield Street and a Clennam Street.

To the south of Newington Causeway can be found the Inner London Sessions House. To the east of the Sessions House is Harper Road. The gardens behind the Sessions House – containing tennis courts and a play area for young children – mark the site of the Horsemonger Lane Gaol, built in 1791 and demolished 90 years later. The poet, Leigh Hunt (to be satirised as Harold Skimpole in *Bleak House*), was imprisoned here between 1812 and 1814 for libelling the Prince Regent. During his confinement he was visited by other poets, Lord Byron and Thomas Moore. There is no longer a Horsemonger Lane, though the name is preserved in Horsemonger Mews two blocks to the east. The gaol was replaced by these gardens, laid out by the Metropolitan Public Gardens Association and opened to the public in 1884 by Mrs Gladstone, wife of the Prime Minister of the time.

In November 1849 Dickens attended the public execution of a couple called Manning for the murder of one of their friends whose body they then buried under the kitchen floor. (**"I never liked him,"** Dickens quoted Manning as saying, **"and I beat in his skull with the ripping chisel."**) Houses across the road – since demolished – were let out so people could witness the hanging from the balconies. Dickens himself paid ten guineas for a ringside view. He was horrified and wrote a moving account of the execution in a letter to *The Times*. **When the two miserable creatures who attracted all this ghastly sight about them, were turned quivering in the air, there was no more emotion, no more pity, no more thought that two immortal souls had gone to judgment**. His letters were reprinted as handbills. Three years later, in an article in *Household Words*, the memory still haunted him (**... those two forms dangling on the top of the entrance gateway – the man's, a limp, loose suit of clothes as if the man had gone out of them; the woman's, a fine shape, so elaborately corseted and artfully dressed, that it was quite unchanged in its trim appearance as it slowly swung from side to side ...**). The letters and article launched a campaign for the ending of public executions – the last taking place in 1868. Horsemonger Gaol was demolished in 1880 but the grave markers for the Mannings are now in the Cuming Museum in Walworth Road. Mrs Manning is believed to be the model for Hortense, the French maid of Lady Dedlock in *Bleak House*.

Today, diagonally opposite the gardens, is the Baitul Aziz mosque, alongside Dickens Square.

In *Little Dorrit* Mr Chivery kept a tobacconist's shop in Horsemonger Lane, his customers being not only the general public but also prisoners. In the novel it is described as a **rural establishment one storey high, which had the benefit of the air from the yards of Horsemonger Lane Jail, and the advantage of a retired walk under the wall of that pleasant establishment.** His son, John, nursed an unrequited passion for Little Dorrit and sat in the backyard of the house, anticipating his death and composing woeful epitaphs for himself.

The north side of the junction of the Borough and Newington Causeway, just past Stones End Street, is where the King's Bench Prison for debtors used to be. Debtors were permitted to leave the prison and circulate within "the rules" of the prison. The rules was an area, sometimes called a liberty, **adjoining the prison, and comprising some dozen streets in which debtors who could raise money to pay large fees, from which their creditors do *not* derive any benefit, are permitted to reside.** Here Mr Micawber in *David Copperfield* was detained in the prison and arranged to meet David and Tommy Traddles **on the outside of the south wall of that place of incarceration on civil process.** Inside the prison life was relaxed for the institution had all sorts of facilities, including reading rooms, a fives court and up to 30 gin shops.

If we turn west and go along Borough Road we come to St George's Circus. An obelisk stands in the middle of this junction of six roads. Erected in 1771, it records the distances to Fleet Street, Palace Yard Westminster and London Bridge. When David Copperfield was about to walk to Dover to see his aunt, Betsey Trotwood, he arranged for **a long-legged man with a very little empty donkey-cart** to take his possessions wrapped in a box to Dover for sixpence. He handed over the box and never saw it again.

At the beginning of Blackfriars Road and on the left there used to be the Surrey Theatre, where Little Dorrit's sister, Fanny, was a dancer while her uncle, Frederick, played **a clarionet as dirty as himself** in the orchestra. The theatre has been replaced by McLaren House, part of the South Bank University. A small plaque commemorates, not the theatre nor Fanny Dorrit, but the deaths of 11 London firemen who were killed by enemy action while relaying water from the basement of the former theatre, which had been pulled down in 1934 having served as a cinema and a scenery paint shop.

On the opposite side, on Lambeth Road and set in

extensive parkland gardens, is the Imperial War Museum. The museum was founded during the First World War and took over buildings previously occupied by the old Bethlehem Hospital for the mentally afflicted, known as Bedlam. Its history went back to the Middle Ages. Much of the central part of the building, including the impressive dome and six-column portico, was built in 1838–40 to the design of Sydney Smirke. It was still a mental hospital in Dickens's time. In an article he wrote for *All the Year Round* in 1860, he reflected: **Are not the sane and the insane equal at night as the sane lie a dreaming? Are not all of us outside this hospital, who dream more or less in the condition of those inside it, every night of our lives?**

Two blocks to the south of the Imperial War Museum is Walcot Square. On his second proposal to Esther Summerson in *Bleak House* Mr Guppy declared that one of his assets was **"a house in that locality, which, in the opinion of my friends, is a hollow bargain (taxes ridiculous, and use of fixtures included in the rent) … It's a six-roomer, exclusive of kitchens," said Mr Guppy, "and in the opinion of my friends, a commodious tenement."** Walcot Square, built in 1837–39, still survives, and was perhaps a social advance on Mr Guppy's previous lodgings in Pentonville when he made his first offer of marriage.

We head westward to the roundabout before Lambeth Bridge, where we turn right along Lambeth Bridge Road, past the church, now a gardening museum, and past Lambeth Palace, the official residence of the Archbishop of Canterbury. We sweep away from the river with, on the left, St Thomas's Hospital. After that we come to another large roundabout. Left leads us to Westminster Bridge. A Florence Nightingale Museum on the left is roughly on the site of Astley's Theatre, demolished in 1896. It was here that Christoper ("Kit") Nubbles, in *The Old Curiosity Shop*, used to come to a performance once every three months when he had received his quarterly salary. And in *Bleak House* Trooper George came here and was **much delighted with the horses and feats of strength; looks at the weapons with a critical eye; disapproves of the combats, as giving evidence of unskilful swordsmanship; but is touched home by the sentiments.**

If we double back along the Lambeth Bridge Road and cross the Thames by Lambeth Bridge, we come to Millbank. There used to be a large penitentiary facing the river, on the site of which today stands the Tate Gallery. David Copperfield and Mr Peggotty searched the area for the fallen Martha, **near the great blank prison.**

Proceeding north, we come to Dean Stanley Street that takes us to Smith Square. Jenny Wren, the Dolls' Dressmaker in *Our Mutual Friend*, lived in this street, formerly Church Street. Lizzie Hexam also lodged here between the death of her father and her marriage to Eugene Wrayburn. Dickens's view of St John's Church, Smith Square, would not be echoed by many today: **In this region are a certain little street called Church Street, and a certain little blind square called Smith Square, in the centre of which last retreat is a very hideous church, with four towers at the four corners, generally resembling some petrified monster, frightful and gigantic, on its back with its legs in the air.** The crippled Jenny Wren was teased for her disability by children. Her revenge was to push them in the church crypt. **"I'd cram 'em all in, and then I'd lock the door and through the key hole I'd blow in pepper."** The church, built between 1713 and 1728, is today famous for regular concerts and the crypt has been transformed into a restaurant, popular with parliamentarians.

Millbank leads by Abingdon Street to Old Palace Yard, with St Stephen's Tower on the right – part of the buildings of parliament, known as the Palace of Westminster. In *Our Mutual Friend* Julius Handford, alias John Harmon, gave as his address The Exchequer Coffee House, Palace Yard, Westminster.

The present buildings of the Houses of Parliament were

erected after the old buildings were destroyed by fire in 1834. Dickens's father had been a reporter here, transcribing debates for the record. When he was only 20, Dickens was introduced by his father to the same work. Dickens had already taught himself shorthand and immediately became a star reporter, making, as he later put it, **quite a splash**. The Reform Act of 1832 was the first step towards a parliament that was more representative of the people, and the first election after the reform returned a galaxy of parliamentary and intellectual talent: Sir Robert Peel, Lord John Russell, William Cobbett, Daniel O'Connell, Lord Stanley ("the Rupert of Debate"), and of a young generation, Macaulay and Gladstone. But Dickens, strangely, was unimpressed and professed a **hatred of the falseness of talk, of bombastic eloquence**. In 1841 he declined an invitation to stand as a Radical Liberal candidate for Reading – his friend, lawyer, playwright and dedicatee of *The Pickwick Papers*, Sir Thomas Talfourd, was already a Member of Parliament for that borough.

Westminster Hall, the cavernous barn-like structure that dates back to the eleventh century and was spared the fire of 1834, housed law courts from the thirteenth century until 1882. One was the Court of Chancery and it was here in *Bleak House* that the final verdict of the Jarndyce vs Jarndyce case was concluded. Here too Lord George Gordon was tried for High Treason – and acquitted – in *Barnaby Rudge*. Dickens was 21, when his first story, "A Dinner at Poplar Walk", was accepted for publication by *Monthly Magazine*. When he heard the news of his first publication, **I walked down to Westminster-hall, and turned into it for half an hour, because my eyes were so dimmed with joy and pride that they could not bear the street, and were not fit to be seen there.**

To the left lies Westminster Abbey, one of the two major churches of the capital, the other being St Paul's Cathedral. In it rest the bodies of kings and queens, statesmen and soldiers. One area in the south transept is set aside for the graves of artists and writers – Poets' Corner. The first poet to be buried here was Geoffrey Chaucer in 1400 – and the last was an actor, Laurence Olivier. Charles Dickens was buried here near to the dramatist, Robert Brinsley Sheridan, and the actor, David Garrick, on 14 June 1870. Dickens had wanted to be buried in Rochester Cathedral, but the graveyard there was closed for further burials.

Dickens died of a cerebral haemorrhage on Friday, 9 June 1870. On the following Monday, *The Times* thundered that only Westminster Abbey would be fitting to receive a writer of such distinction. Later on the same morning Dean Stanley, after whom Church Street was later renamed and the clergyman in charge of all that went on in the Abbey, had a visit from one of Dickens's sons and his biographer, John Forster. They explained that if Dickens was to be buried in the Abbey, it had to be a modest and private burial early in the morning. So the body was brought by train from Rochester to Charing Cross station on the morning of Wednesday 14 June and three mourning coaches and the hearse came to the Abbey. There was none of what Dickens's old newspaper, *The Daily News*, called *the dismal frippery of the undertaker*. The only attendants were his immediate family, his doctor, his solicitor, and two friends – John Forster and the novelist Wilkie Collins.

It was all over quite early and when later in the morning a journalist asked the Dean about the funeral he replied, "It has already taken place." The grave was left open for the rest of the day, and the spot was visited by thousands of mourners, many of whom strewed flowers over the plain but polished oak coffin. In the following days many thousands also came to pay their respects.

Parliament Street, leading to Whitehall, exits Parliament Square to the north at the north-east corner. In Derby Gate, on the left, is The Red Lion, where Dickens, aged 12, and with money in his pocket, asked the landlord for a drink.

"What is your very best, the VERY *best* – ale a glass?" ... "Twopence," says he.

"Then," says I, "just draw me a glass of that if you please, with a good head to it."

The landlord looked at me, in return over the bar, from head to foot, with a strange smile on his face, and instead of drawing the beer, looked round the screen and said something to his wife, who came out from behind it, with her work in her hand, and joined him in surveying me ... They asked me a good many questions, as to what my name was, how old I was, where I lived, how I was employed, etc., etc. To all of which, that I might commit nobody, I invented appropriate answers. They served me with the ale, though I suspect it was not the strongest on the premises; and the landlord's wife, opening the little half-door and bending down, gave me a kiss that was half-admiring and half-compassionate, but all womanly and good, I am sure.

The story, without a reference to the inn, was replicated in *David Copperfield*.

As we continue along Whitehall we pass the Horse Guards, with two horsemen in nineteenth-century military dress at the gates. We can walk through the Horse Guards to Horse Guards Parade, where the Queen "troops the colour" on her official birthday in June each year. St James's Park lies beyond. On the eastern side, Martin Chuzzlewit arranged to meet Mary Graham just before his departure to the United States. The rendezvous had been orchestrated by Martin's servant, Mark Tapley, who timed it precisely according to the clock on the Horse Guards.

If we pass through Admiralty Arch at the north-east end of The Mall, turn left into Spring Gardens, left again into Cockspur Street, we come to the junction of Pall Mall and Haymarket. On the east side of Haymarket once stood Her Majesty's Theatre. There have been a succession of theatres on the site. In *Nicholas Nickleby* the dastardly Sir Mulberry Hawk, with his acolytes, Pluck and Pyke, brought Mrs

Nickleby to a box here. By prior arrangement, Kate Nickleby was brought to the adjacent box with the Wititterleys. It was a humiliation for Kate.

Trafalgar Square to the north of Whitehall is where this walk ends – and where we started with Walk One.

The First Suburbs

1. Camden Town

The inner Ring Road from Paddington to Islington, made up today of Marylebone Road, Euston Road, Pentonville Road and City Road, was a new road, built by order of an Act of Parliament in 1757, and was known as "The New Road" until 1857. It marked a line on the northern expansion of London, but not for long. Regent's Park was designed during the Napoleonic Wars and urban development crept north of the road during the first half of the nineteenth century. There was a decided class distinction south and north of the line. To the south were the aristocratic estates of Bloomsbury and what later became known as Fitzrovia. Only Clerkenwell was a more plebeian enclosure south of the New Road. To the north, Somers Town was developed on land owned by Lord Somers between what is now Euston and King's Cross. Further north, Camden Town grew up on land owned by Lord Camden. Somers Town and Camden Town – and Pentonville to the east – were residential areas for the burgeoning lower middle class that worked in the cities of Westminster and London.

These were districts of uncertain and changing social composition. Somers Town in the early part of the nineteenth century became a home for French and Spanish migrants. Terraced houses were smaller as you went north. Most people walked to their work, two, three or four miles each day. Public transport was limited and expensive, and only expanded and became cheaper after the middle of the century. Just as Dickens himself used to walk from Camden Town to Hungerford Stairs each morning, so Bob Cratchit in *A Christmas Carol* went from Camden Town to the City. During the rush hours of mornings and evenings the streets would have been thronged with pedestrians.

Camden Town was still semi-rural when the Dickens family moved into Bayham Street in 1823 from Chatham. A Veterinary College was founded in Camden Town in 1791 to improve animal husbandry. It specialised in dealing with cavalry horses during the Napoleonic Wars. The College still exists on Royal College Street and is now part of the University of London. North of Camden Town were the wooded uplands of Hampstead and Highgate.

In his childhood and early teens Charles Dickens had several homes in this area, thanks to the unstable nature of his family's finances. In 1823 the Dickens family lived at number 16 (later numbered 141) Bayham Street for a year. It was **a small mean tenement, with a wretched little back-garden abutting on a squalid court**. Demolished before the First World War, it had been built in about 1812 and was rented for £22 a year. The house had four rooms, a basement and a **little back-garret**, all quite cramped for the Dickens family that in 1823 included six children. The window frame from the little back-garret room that Charles Dickens occupied has been salvaged and can be seen at the Dickens Museum in Doughty Street. In his room Dickens had a toy theatre that he had brought from Chatham. There was a meadow at the back – **frowzy fields, and cow-houses, and dung-hills, and dust-heaps, and ditches, and gardens, and summer-houses, and carpet-beating grounds**. On arrival Dickens, aged 11, did not go to school. **I degenerated into cleaning his boots of a morning, and my own; and making myself useful in the work of that little house; and looking after my younger brothers and sisters; and going on such poor errands as arose out of our poor way of living**. A plaque marks the site of the house on the north-eastern part of the road.

Tommy Traddles in *David Copperfield* lived in this area **in a little street near the Veterinary College at Camden Town, which was principally tenanted, as one of the clerks who lived in that direction informed me, by gentlemen students, who bought live donkeys and made experiments on those quadrupeds in their private apartments ... The inhabitants appeared to have a propensity to throw any little trifles they were not in want of, into the road: which not only made it rank and sloppy, but untidy too, on account of the cabbage leaves. The refuse was not wholly vegetable either, for I myself saw a shoe, a doubled-up saucepan, a black bonnet, and an umbrella, in various stages of decomposition, as I was looking for the number I wanted.**

Bayham Street today has a few terraced houses that date from Dickens's time. A building to the south of Dickens's old home houses the main office of the Variety Club of Great Britain. This would have pleased Dickens. The Variety Club started in Pittsburgh, Pennsylvania, as a charity for sick, disabled or disadvantaged children, and is promoted by show business personalities. The British branch was launched in 1949. Their most visible activity is the fleet of Sunshine Coaches that take children and their families on outings to places of amusement and interest.

As a boy Dickens wandered all over the area, observing everything. His real world was circumscribed by poverty, humiliation, his father's debts and his own demeaning work in the blacking factory. His imaginative world, however, was stimulated by the realm of marginal London; newly arrived migrants from the countryside who lived on their wits and provided basic services – food, drink, clothes – to others also living on the margin. His observations were stored up to be recycled in his mature fiction.

Although the Bayham Road house was his main home in

the area, his family moved around and rented accommodation south of the New Road in Gower Street, and in Somers Town. Other temporary homes were in Johnson Street (now Cranleigh Street) off Eversholt Street – **a charming little villa** – and in the Polygon, an arrangement of houses in the form of a circle within Clarendon Square. On Seymour Street (now Eversholt Street) stands St Mary's Church, known as Somers Chapel in the early nineteenth century, which Dickens occasionally attended. Johnson Street was then at the northern fringe of Somers Town and was separated from Camden Town by fields. In *Bleak House* Harold Skimpole had a dysfunctional family home in the Polygon. The older pattern of roads here has disappeared and only Polygon Road survives as a reminder. In Somers Town, Dickens noted, **there was at that time a number of poor Spanish refugees walking about in cloaks, smoking little paper cigars.** While his father was in the Marshalsea with the rest of his family, the young Charles was a lodger in Little College Street, a few roads to the east of Bayham Street with **a reduced old lady**, Mrs Roylance, who became a model for Mrs Pipchin in *Dombey and Son*.

After a legacy allowed John Dickens to pay off his debts and obtain release from the Marshalsea Prison Charles was able to leave work at the blacking factory and – joy of joys! – attend school. The school chosen was Wellington House Academy in Hampstead Road, at the junction of Granby Street (now Terrace) and Hampstead Road. The whole configuration of streets, as well as many of their names, has changed since the 1820s. No trace of the school exists today. (But just north of Granby Terrace at 263 Hampstead Road, on the wall of a faded house that has seen better days, a plaque tells us that this was once the home of George Cruikshank (1792–1878), who did illustrations for *Sketches by Boz* and *Oliver Twist*.) Dickens used the school as a model for Salem House in *David Copperfield*. It was his only secondary schooling and he left when he was 15. Education does not seem to have been taken very seriously. The pupils kept many pets. **Red-polls, linnets, and even canaries were kept in desks, drawers, hat-boxes and other strange refuges for birds; but white mice were the favourite stock. The boys trained the white mice much better than the masters trained the boys.**

In the 20 years after Dickens's schooldays in Hampstead Road the whole area was totally transformed, physically and socially, by the building of the railways from two termini – Euston and King's Cross. Two railway lines were built by two different railway companies, the London and Birmingham (from 1846 the London and North Western) and the Midland, to the Midlands and the north of England. There were geographical problems in driving the railway lines north. Already the areas immediately north of the two stations were being built up, and it would have been too expensive to buy the land and compensate the people who lived there. Anyway the hills of Hampstead and Highgate were in the way. Tunnels were very expensive and had to be avoided if possible. So the lines swing off to the west. Poorer (and, for the railway companies, cheaper) quarters were cleared and only one major tunnel, under Primrose Hill, was built.

In *Dombey and Son* Paul Dombey's nanny, Mrs Toodle, lived at Staggs's Gardens, Camden Town – or **Camberling Town** as the inhabitants called it. Staggs's Gardens cannot be located. It or its inspiration has probably been swept away with the railway developments. It was still semi-rural in the novel. Staggs's Gardens **was a little row of houses with squalid patches of ground before them, fenced off with old doors, barrel staves, scraps of tarpaulin, and dead bushes; with bottomless tin kettles, and exhausted iron fenders, thrust into the gaps. Here the Staggs's Gardeners trained scarlet beans, kept fowls and rabbits, erected rotten summer-houses, dried clothes, and smoked pipes.**

Mrs Toodle's husband worked for the railways and his language is full of railway imagery. He was constructing Primrose Hill tunnel, a thousand-metre tunnel between Chalk Farm and Swiss Cottage. In *Dombey and Son* Dickens has an apocalyptic description of the changes to the physical environment.

The first shock of a great earthquake had, just at that period, rent the whole neighbourhood to its centre. Traces of its course were visible on every side. Houses were knocked down, streets broken through and stopped, deep pits and trenches dug in the ground, enormous heaps of earth and clay thrown up, buildings that were undermined and shaken propped up with great beams of wood. Here a chaos of carts, overthrown and jumbled together, lay topsy-turvy at the bottom of a steep, unnatural hill; there, confused treasures of iron soaked and rusted in something that had accidentally become a pond. Everywhere were bridges that led nowhere, thoroughfares that were wholly impassable ... There were a hundred thousand shapes and substances of incompleteness wildly mingled out of their places, upside down, burrowing in the earth, aspiring in the air, mouldering in water, and unintelligible as any dream.

The railway, or **railroad**, as Dickens called it, is invisible today. It is in a deep trench alongside Hampstead Road with walls too high to see passing trains. Even passengers on those trains travelling north are unable to appreciate the magnificent entry into the Primrose Hill tunnel, designed in 1837 by Robert Stephenson.

2. Chelsea

In the 1830s Chelsea was a fishing village on the River Thames with its own identity separate from London. In the previous century it had been a dangerous place. In *Barnaby Rudge*, **few would venture ... to Chelsea, unarmed and unattended.**

During the eighteenth century some smart houses were being built in the orchards to the north of the river. In 1838, in a letter to Leigh Hunt, Dickens could describe Chelsea as **in the country**. In the 1820s and 1830s it became a place that attracted artists and writers, people who wanted some detachment from the social whirl of the metropolis. Dickens located two of his secondary characters in Chelsea – Mr Bayham Badger, cousin of Mr Kenge, in *Bleak House*, and Miss Sophie Wackles, object of Dick Swiveller's passion, in *The Old Curiosity Shop*.

St Luke's Church was built in 1818–20 in an unselfconscious Gothic Revival style. Light and spacious, it catered for the smart new bourgeoisie who distanced themselves from the river folk around Chelsea Old Church. The first rector of St Luke's was a brother of the Duke of Wellington. The rector in 1836 was Charles Kingsley, namesake and father of the novelist. The Old Church, where Sir (St) Thomas More is buried, was bombed in the Second World War and has been largely rebuilt, and so is not "older" than St Luke's. Henry James, the American-born novelist, died in Chelsea. His funeral was held at the Old Church in 1916. The cremation was at Golders Green and the ashes taken to Cambridge, Massachusetts. There is a memorial to James in the Old Church churchyard.

The family of Dickens's wife, Catherine Hogarth, lived at 18 York Place, to the south of Fulham Road. Her father, George, was Scottish and had known Sir Walter Scott. He had come to London in 1834 as the music and drama critic of the *Morning Chronicle*, thereby becoming a colleague of Dickens. Hogarth and Dickens got on well together – then. Dickens was invited to the house where he met Catherine, one of several daughters, and fell in love. He was a regular visitor. He was always a practical joker. On one occasion, he himself recalled, **a young man dressed as a sailor jumped in at the window, danced a hornpipe, whistling the tune, jumped out again, and a few minutes later Charles Dickens** walked gravely in at the door, as if nothing had happened, shook hands all round, and then, at the sight of their puzzled faces, burst into a roar of laughter. York Place has disappeared and the Royal Brompton Hospital occupies its site. Dickens's engagement lasted a year, and to be nearer his fiancée he rented 11 Selwood Terrace nearby for several months, a house in a recently built terrace, that was then surrounded by open country. (There is no plaque on the house; nor is there one on number 9, where DH Lawrence lodged before his marriage in 1914.) Dickens's finances were being stretched for he was also paying rent on the flat in Furnival's Inn, Holborn.

Charles Dickens and Catherine Hogarth were married at St Luke's Church on 2 April 1836. Apart from members of the Hogarth and Dickens families, the only others present were the best man, Thomas Beard, another parliamentary reporter and fellow-journalist, and John Macrone, a publisher who had bought the copyright of *Sketches by Boz*. Dickens's financial situation was about to be changed dramatically, for the first number of *The Pickwick Papers* had appeared just two days before. The reception was at York Place, then facing orchards and market gardens. The couple went off to Chalk, near Rochester in Kent, for their honeymoon.

Dickens walked all over London and in 1861 walked through Chelsea by the river. He set out from the offices of *All the Year Round* in Wellington Street North. The day was so beautifully bright and warm that I thought I would walk on by Millbank, to see the river. I walked straight on for three miles on a splendid broad esplanade overhanging the Thames, with immense factories, railway works, and whatnot erected on it, and with the strangest beginnings and ends of wealthy streets pushing themselves into the very Thames. When I was a rower on that river, it was all broken ground and ditch, with here and there a public-house or two, an old mill, and a tall chimney. I had never seen it in any state of transition, though I suppose myself to know this rather large city as well as anyone in it.

Half a mile to the south of St Luke's Church is Upper Cheyne Row. On the north side at number 22 lived Leigh Hunt, the gifted, feckless dilettante. Dickens portrayed him as the gifted, feckless dilettante Harold Skimpole in *Bleak House*. Leigh Hunt did not recognise himself at first and when he did find out he was deeply upset.

Between Upper Cheyne Row and the river is Cheyne Row where, at number 24, the National Trust owns Carlyle's House, built in 1703. The Carlyles had known Leigh Hunt and visited him here in Chelsea. In Carlyle's view, Chelsea was *unfashionable; it was once the resort of the Court and great, however; hence numerous old houses in it, at once cheap and excellent*. He saw the house in Cheyne Row, liked it and leased it at a rent of £35 a year. The Carlyles stayed there for the rest of their lives. Thomas Carlyle died here in 1881.

Carlyle was 17 years older than Dickens who hero-worshipped him: **I would go at all times farther to see Carlyle than any man alive.** Dickens wrote to one of his sons that Carlyle was **the man who had influenced** him **most.** Carlyle had a respect and affection for the younger man, though he was suspicious of what he called "fiction-eering". Carlyle was one of the select handful who came to listen to Dickens reading *The Chimes* in 1844 at John Forster's house in Lincoln's Inn Fields. Both men professed a tough radical humanitarianism. (In both men the toughness could manifest itself in a brutal racism.) Each developed a literary style of his own, a style that was creatively journalistic rather than traditionally literary. Both were outsiders, and Dickens owed much to Carlyle's *French Revolution* in his writing of *A Tale of Two Cities*. Indeed Carlyle helped him with the writing of the book and used to lend him a "cartload" of books from the London Library. Dickens was a frequent visitor to Carlyle's house in Cheyne Row but there was never the reciprocal entertainment on the scale that Dickens hosted in his successive London homes. Carlyle was not, as his wife Jane was, an extrovert. Nor was the house suitable for entertaining. In 1852 the Carlyles did extend one room on the first floor when the attic was adapted for use as Carlyle's study.

Mrs Carlyle died in 1866 and when Dickens died four years later, Carlyle was heartbroken: *No death since 1866 had fallen on me with such a stroke ... The good, the gentle ... noble Dickens – every inch of him an honest man.*

The Chelsea Embankment was built in the 1870s. Gardens and a road flank the river, and a statue of a seated and brooding Carlyle looks over it. A few yards to the right is a statue of Sir Thomas More.

3. Greenwich

Greenwich was a separate town in the early nineteenth century, with a history of royal patronage and associations with the Royal Navy. In the early 1830s it had a population of about 25,000. Originally a fishing village, it became a favoured royal residence from the fifteenth century. Two of England's best-known monarchs, King Henry VIII and Queen Elizabeth I, were born here. The former married two of his wives in Greenwich. King Henry VIII is also popularly seen as the founder of the Royal Navy and until the nineteenth century ships were built at nearby Woolwich and Deptford. King Charles II laid out Greenwich Park in the 1660s and, patron of scientific learning that he was, established the Royal Observatory there, through which the meridian line passes.

The town near the river and the pier is dominated by the royally sponsored buildings, Greenwich Hospital, the Royal Naval College and the Queen's House, designed in the early seventeenth century by Inigo Jones.

Dickens, born at Portsmouth and reared in Chatham, two

other towns associated with the Royal Navy, felt at home in Greenwich. The vernacular architecture – the smart terraced housing built for navy personnel – would remind him of the other two towns.

The best approach to Greenwich from London is not by the railway (first built in the 1830s, making the town the earliest of the commuter suburbs), nor by the congested roads. Not even by the Docklands Light railway that disgorges passengers near the *Cutty Sark*, the last of the tea clippers that sailed to the Far East in the nineteenth century. The best approach is by river. Boats regularly ply from Westminster Pier and call at Tower Pier. It is possible to see parts of London associated with Dickens's novels – the Temple, Southwark, the area of Jacob's Island, the Grapes Tavern at Limehouse – in a way that would have been more familiar to Dickens and his contemporaries.

Greenwich was a favourite place for holiday excursions for Londoners. From the eighteenth century a regular Greenwich Fair was held in the park which lasted three days in May. It became a riotous event. Roads from London, as well as the river, were crowded with traffic.

In 1835, two years before the railway arrived, the 23 year-old Dickens wrote a report on his journey to the Fair. It became one of the *Sketches by Boz*: **We cannot conscientiously deny the charge of having once made the passage in a spring van accompanied by thirteen gentlemen, fourteen ladies, an unlimited number of children, and a barrel of beer; and we have a vague recollection of having, in later days, found ourself the eighth outside, on the top of a hackney coach, at something past four o' clock in the morning, with a rather confused idea of our own name, or place of residence. We have grown older since then, and quiet, and steady.** (His style of reportage matured too.)

Dickens loved it all. He noted people playing "Kiss in the Ring" and "Threading my Grandmother's Needle". But **the principal amusement is to drag young ladies up the** steep hill which leads to the observatory, and then drag them down again, at the very top of their speed, greatly to the derangement of their curls and bonnet-caps, and much to the edification of lookers-on from below. The fair was a periodical breaking out, we suppose; a sort of rash; a three days' fever which cools the blood for six months after. But the Regency riotousness also attracted righteous preachers who denounced the licentiousness of the fair. The citizens of Greenwich too were not keen on this annual invasion and campaigned to have it stopped. Nathaniel Hawthorne in the 1850s found the Fair *little more than a confusion of unwashed and shabbily dressed people ... The common people of England*, he went on to observe prissily, *have no daily familiarity with even so necessary a thing as a washbowl, not to mention a bathing-tub.* Cleanliness and godliness finally triumphed and the last Fair was held in 1857.

Greenwich became celebrated also for its riverside taverns that provided whitebait allegedly from the Thames. Dickens himself used to patronise The Ship, which was bombed in the Second World War. Its site is now occupied by the *Cutty Sark*. A party for Dickens was hosted here on his return from America in 1842, and another when *Martin Chuzzlewit* was published. In his last novel, *Our Mutual Friend*, Bella Wilfer and her father have dinner at The Ship, overlooking the river ... looking at the ships and steamboats. She later was married to John Rokesmith at the Greenwich Parish Church of St Alfege. The church has a history going back a thousand years, but the present building was designed by Nicholas Hawksmoor, also responsible for St Anne's Limehouse, St George's-in-the-East Shadwell and the western towers of Westminster Abbey. The church porch, having swallowed up Bella Wilfer for ever and ever, had it not in its power to relinquish that young woman but slid into the happy sunlight Mrs John Rokesmith instead. The newlyweds went on to have dinner at The Ship. The marriage dinner was the crowning success, for what had bride and bridegroom plotted to do, but to have and hold that dinner in the very room of the hotel where Pa and the lovely woman had dined together! ... And the dishes being seasoned with Bliss – an article which they are sometimes out of at Greenwich – were of perfect flavour, and the golden drinks had been bottled in the golden age and hoarding up their sparkles ever since.

Only one of the famous Greenwich riverside taverns has survived. The Trafalgar Tavern to the east of Greenwich Hospital is crowded and still serves whitebait. There is a classless buzz about the place, reminding one of a popular seaside resort. You have the benefit of piped music and on Wednesday nights there is "an evening of acoustic music, featuring musicians from Greenwich and beyond", perhaps the twenty-first century equivalent of the Greenwich Fair.

Mr and Mrs Rokesmith took **a modest little cottage, but bright and fresh** at Blackheath. Blackheath is above Greenwich, and was on the old road to Rochester and Canterbury, **at the end of the long vista of gnarled old trees in Greenwich Park**. In *David Copperfield* Salem House, the school attended by David, Traddles and Steerforth and headed by Mr Creakle, was **down by Blackheath**. David, on his walk from London to Dover, sleeps rough for a night behind the school, **in a corner where there used to be a haystack. I imagined that it would be a kind of company to have the boys, and the bedroom where I used to tell the stories, so near to me.**

Beyond Blackheath to the east, is Shooter's Hill, the location for the opening chapter of *A Tale of Two Cities*, when the Dover mail coach is stopped. The area was notorious for its highwaymen and when Jerry Cruncher stopped the coach, passengers and crew were much alarmed. And Shooter's Hill is where Tony Weller finally retires in *The Pickwick Papers*, taking a public house, **where he is quite reverenced as an oracle.**

4. Hampstead

The uplands of Hampstead and Highgate have retained the role that they have had for centuries. Near enough to the capital for convenience, far enough away to enjoy the open country. Hampstead, swathed and protected by the Heath, can still kid itself that it is a "village". It has always attracted residents who were artistically inclined or politically radical. It was the home of the Labour Party leaders, Hugh Gaitskell and Michael Foot.

Hampstead was important for Dickens. After the traumatic death of his sister-in-law, Mary Hogarth, in 1837, while he was writing simultaneously *The Pickwick Papers* and *Oliver Twist*, he retreated to a Hampstead farmhouse, Wyldes Farm. This is located just off Hampstead Way. The farmer used to occupy a converted barn and to let out the farmhouse – often to artists and writers. But Dickens did not acquire that familiarity with the place and people which he had with the parts of London nearer the centre. Hampstead was a place of retreat and recreation. It was a favourite resort for Dickens, who would persuade friends to ride a horse out there energetically to the public house, Jack Straw's Castle. **I knows a good 'ouse there**, he wrote to John Forster, **when we can have a red-hot chop for dinner and a glass of wine**.

Washington Irving commemorated the same inn in his *Tales of a Traveller*, and Thackeray and the painter, Lord Leighton, were later regulars. Jack Straw's Castle has had its present name only for two centuries, before when it was known just as "the castle". The fourteenth-century leader of the Peasants' Revolt is alleged to have sought refuge in the area. Jack Straw's Castle is no longer a pub, but a "personal training club", whatever that means. The present building is of no great antiquity. It was destroyed in the Second World War and rebuilt in the 1960s in what has been described as Georgian Gothic. In the nineteenth century John Sadleir, a financier and swindler, committed suicide behind Jack

Straw's Castle. The **immensely rich** Mr Merdle MP in *Little Dorrit* was based on Sadleir.

A mile to the east, also on the edge of the Heath, is Spaniard's Inn, an eighteenth-century construction. It is still a pub. In the eighteenth century some of the Gordon Rioters were detained there, diverted from the sacking of Kenwood (then Caen Wood), the home of the liberal lawyer, Lord Mansfield, as described in *Barnaby Rudge*. And in *The Pickwick Papers* Mrs Bardell had tea here with her son and some friends before being lured into custody by an employee of the solicitors, Dodson and Fogg, to be detained at the Fleet prison.

Hampstead features in several of Dickens's other novels; David Copperfield used to stride out to Hampstead and Dick Swiveller in *The Old Curiosity Shop* had a cottage there **which had in the garden a smoking-box, the envy of the civilised world**. Bill Sikes, after the murder of Nancy in *Oliver Twist* wanders around Hampstead Heath near Kenwood. Like Dick Whittington four centuries earlier, he went to Highgate and turned back but, **unsteady of purpose and uncertain where to go, struck off to the right again almost as soon as he began to descend it, and taking the footpath across the fields that skirted Caen Wood, and so came out on Hampstead Heath. Traversing the hollow by the Vale of Health, he mounted the opposite bank, and crossing the road which joins the villages of Hampstead and Highgate, made along the remaining portion of the Heath to the fields at North End**. He continued to wander – to Hendon and Hatfield before he returned to central London and his eventual death in Bermondsey.

5. Highgate

Highgate has many of the qualities of Hampstead and with, if anything, more literary associations. Dickens lived here briefly in 1832 at 92 North Road – a plaque is on the wall. In the same road the poet AE Housman (1859–1936) had a house and the former Poet Laureate, John Betjeman (1906–84), went to school here. The parish church of St Michael was being built while Dickens was in North Road. There had been no parish church until then, and the chapel at Highgate School was used for Anglican worship. Opposite the church at 3 The Grove is a house with two plaques noting earlier literary occupiers – Samuel Taylor Coleridge (1772–1834), author of *The Ancient Mariner* and the twentieth century novelist, journalist and broadcaster, JB Priestley (1894–1984).

St Michael's Church looks down on the extensive Highgate Cemetery on both sides of Swain's Lane. The eastern cemetery hosts the graves of Karl Marx and Dickens's novelist contemporary, George Eliot. The more extensive western cemetery has the graves of Dickens's parents, Elizabeth and John Dickens. He wrote the epitaph for his father, describing him as a **zealous, useful, cheerful spirit**. Also buried in the family grave is his daughter, Dora, darkly named after the wife of David Copperfield – he was writing this novel at the time of her birth. The real Dora died as an infant the following year.

Between St Michael's Church and the Highgate Literary and Scientific Institution is Church House, 10 South Grove. This is reckoned to be the home of David Copperfield's overbearing and amoral school friend, James Steerforth. In the same novel, Dr Strong, the old Canterbury teacher and scholar, retired with his daughter, Annie, to Highgate – precise location unknown – and David and Dora had their marital home next door, accommodating also Betsey Trotwood and Mr Dick.

As with Hampstead, Dickens never *internalised* Highgate. It is a retreat from the city for his characters, outsiders who settle there. Similarly it is a place of transit for other characters. Noah Claypole and Charlotte in *Oliver Twist* pass under Highgate Archway on their way to the city of London. It is at the Archway that Inspector Bucket picks up the trail of the fugitive Lady Dedlock in *Bleak House*, and in *Barnaby Rudge* Joe Willett, after saying farewell to Dolly Varden, wanders up to Highgate to meditate **but there were no voices in the bells to bid him turn.**

6. Limehouse

Until the nineteenth century, the "East End" of London (immediately north of the river Thames and to the east of the Tower of London) consisted of a string of villages – Wapping, Shadwell, Limehouse and Ratcliffe – surrounded by marshy land and market gardens. There was a tradition of sea-faring and boat-building among the village menfolk going back to the early sixteenth century. It became an area of migration from overseas in the nineteenth century. In the first decade of the century the East and West India Docks were built and a private company constructed the Commercial Road to facilitate the bringing of goods from the new docks to central London. These were followed in the next half century with a chain of docks, along with vast warehouses and offices. All were contained behind grim brick walls. One of the last, the Royal Victoria Dock, begun in 1850, covered 94 acres of water and was then the largest such dock in the world. North and south of the river there are swing bridges on canals that lead from the river to the docks. **Captain Cuttle,** in *Dombey and Son*, lived at Limehouse **on the brink of a little canal near the India Docks, where there was a swivel bridge which opened now and then to let in some wandering monster of a ship come roaming up the street like a stranded leviathan.**

The east end of the city, around Bevis Marks synagogue, was already a Jewish (mainly Sephardic) quarter. From 1850 and increasingly after the 1870s, Jews, mostly Ashkenazi, migrated here from central and eastern Europe, creating the

Jewish East End. During the nineteenth century communities of Chinese and of Lascars, a generic term for sailors from the lands bordering the Indian Ocean, settled here. And during the same period the villages were absorbed into the expanding urbanisation of London. In the last hundred years it became peopled by later immigrants. Today Bengali has replaced Yiddish as the language of the streets and the Chinese commercial contribution has been take-away restaurants rather than opium dens. But an aroma of curry pervades Cable Street, which marks a social and ethnic frontier. To the north is international Limehouse. To the south, as far as the River Thames, is another world. Warehouses have been converted into flats and offices. This is a world of global capitalism, an extension of Wapping and Canary Wharf.

Dickens, with a father who worked for the Naval Pay Board, Portsmouth as a birthplace and happy childhood memories of Chatham, had a particular affection for sailors and people connected with the sea. Though some may be eccentric, none of his villainous characters is associated with seafaring. In his childhood he called on his godfather, Christopher Huffam, a ship's chandler, who lived at Church Row, now Newell Street, perhaps in one of the handful of eighteenth-century terraced houses that run south-west of the splendid early eighteenth-century church of St Anne, designed by Nicholas Hawksmoor. These are all that are left to suggest even to the most sensitive social archaeologist that here was once a village centre.

Dickens's visits to Limehouse may have been recreated in *Dombey and Son*, when Walter Gay went to see Captain Cuttle in Limehouse past **slopsellers' shops ... anchor and chain-cable forges ... rows of houses, with little vane-surmounted masts uprearing themselves from among the scarlet beans. Then, ditches. Then, pollarded willows. Then, more ditches ... Then, the air was perfumed with chips, and all other trades were swallowed up in mast, oar,**

and block making, and boat building. Captain Cuttle may have been modelled on Christopher Huffam.

Lizzie Hexham in *Our Mutual Friend* lived in Limehouse. **The low building had the look of having once been a mill. There was a rotten wart of wood upon its forehead that seemed to indicate where the sails had been.**

If we continue south along Newell Street and turn right into Three Colt Street we reach the eastern end of Narrow Street. All around sanitised warehouses and former wharves have been converted into marinas. On the left at number 76, opposite Ropemakers Fields, is the Grapes Public House, generally accepted as the original for the Six Jolly Fellowship Porters tavern in *Our Mutual Friend*. Dickens described it as being **like a handle of a flat iron set upright on its broadest end.** (This was an image Dickens also used to describe his old school in Hampstead Road.) **It had long settled down into a state of hale infirmity. In its whole constitution it had not a straight floor, and hardly a straight line; but it had outlasted, and clearly would yet outlast, many a better-trimmed building, many a sprucer public-house. Externally it was a narrow, lopsided wooden jumble of corpulent windows heaped one upon another as you might heap as many toppling oranges, with a crazy wooden verandah impending over the water; indeed, the whole house, inclusive of the complaining flag-staff on the roof, impended over the water, but seemed to have got into the condition of a faint-hearted diver who has passed so long on the brink that he will never go in at all.** Today the pub is recognisable from Dickens's description. Framed pictures of Bill Sikes and Mr Pickwick – neither of whom had connections with the Six Jolly Fellowship Porters – adorn the walls, and peppermint and camomile tea is available in the bar. A pricey restaurant is upstairs, specialising in fish described – what a relief! – as fresh, but booking is recommended. The pub is best seen from the river.

One mile to the west, south-east of Shadwell station, are

the Blue Gate Fields schools. In the 1860s one of the most celebrated Chinese opium dens was located here, described as "a model of respectability" even though it was surrounded by brothels. In the company of his American friends, James T and Annie Adam Fields, Dickens visited an opium den here. He used the experience in the opening chapter of *The Mystery of Edwin Drood*.

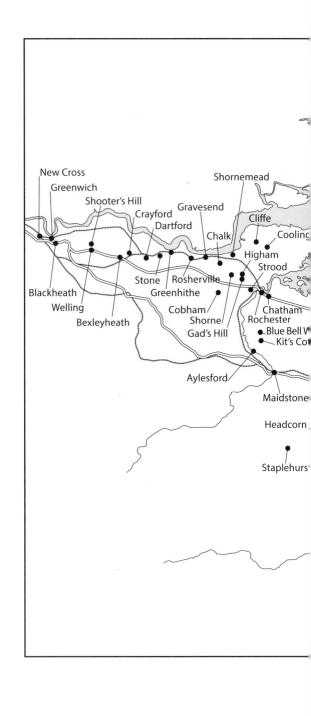

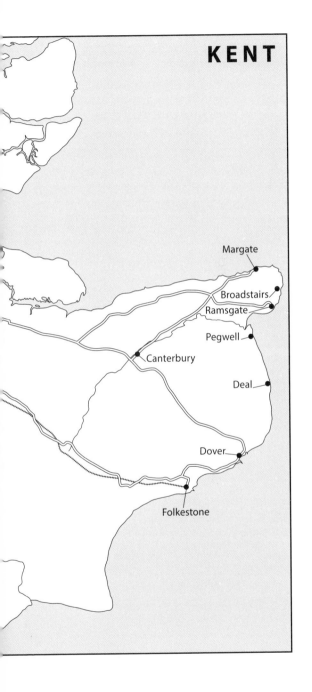

KENT

Margate

Broadstairs

Ramsgate

Pegwell

Canterbury

Deal

Dover

Folkestone

London into Kent

MY LAST SPECIAL FEAT was turning out of bed at two, after a hard day, pedestrian and otherwise, and walking thirty miles into the country to breakfast. The road was so lonely in the night that I fell asleep to the monotonous sound of my own feet, doing their regular four miles an hour. Mile after mile I walked, without the slightest sense of exertion, dozing heavily and dreaming constantly. It was only when I made a stumble like a drunken man, or struck out into the road to avoid a horseman close upon me on the path – who had no existence – that I came to myself and looked about.

Thus wrote Charles Dickens, in an 1860 article "Shy Neighbourhoods", which appeared in the magazine he edited (or, as he said, "conducted"), *All the Year Round*. The 30-mile walk referred to a trek he made from central London in October 1857 to his recently acquired house at Gad's Hill between Rochester and Gravesend. Dickens was 45 years old, at the height of his fame. The timing of the walk is significant.

It seems probable that Dickens undertook the walk – the authorities are not unanimous – on the night of either Tuesday 14 or Wednesday 15 October 1857. The moon would have been entering its last quarter, and meteorological records indicate that it was foggy at dawn and overcast later in the day. But then, as Dickens himself has described, London was notorious for its fogs. Dickens always walked briskly, maintaining a steady pace and rarely stopping. We have a description of the way Dickens walked from a resident of Strood who often saw him walking from Gad's Hill into Rochester. He usually wore *low shoes not over-well mended, loose large check-patterned trousers that sometimes got entangled in those shoes when walking, a house coat thrown open, sometimes without waistcoat, a belt instead of braces, a necktie which now and then got round towards his ear, and a large-brimmed felt hat, similar to an American's, set well at the back of his head. In his hand he carried by the middle an umbrella, which he was in the habit of constantly swinging ... he walked in the middle of the road at a rapid pace, upright, but with his eyes cast down as if deep in thought.*

His eldest son, Charley, also recalled walking with him: *Many a mile have I walked with him thus – he striding along with his regular four-miles-an-hour swing; his eyes looking straight before him, his lips slightly working, as they generally did when he sat thinking and writing; almost unconscious of companionship, and keeping half a pace or so ahead. When he had worked out what had come into his mind he would drop back again into line – again, I am sure, almost unconsciously – and the conversation would be resumed, as if there had been no appreciable break or interval at all.*

There was, however, something special about the night walk of the autumn of 1857. In August that year he had become infatuated with the actress, Ellen (Nelly) Ternan. In September he had gone on a walking tour in the north of England with Wilkie Collins, **the walking tour of two idle apprentices**, and just happened to turn up for the races at Doncaster where Nelly was performing in the theatre. A few days before the walk he instructed his wife's confidential maid to convert his dressing room at his house at Tavistock Square into his bedroom and to block the door between that room and his former marital bedroom with bookshelves. This was a most symbolic gesture after years of increasing alienation from his wife, Catherine. There had been flirtations for ten years or more, and in 1855 Maria Beadnell, his first flame, now Mrs Winter, had got in contact with him. Memories of his first love excited him but meeting up with her was a bitter disappointment and Dickens portrayed her with callous savagery as Flora Finching in *Little Dorrit*.

In the late spring of the following year, 1858, Dickens formally, publicly and brutally dumped Catherine.

Edgar Johnson's biography of 1952 summarises Dickens's life with the subtitle, *His Tragedy and Triumph*. Until the late 1850s his adult life had been constant triumph. With the serialisation of *The Pickwick Papers* at the age of 24 he became instantly famous, and celebrity followed him for the rest of his life. The 12 years before his death were the years of tragedy. Although Nelly became his lover, Dickens had to keep it secret and was sometimes furtive in his public movements, and with the collapse of his marriage he lost friends. There were several other personal changes. In the years of his triumph his closest friend was John Forster, his biographer. Like Dickens, Forster was a lower-middle class lad from the provinces – in his case Newcastle-upon-Tyne – who arrived in London and immediately became an important figure in the literary world. He was an excellent man of business, with a legal training, who gained the confidence of writers a generation or so older – such as Charles Lamb and Walter Savage Landor – and looked after their affairs. Both Dickens and Forster walked tall in literary London while still in their midtwenties. Forster was distressed at the marital breakdown and Dickens did not always follow his advice. Relations cooled in the late 1850s, and Forster was replaced as an intimate by the novelist, Wilkie Collins, Dickens's junior by 11 years. Collins was the son and brother of Royal Academicians. He responded to the raffish side of Dickens's character, managing a life with two mistresses simultaneously. Dickens and Collins spent holidays together in Paris, and collaborated on writing. Dickens never cut off relations with Forster, who wrote the affectionate early biography, but was impatient with a prissiness in Forster's character; the character of Podsnap, the self-righteous and insular character in *Our Mutual Friend*, is generally believed to have been based on Forster.

In the years after 1857 Dickens took up, against the advice of John Forster, his new career of paid public readings. Thereafter he was constantly on the move. He found homes for Nelly first in Slough and then in Peckham, adopted false names and really behaved like a character in one of his own novels. It was at this time that he grew the beard. He had grown a beard before for theatrical performances or temporarily on holiday, but after 1857 his beard became a fixed feature. Although beards had become more fashionable after the Crimean War, it was as if Dickens was adopting a disguise from the familiar open and sensual features of his early manhood, so iconically captured in Daniel Maclise's portrait of 1839.

The route of the 1857 walk was symbolic. Dickens had leased Tavistock House, Tavistock Square, since 1851. The building has since been replaced by the current headquarters of the British Medical Association. Tavistock House had been the family home, where his ten children – of whom one died as an infant – lived and where he entertained. It was the domain of his wife, Catherine. In 1855 he bought Gad's Hill Place, the house of his childhood dreams. He spent much of the following year making changes to the house, often staying at the Sir John Falstaff inn opposite. Although Catherine stayed at Gad's Hill once, it was very much Charles's house and was to become his base for the rest of his life. So the walk was a move from one building that represented his life of the previous 21 years, to another building that was to represent the following 13.

Dickens was not alone among the great Victorians in being a strenuous walker, others also used to eat up the miles. George Borrow could walk up to 60 miles in a day, striding along at six miles an hour. The Prime Minister William Gladstone walked dozens of miles across England and Scotland. He would record the distances covered in his journal with obsessive precision – *34¾ miles*. Gladstone also walked around London at night, rescuing prostitutes. An older contemporary, the historian Thomas Macaulay (born in 1800), also used to pace the streets of the capital. Macaulay reckoned that in his youth he had walked along every London street. In the years after 1820 London underwent a rapid expansion and such a claim would no longer have been plausible.

In the previous century, long-distance cross-country walking was regarded as a bit odd, a socially inferior practice. Before the coming of the railways there were four principal methods of long distance journeying. The socially superior would have their own vehicles of various degrees of expense and elaborateness. Below that, the highest form of public transport was the stagecoach, which had its glory days in the first 30 years of the nineteenth century, between the organisation of roads through the turnpike trusts and the coming of the railways (or **railroads**, as Dickens called them). Dickens recorded and celebrated this final age of the stagecoach in many of his early works such as *The Pickwick Papers* and *Nicholas Nickleby*. Travel was exhausting, uncomfortable, hazardous and time-consuming, but there was a network of support, with the coaching inns, relays of horses and coach craftsmen ready to repair or replace. Below the stagecoaches – socially – were the wagons: slow, friendly and also uncomfortable. And below all of them were the pedestrians. This was particularly the case in England; less so in Wales or Scotland.

One visitor to England at the end of the eighteenth century observed that a *traveller on foot in this country seems to be considered as a sort of wild man, or an out-of-the-way being, who is stared at, pitied, suspected, and shunned by everybody that meets him.*

The traveller on foot did not eat in the main dining room of a public house but was often directed to eat in the kitchen with the domestic staff. This had clearly changed by the 1830s; it is hard to imagine the young Gladstone being directed to the kitchen. But by then walking long distances had become more socially acceptable for middle class intellectuals. The cause may have been the influence of William Wordsworth, who was Poet Laureate from 1834 to 1850. He had drawn attention to the beauties of Britain and his rambles, whether past Tintern Abbey or in the Lake District, chimed with a romantically inclined reading public.

For many in London, however, walking was an essential part of daily life. In the years after the Napoleonic wars London expanded and new inner suburbs grew north of what was known as New Road, now the road that passes by the northern railway termini – Marylebone, Baker Street, Euston and Kings Cross/St Pancras. People lived here and walked to offices in the cities of London and Westminster. In an early paper that appeared in *Sketches by Boz*, Dickens noted how **the early clerk population of Somers and Camden towns, Islington, and Pentonville, are fast pouring into the city; or directing their steps towards Chancery-lane and the Inns of Court. Middle-aged men, whose salaries have by no means increased in the same proportion as their families, plod steadily along, apparently with no object in view but the counting-house; knowing by sight almost every body they meet or overtake, for they have seen them every morning (Sundays excepted) during the past twenty years, but speaking to no one.**

In Dickens's novels there are several accounts of long walks; there was nothing exceptional about them. Sam Weller, when he goes to see his father and stepmother in Dorking, walks all the way back to London. Traddles in *David Copperfield* almost incidentally mentions that he walked from London to Devonshire to see his fiancée, the **dearest girl in the world**. Oliver Twist at the age of 11 walked from Mudfog, 70 miles north of London, to the capital, covering 20 miles in the first day. David Copperfield at about the same age walked from London to Dover, walking 23 miles in one day from Blackheath to Chatham. Pip in *Great Expectations*, when he learnt that Estella was to marry Bentley Drummle, walked

in despair back to London from – one presumes – Rochester. Later in the book he travelled by stagecoach but alighted
at the Half-way House, and **breakfasted there, and walked
the rest of the distance**. Nell and her grandfather in *The
Old Curiosity Shop* wander largely on foot from the capital
to the West Midlands. Nicholas Nickleby and Smike walk
the greater part of the way from London to Portsmouth. On
the first day they walked 30 miles from London to Godalm-
ing. Given Smike's physical frailty this seems improbable.
More improbable is the 25 miles alleged to have been walked
by Mr Pickwick and his companions, after having enjoyed
a lavish and bibulous wedding breakfast at Dingley Dell in
December.

Apart from that night in 1857 I do not think Dickens
walked 30 miles in one day (or night). Regularly he walked
10 or 12 miles in a day; sometimes 20. A methodical man,
his habit was to write every morning for four hours, and
then walk for four hours. He had the idea that hours given
to intellectual labour should correspond to hours spent in
strenuous physical exercise, in his case, walking. But there
was, even for Dickens, something exceptional about the
night walk into Kent in October 1857. I think it was, in fact,
the turning point of his life. In spite of his assertion that he
was half-asleep during the walk, I think his mind may well
have been actively reassessing his life.

As I read about and reflected on Dickens's walk, I decided
that I would like to repeat it, also leaving Tavistock Square at
two in the morning. I suggested the idea to my wife, Theresa.
She was alarmed and thought that I was crazy to walk in the
middle of the night through what she saw as some of the
dodgiest parts of London. I did some research. It appears
that the London boroughs with the lowest crime rate were
Greenwich and Bexley. By contrast, the Cities of London
and Westminster and the Royal Borough of Kensington
and Chelsea were the most crime-ridden boroughs. Southwark and Lambeth were average. But I also sought advice. I

telephoned Southwark Police to discuss the idea of the walk. I explained that it was in the steps of Charles Dickens and they were immediately empathetic and helpful. I should not go alone, they advised. Nor at the weekend. The Elephant and Castle area was notorious for muggings. The riskiest time was when the clubs closed – about 3:00 am along the Old Kent Road. The clubs were usually open at weekends. I found two friends to go with me – Robin and Les – and we agreed to go mid-week. Meanwhile I did a recce of the area during the daytime. I went to the Elephant and Castle to check where we could best cross the roads, avoiding the subway, and I dropped in on shops and cafes on the Old Kent Road to ask what it was like there at 3:00 and 4:00 in the morning. There was always a trickle of traffic and people around, I was told. This was reassuring, at least for me, even if Theresa was not totally convinced.

In determining which route to take, I consulted Victorian maps. I wanted to follow the route Dickens was most likely to have taken. Although Tavistock Square was where he had his family house, he also kept a bachelor pad above the offices of his magazine, *Household Words*, in Wellington Street off the Strand. On Pip's walk in the opposite direction in *Great Expectations*, he crossed over London Bridge, but Blackfriars Bridge or Waterloo Bridge would have made sense if Dickens was setting out either from Wellington Street or Tavistock Square. Dickens was always careful with his money and in 1857 Waterloo Bridge was still levying a toll on pedestrians crossing. Dickens would, I guessed, have opted for the free bridge. We therefore decided to cross the river by Blackfriars Bridge. He probably went by St George's Obelisk, the junction south of the Thames of roads going to London Bridge, Blackfriars and Westminster. The route from there to Gad's Hill is straightforward – to the Elephant and Castle, the Bricklayers' Arms, along the old Watling Street to Blackheath, Shooter's Hill, Welling, Bexleyheath, Crayford, Dartford and by the Old Dover Road skirting the south of Gravesend.

So one night in November 2011 Robin's wife dropped the three of us off at Tavistock Square at 2:00 in the morning and we set off, walking past Dickens's earlier home in Doughty Street, by Ludgate Circus, and crossing the Thames by Blackfriars Bridge. St George's Circus was on the edge of the built-up area in the 1850s. There were a few buildings to the south, including Walcot Square, where Mr Guppy in *Bleak House* lived.

We sped by the Elephant and Castle and along the Old Kent Road, the old Watling Street. There was indeed a constant flow of traffic and few pedestrians in these wee hours. Busses passed by, their passengers mostly asleep. It was as if zombies were being transported across the capital. Shops indicated a culturally diverse population and the Old Kent Road seemed to be full of Pentecostal churches. Signs pointed to Peckham on the right, and we thought of the house Dickens bought for Nelly. It was on a good train line – into central London and also handy for Rochester. In her biography of Ellen Ternan, Claire Tomalin speculates on one story that Dickens's fatal stroke occurred there and not at Gad's Hill, the body being transported by cart to Gad's Hill in the dead of night, if that is not too inappropriate a phrase.

We were getting into our stride. There wasn't much conversation along a road that was unfamiliar to any of us. At New Cross we entered the old county of Kent and started to climb. Suddenly we came to the open level space of Blackheath. We had left the dodgier parts of London and were about to enter gracious inner suburbia. We had met no potential muggers but were accosted, I think, by a lady of the night, although Les firmly (and perhaps gallantly) denied she was. We were ready for a break – we had walked seven or eight miles and it was nearly 4:00am. To our surprise and delight we found the Blackheath Tea Hut, an all night café. We joined some jolly policemen celebrating the birthday of one of their colleagues with tea and baps.

Opposite the Tea Hut was the walk down to Greenwich,

the long vista of gnarled old trees in Greenwich Park, as Dickens called it in his Christmas story "The Seven Poor Travellers".

David Copperfield also paused at Blackheath on his walk to Dover. The school he had attended, Salem House, where he had met Steerforth and Traddles, was at Blackheath – the exact location is uncertain – and on his walk David spent a night sleeping rough near the familiar buildings of the school. Blackheath overlooks Greenwich Park where Dickens, in 1835 at the age of 23, wrote a delightful early piece, later appearing in *Sketches by Boz*, on the unrestrained enjoyments of Greenwich Fair.

It was still dark when we resumed after our break. Did Dickens have a break? There may have been hostelries where he might have had a glass of something to spur him on.

Blackheath in the eighteenth century – along with Shooter's Hill and Bexleyheath – had a reputation for highway robbery. The road was famed for **the unmerciful plundering of travellers**. Passengers on the night coach to Dover in the second chapter of *A Tale of Two Cities* were nervous of highwaymen when, on a late November night, the coach carrying Jarvis Lorry was **lumbering up** and was stopped by a horseman with an urgent message. Fear gripped crew and passengers, **the guard suspected the passengers, the passengers suspected one another and the guards, they all suspected everybody else, and the coachman was sure of nothing but the horses.** The gradient was steep and passengers had dismounted from the coach, **not because they had the least relish for walking exercise, under the circumstances, but because the hill, and the harness, and the mud, and the mail, were all so heavy, that the horses had three times already come to a stop, besides once drawing the coach across the road, with the mutinous intent of taking it back to Blackheath.** At the summit of Shooter's Hill, just beyond the Victorian Gothic water tower, was a pub, The Bull, rebuilt in the 1880s. Its predecessor was a coaching inn, built in 1749, which would have been familiar to Charles Dickens. Tony Weller, Sam's father in *The Pickwick Papers*, retired to near Shooter's Hill.

The road was as straight as an arrow's flight as we paced along the route of the Roman road through Welling, Bexleyheath and Crayford. I observed a strange phenomenon in these dormitory towns: an extraordinary number of *nail bars*. We passed three in Welling and five in Bexleyheath but only one in Crayford. Dawn was beginning to break and we were heartened by a phone call from my wife, Theresa, at 6:30am. She was relieved to learn that we had not been beset by footpads. We were cheered on for the rest of the walk.

We wondered how the dawn would have been for Dickens. He does describe a similar dawn as Oliver Twist walked into London from Bethnal Green with Bill Sikes, en route to the burglary in Chertsey: **The day had fairly begun to break. Many of the lamps were already extinguished, a few country wagons were slowly toiling on towards London, and now and then a stage-coach, covered with mud, rattled briskly by ... The public-houses, with gas-lights burning inside, were already open. By degrees other shops began to be unclosed, and a few scattered people were met with. Then came struggling groups of labourers going to their work; then men and women with fish-baskets on their heads, donkey-carts laden with vegetables, chaise-carts filled with live-stock or whole carcasses of meat, milkwomen with pails, and an unbroken concourse of people trudging out with supplies to the eastern suburbs of the town.**

There are several points to make here. *Oliver Twist* was written 20 years before the 1857 walk and Bethnal Green is described as if it is in the country, whereas maps of the time show a continuous built up area. The Oliver walk was, I think, in late spring, rather than October. And between the 1830s and the 1850s the railways had arrived. (Indeed, during our walk, we were comforted by the fact that if it was too much for us, we were never more than two miles from a railway station and that from 6:00 in the morning there would be commuter trains that could take us into central London.) Dickens might well have encountered carts bringing fresh produce into London or to the market centres in the southeast of the metropolis. Although the railways totally changed the transportation of fresh milk, fruit and vegetables, it was not always on an industrial scale; smaller cultivators continued to use horse-drawn carts. So the account in *Oliver Twist* might broadly have described Dickens's walk in 1857.

Dickens was familiar with this route, which gets several mentions in his novels. Mr Dorrit, after his release from Marshalsea, set out on this road. In *The Pickwick Papers*, Dickens tells a story – or Tony Weller does – about two coachmen who saluted each other with a **jerking round of the right wrist and a rising of the little finger into the air at the same time. They were twins, between whom an unaffected and devoted attachment existed. They passed each other on the Dover Road, every day, for twenty-four years, never exchanging any other greeting than this; and yet, when one died, the other pined away, and soon afterwards followed him**.

I had arranged to call at the house of my friend Hassan at Crayford at about 7:00am. We were half an hour late, but what a welcome break it was. We sat in comfortable chairs, sipping Somali coffee – Hassan's wife is Somali. We asked Hassan about the nail bars. There was a simple explanation, he told us. Vietnamese refugees had been settled at Thamesmead, east of Greenwich. They had cornered such a market as there was in nail bars in north-west Kent.

We had to tear ourselves away from the armchairs and move on; Crayford and then on to Dartford. Though traffic is diverted away from the centre, Dartford is the first place east of London which seemed to have its own character, rather than being just a dormitory suburb of the capital. Like Rochester, it has a Royal Victoria and Bull Hotel, where, a plaque declares, the steam locomotive pioneer, Robert Trevithick, lived and died. We were entering Dickens country, for Dart-ford has a Copperfield Market and a Pickwick Pawnbrokers.

The north Kentish coast has reminders of a medieval royal importance. Greenwich and Eltham had palaces, and travellers, royal and common, used to travel to continental Europe by the River Thames in boats that hugged the shore, landing for supplies or ceremonies. At Dartford, King Henry V stopped to give thanks in the church for his victory at Agincourt.

Today the coastline has been disfigured by the chalk quar-ries and half-abandoned industrial sites. The industries were mostly for the production of cement and paper. Cement was developed here from the late eighteenth century, the indus-try being fed from the local chalk. Unruly capitalism had its wicked way with the virgin landscape and moved on. Today huge acres consist of a jungle of squalor, though in some of the old villages near the shore are blocks of flats that would wish to be seen as luxury accommodation.

Walking on a high bridge over the M25 seemed to be sym-bolic, though this stretch of the orbital road is not actually a motorway. We were breaking through the chain that fet-tered the capital. On the eastern side we could look across meadows where horses were grazing, arched by the Dartford Bridge, with an oil refinery on the northern bank of the River Thames, busy with freight-bearing craft – a mix of rural England, industry and modern transport networks.

Beyond the bridge is another area of sad development that conceals the treasure of the church at Stone and the old coastal village of Greenhithe. The landscape is post-industrial, the last factory having been closed down in 2010. Greenhithe has two parts – a residential area and a marina dating from not earlier than the 1980s. It was once a pretty little fishing village, with a pier in the eighteenth century. In Dickens's time it attracted visitors who arrived by paddle-steamer to enjoy what one tourist book described as Green-hithe's *rural and sylvan scenes*. It provided moorage for a yacht owned by Mr Tartar in *The Mystery of Edwin Drood*. Beyond the pier an older village spreads round the Sir John Franklin public house. Franklin was a Lincolnshire man, a naval officer, and an explorer who died with his men in seeking the North West Passage in 1845. The whole expedition perished. Local people, Eskimos – First Nations is the culturally sensitive term used nowadays in Canada – maintained that the expedition resorted to cannibalism before perishing. These reports led, understandably, to huge controversy in Britain. Franklin's widow repudiated the notion; her husband was *clean, Christian and genteel*, she declared. Dickens entered the controversy, repudiating the Inuit evidence. **We believe every savage in his heart to be covetous, treacherous, and cruel: and we have yet to learn what knowledge the white man – lost, houseless, shipless, apparently forgotten by his race, plainly famine-stricken, weak, frozen and dying – has of the gentleness of Exquimaux.** The story of Franklin inspired Wilkie Collins and Dickens to write a play, *The Frozen Deep*. This was put on in early 1857 with an amateur cast, including Dickens's daughters. It had huge social success. When Dickens's friend, Douglas Jerrold, died later that year, Dickens came up with the idea of performing the play to raise funds for Jerrold's widow and family. He, of course, played the central character. One performance was attended by Queen Victoria. Collins and Dickens decided to put on money-spinning performances at the Free Trade Hall, Manchester, in August. A larger venue called for the employment of professional actresses rather than Dickens's own daughters. One of the actresses recruited was Ellen Ternan. This was the genesis of Dickens's infatuation and the beginning of the upheavals in his life.

Seven or eight miles after leaving Crayford, we stopped for a third breakfast at a greasy spoon on the western outskirts of Gravesend, before the final haul. The Old Dover Road took us along the southern fringes of Gravesend. Between this road and the Thames was Rosherville Gardens, pleasure gardens in Dickens's time. **Ah Rosherville! That fated Rosherville, when shall we see it?** Dickens wrote in a letter in 1847, when the gardens had been open for ten years, replacing disused chalk quarries. Paddle-steamers brought day trippers from London to a special pier. The gardens, with an archery ground, a maze, a conservatory, and a "bijou" theatre were there for the delight of trippers. There was even a zoo with elephants and a bear pit. The gardens were founded in 1837 and lingered on until the 1930s, but the heyday was late Victorian times. Rosherville later became another insensitive industrial site and there is little to see of its earlier glories. All that is left of the pier are stumps in the ground with a commemorative plaque. One of the industries that took over the area was Henley's Electric Cable Works. Their Art Deco headquarters survives but is boarded up, ripe for demolition.

Gravesend featured in Dickens's life and work, but not to the extent that Rochester did. The docks at Tilbury were built in the 1880s, but early in the century Gravesend had been a resort and a major port. It features occasionally in Dickens's work. Mr Pickwick and his colleagues walked to Gravesend from Cobham. It was one of the places the law clerks in *Bleak House* would visit as day trippers from London. The tripper traffic expanded enormously during Dickens's youth. In 1821 27,000 people disembarked each year at Gravesend. Ten years later the figure was almost a quarter of a million. The elegant Town Pier built in 1834 to deal with this traffic still survives. It was also a port for boats from other parts of the east coast of Britain. When Peggotty and Ham visited David Copperfield at Blackheath they came to Gravesend from Yarmouth **in one of our Yarmouth lugs**. It was also a port of embarkation for places abroad. Gravesend was where Walter Gay and his bride, Florence, in *Dombey and Son*, set off on their honeymoon. When Mr Peggotty emigrated to Australia with Mr Micawber, it was from Gravesend that they set off. Australia was, in Dickens's imagination, a continent of adventure and opportunity. Both Micawber and Magwitch transformed their lives and prospered in Australia. Micawber went as a voluntary emigrant, Magwitch as a transported criminal. Dickens, who despaired of what he saw as the fecklessness of his sons – inherited, he claimed, of course from their mother – sent two of his sons to Australia to farm and trade. In the 1860s he entertained the idea of visiting Australia himself to give readings and make money.

Gravesend was more than a people's port of embarkation or disembarkation. Here in 1863 Princess Alexandra of Denmark came onto English soil to marry Queen Victoria's eldest son, the Prince of Wales. The second pier, the Terrace Pier, became the Royal Terrace Pier thereafter.

Dickens knew Gravesend as a boy, living at Chatham, and as a newly-wed, honeymooning at Chalk nearby. On the shore near the canal built to connect the Thames and the Medway he would have seen a house that had an upturned boat serving as a roof. This clearly stuck in his mind when in 1849 he wrote in *David Copperfield* of the Peggotty household in Great Yarmouth. The house lasted until 1924. When his house at Gad's Hill was undergoing the changes he insisted on, Dickens stayed at Waits Hotel in the town. This later became the Commercial Hotel but no trace survives. The town also has memories of that other great Victorian, General Charles George Gordon, who, as a Royal Engineer in the late 1860s, worked on the Thames fortresses that defended the approach to the capital. He did charitable work, teaching at "ragged schools" and founding a boys' club. Did Dickens and Gordon ever meet?

Dickens was commemorated in the naming of two of the passenger ferry boats that plied between Gravesend and Tilbury at the turn of the twenty-first century: a locally built catamaran was named *Great Expectations* and a trimaran *Martin Chuzzlewit*.

We walked along the southern outskirts of Gravesend, joining the main road to Rochester, built in the twentieth century. We could have gone straight ahead – as Dickens certainly would have done – through the village of Chalk, past the weather-boarded cottage where, in happier marital days, he had spent his honeymoon with Catherine. A plaque on the cottage commemorates the honeymoon. Chalk also claims the origin of the forge in *Great Expectations*; this stands, fittingly, in Forge Lane. It adjoined the house, which **was a wooden house, as many of the dwellings in our country were.** Some early numbers of *The Pickwick Papers* were written in Chalk; hence the freshness of the Rochester chapters.

We were tired and, rather than diverting through Chalk, chose the boring slog up to Gad's Hill, reaching the Sir John Falstaff pub, opposite Dickens's home, Gad's Hill Place.

The walk had taken us 12 hours. When Pip in *Great Expectations* travelled by coach to London, the journey took five hours. Dickens in 1857 had covered the distance on foot in seven. But then Dickens in 1857 was 45 and the combined age of the three of us was 194.

Gad's Hill

IT WAS MIDWAY between Gravesend and Rochester, and the widening river was bearing the ships, white-sailed or black-smoked, out to sea, when I noticed by the wayside a very queer small boy.

"Holloa!" said I, to the very queer small boy, "where do you live?"

"At Chatham," says he.

"What do you do there?" says I.

"I go to school," says he.

I took him up in a moment, and we went on. Presently the very queer small boy says, "This is Gads-hill we are coming to, where Falstaff went out to rob those travellers, and ran away."

"You know something about Falstaff, eh?" said I.

"All about him," said the very queer small boy. "I am old (I am nine), and I read all sorts of books. But let us stop at the top of the hill, and look at the house there, if you please!"

"You admire the house?" said I.

"Bless you, sir," says the very queer small boy, "when I was not more than half as old as nine, it used to be a treat for me to be brought to look at it. And now, I am nine, I come by myself to look at it. And ever since I can recollect, my father, seeing me so fond of it, has often said to me, 'If you were to be very persevering and were to work hard, you might some day come to live in it.'"

Dickens wrote this whimsical account, imagining his own self as a boy, wistfully coveting "the house" in 1860 for *All the Year Round*; it was later reprinted in *The Uncommercial Traveller*. He had bought the house – Gad's Hill Place – in 1855. At first he bought it as much as an investment as a possible residence, and indeed in the first year of ownership did let it out. But after the breakdown of his marriage it became his main home for the rest of his life.

Dickens was thrilled by the literary associations with Gad's Hill. It was on one of the pilgrim routes between London and Canterbury and he savoured the idea that Chaucer's pilgrims passed by the house. Canterbury pilgrims were the potential victims of Falstaff's robbery in Shakespeare's King Henry IV Part One: *Lads, tomorrow morning, by four o'clock, early at Gadshill! There are pilgrims going to Canterbury with rich offerings, and traders riding to London with fat purses.*

The road between Rochester and Gravesend was probably the busiest in Kent in the eighteenth and into the nineteenth century. Gravesend was a major domestic port, conveying merchandise to and from Kent. Travellers for Rochester, Canterbury, Dover and the continent often went by boat to Gravesend and onward by road. It was the second road in the county to be managed by a turnpike trust and so had milestones from the eighteenth century. As Mr F's aunt in *Little Dorrit* said, **"There's milestones on the Dover Road".**

Dickens felt a sense of history about the Dover Road, over which **the old Romans used to march, over where the old Canterbury pilgrims used to go, over the road where the travelling trains of the old imperious priests and princes used to jingle on horseback between the Continent and this Island through the mud and water, over the road where Shakespeare hummed to himself, "Blow, blow, thou winter wind."**

Dickens was an acute observer of the wayfarers on this road. He noted the tramps – scoundrels, men and women living off their wits, the shabby genteel, reduced gentlefolk.

There were also itinerant craftsmen, tinkers, chair-menders, umbrella-menders, clock-menders, knife-grinders. And then the seasonal migrations: haymakers in the early summer and hop-pickers from elsewhere. **Many of these hoppers are Irish, but many come from London.** Kent provided a working holiday for people from East London until the 1960s.

The house, Gad's Hill Place – in his correspondence he often referred to it as **Gad's** – was initially known as Gad's Hill House, and was built in about 1780 by Thomas Stephens, successively ostler, brewer and mayor of Rochester. After he died, the house had several owners and occupiers until 1827 when the Reverend James Lynn acquired the freehold and for a while lived in it. His daughter, Eliza, was a free thinker, wrote a novel – *Joshua Davidson* – based on the Gospel story and wrote for several journals, including Dickens's own *Household Words*. After her father died, she inherited the house. By one of those coincidences that would be stretching credibility if they occurred in a Dickens novel, Miss Lynn met WH Wills, the assistant editor of *Household Words* at a dinner party at the beginning of February 1855. She told him she had just inherited Gad's Hill Place and wanted to sell it. Wills immediately told Dickens, who he knew was interested in the property. Dickens entered negotiations to purchase the place. The house had already appeared – it is reasonable to surmise – in his own fiction. In *A Christmas Carol*, written in 1843, Scrooge and the Spirit of Christmas Past visited the scenes of Scrooge's childhood and **approached a mansion of dull red brick, with a little weathercock – surmounted cupola on the roof, and a bell hanging in it.**

Dickens's younger sister, Letitia, had married an architect and surveyor, Henry Austin. He came to Gad's Hill and checked the foundations, roof and drainage. All seemed to be in order but negotiations were prolonged. Miss Lynn wanted £2,000, Henry Austin suggested £1,700. They agreed on £1,790 – £1,700 for the house and £90 for an area of derelict land on the other side of the road.

Gad's Hill Place

In March 1856 Dickens became the owner of **my little Kentish free-hold**. The house was already occupied by a tenant, the Rector of Higham, the Reverend Joseph Hindle. His lease did not expire for another year. Dickens agreed for him to see out the lease. Dickens had big plans for decorating and furnishing the house. **It is so old-fashioned, plain, and comfortable**, he wrote to his friend, Baroness Burdett-Coutts. **On the summit of Gad's Hill, with a noble prospect at the side and behind, looking down into the Valley of the Medway. Lord Darnley's Park at Cobham (a beautiful place with a noble walk through the wood) is close by it; and Rochester is within a mile or two. It is only an hour and a quarter from London by the Railway.** (One hundred and fifty years later the train from Higham to Charing Cross takes an hour and four minutes.) **To crown all, the sign of** the Sir John Falstaff is over the way, and I used to look at it as a wonderful Mansion (which God knows it is not), when I was a very odd child with the first faint shadows of all my books in my head – I suppose.

Initially he moved in only for the summer, retaining Tavistock House until 1860. After that Gad's Hill became his principal residence.

Dickens had the plot of land across the road planted as a shrubbery and it became known as the Wilderness. In Dickens's time it was dominated by two huge cedar trees, planted about the time the house was built. In 1907 storms severely damaged them and they were felled. Fresh cedars have been planted to replace them. One of Dickens's favourite dogs, the St Bernard Linda, is buried in the Wilderness. And it was in the Wilderness that Dickens placed the chalet that had been a gift from the French actor, Charles Fechter, in 1864. It arrived at Gad's Hill in 58 packing cases, containing 94 pieces and, like a complex piece of IKEA furniture, had to be assembled. **My room is up among the branches of the trees,** he wrote to an American friend, **and the birds and the butterflies fly in and out, and the green branches shoot in at the open windows, and the lights and shadows of the clouds come and go with the rest of the company.**

Dickens had a tunnel constructed under the road connecting the front garden of the house to the Wilderness in 1865. It is no longer used but the entrance and steps can be seen from the public footpath. During the Second World War it became a comfortable First Aid Post.

As soon as he moved into the house Dickens organised a house-warming party, arranging for guests to come from London by train, to Higham Station, a mile and a quarter away. (The station is undistinguished but the train, heading for Rochester, plunges into a long two-mile tunnel. Whereby hangs a tale. This tunnel was originally built between 1819 and 1824 for a canal. The designer was William Tierney Clark, the architect-engineer who also designed the suspension bridge over the Thames at Marlow, which was a prototype of his internationally best-known work, the 1839 iron suspension bridge over the Danube at Budapest. The South Eastern Railway Company bought up the canal in 1844, filled it in and laid the railway line in its place. Traces of the canal that linked Gravesend with the Medway at Strood can still be seen in Lower Higham village.)

Dickens had brought his books and other personal effects from Tavistock House. Among these were the dummy bookcases, concealing the entrance to his study. The book titles on the dummy bookcase included *The History of a Short Chancery Suit* in twenty-seven volumes and *Cat's Lives* in nine volumes. Another set of dummy books was the *Catalogue of Statues of the Duke of Wellington* in ten volumes. This reveals one of Dickens's prejudices – not against the Duke of Wellington, but against such memorials to the living or the dead. In his will he conjured **my friends on no account to make me the subject of any monument, memorial, or testimonial whatever. I rest my claims to the remembrance of my country upon my published works, and to the remembrance of my friends upon their experience of me in addition thereto.** In accordance with his wishes no statue was erected to Dickens after his death. That is, until the summer of 2013 when, in defiance of his wishes, a statue was erected and unveiled at the city of his birthplace, Portsmouth. This is the first in Britain – though there are statues of Dickens in Sydney, Australia, and Philadelphia, in the United States.

When he was at Gad's Hill he wrote in the library, the room that is on the ground floor to the right of the porch as you face the building. After 1865 when he had the chalet he worked there during the summer mornings. He was methodical, and wrote with a quill on blue paper. He was short-sighted and wore gold-rimmed spectacles when at work; curiously, none of the pictures of him show him wearing glasses – unlike Thackeray, for example.

He brought other things from Tavistock House. He was almost fetishistic in his insistence on writing only when there were certain objects on his writing desk. These included a French bronze of two fat toads fighting a duel with swords; one of them lunges forward and appears to be fatally piercing his adversary in the stomach. Another was a statuette of a dog-fancier with little dogs under his arms and pouring out of his pockets. And there was always a huge paper-knife, that he often held in his hand during his public readings. A small vase, ornamented with cowslips, would contain fresh flowers. Nearby was a register with his commitments for the week and month. Whenever he was in residence he had a flag hoisted at the top of the house.

Today the premises are usually closed to visitors. It has to be remembered that the house is the working environment of a school. Occasionally there are open days for Dickens enthusiasts but the school's privacy should be respected. Much can be seen and appreciated from the public highway. On the open days it is possible to explore the garden at the back. In it is a replica of the grave of Dick, the canary, a favourite of Dickens. Dick came from Broadstairs, lived to the age of 15 years and used to be provided with a thimbleful of sherry at 11:00 every morning.

In the garden can also be found part of the balustrade of the medieval Rochester bridge, demolished in 1859. It was presented to Dickens who had it **set up on the lawn behind the house. I have ordered a sundial for the top of it, and it will be a very good object indeed.**

To the west of the house were meadows. Each year Dickens collected hay from them, but they were also used for open air parties and gatherings for popular sports. In 1866 the meadow was filled with over 2,000 people attending sports and games. **I allowed the landlord of the Falstaff to have a drinking-booth on the ground. Not to seem to dictate or distrust, I gave all the prizes (about ten pounds in the aggregate) in money. The great mass of the crowd were** labouring men of all kinds, soldiers, sailors, and navvies. They did not between half-past ten, when we began, and sunset, displace a rope or a stake; and they left every barrier and flag as neat as they found it. There was not a dispute and there was no drunkenness whatever ... Among other oddities we had a Hurdle Race for Strangers. One man (he came in second) ran 120 yards and leapt over ten hurdles, in twenty seconds, *with a pipe in his mouth, and smoking it all the time*. "If it hadn't been for your pipe," I said to him at the winning post, "you would have been first." "I beg your pardon, Sir" he answered, "but if it hadn't been for my pipe, I should have been nowhere."

One area was set aside as a cricket ground. Although he was never a hearty sportsman, Dickens enjoyed cricket. If there was a deficit in the funds of the Higham Cricket Club at the end of the season he used to make it up. Indeed the last cheque he ever signed was for the Club. The Club used to play regularly in the meadow at the back of the house. Dickens stipulated that this privilege would be withdrawn if there were cases of drunkenness or bad language. He often hurried back to Gad's Hill from London in order to attend a match and keep the score.

While the changes were being undertaken Dickens sometimes stayed at the Sir John Falstaff – and occasionally at Gravesend – so as to supervise the improvements and repairs on the spot. The inn went back centuries, though the building in Dickens's time – and in ours – dates probably from the eighteenth century. In the 1860s the landlord was a Mr Trood, a name suggestive of Drood. A few days after Dickens's death in 1870, a fan made a pilgrimage to Gad's Hill and called at the inn and shared his loss with the waiter.

"A great loss this of Mr Dickens," said the pilgrim.

"A very great loss to us, sir," replied the waiter, shaking his head; "he had all his ale sent in from this house!"

When the Dickens family moved into Gad's Hill Place in the summer of 1857, it consisted of Catherine, his sister-in-law

Georgina, his daughters, Mary (always known as Mamie), then nineteen years old, and Catherine (Katey), aged eighteen; and his seven sons – Charley, twenty, Walter, sixteen, Frank, thirteen, Alfred, twelve, Sydney, ten, Henry (Harry), eight, and Edward (known as Plorn), four. His wife, Catherine, only came to Gad's Hill once, in the summer of 1857. Georgina was taking over much of the household management as relations between Charles and his wife were heading towards disaster and separation – this was the summer Charles met Ellen (Nelly) Ternan. After the separation Georgina stayed on with her brother-in-law, sharing the honours as hostess with the eldest daughter, Mamie. One of the merits of Georgina, in Dickens's eyes, was that she was one of the few people – and certainly the only woman – who could keep pace with him on his energetic walks.

One of the first of Dickens's guests at Gad's Hill Place was the Danish writer, Hans Christian Andersen. The stay was a disaster. He expected to be waited on in bed and demanded that he be shaved by Dickens's eldest son, Charley, to the latter's *intense indignation*. Charley, who was no trained barber, declined the office. *The whole day*, Andersen recorded pitifully in his diary, *I went with a great growth of beard*. Charley had spent time in Germany and knew the language but was unable to understand Andersen's German; his English was unintelligible and none of the family spoke Danish. He was quarrelsome, and could not keep up with his host as a walker. Dickens, normally most forbearing towards his guests, confided to Lady Burdett-Coutts, **We are suffering very much from Andersen.** He was finally taken to Maidstone where he took a train to Folkestone, going from there back to Denmark. Such was relief of the family that Dickens had a placard placed on a table his guest had used, with the words, **Hans Andersen slept in this room for five weeks which seemed to the family ages.** But not all the family, for the soon-to-be-dumped Mrs Dickens got on very well with him.

Charley was in awe of his father and used to address him

as Sir. Other sons brought friends along from school. His son Alfred brought some of his mates who had been a bit anxious about meeting the great man, but were won over. *By Jove, Dickens,* one said to Alfred afterwards, *your governor is a stunner and no mistake.* The sons joined him on outings. Sometimes they rowed him up the Medway from Rochester to Maidstone. At other times they strode with him, usually a pace or so behind. He seemed to need their company but he was often quite silent. Sometimes his lips would be at work as if he was composing speeches.

Dickens was a great host and within a few years there emerged a pattern in his hospitality. He would often meet his guests personally at Higham railway station and drive them in his pony-drawn **jaunting car** – one of his ponies was called Newman Noggs, after the character in *Nicholas Nickleby*. On arrival at the house his guests were given a cider cup, a cooling drink with a mixture of cider, soda water, sherry, brandy, lemon-peel, sugar and ice, topped with a sprig of borage. Guest rooms were always comfortable, provided with a small library, warm fires and tea-making facilities. The Sir John Falstaff inn was used as an overflow for guests when all the bedrooms in the house were occupied. A buffet breakfast was provided – but Dickens would have got up early and regularly worked in the library on correspondence or on stories. He was not to be disturbed and the house was expected to be quiet. Guests had to amuse themselves. Lunch was served at 1:30 pm after which came a systematic programme of entertainment, with boisterous din and bustle. This might include energetic walks to Cobham Park, accompanied by his dogs, or to other villages around. Sometimes, with scrupulous attention to detail, Dickens would organise picnics. After leaving the picnic site, Dickens would ensure that no litter was left behind – in some ways he was a very modern man. Or Dickens might take guests in his barouche (a type of smart horse-drawn carriage) to look at Rochester Castle. This took up the time until dinner, a more formal occasion. Dickens used to provide his male guests with a button-hole, a scarlet geranium – his favourite flower. Dickens did not like the custom of ladies withdrawing after dinner; he would lead the way after only a few minutes to the drawing room. Some time might be spent with daughter Mamie and sister-in-law Georgina but then, if there were no party games, men withdrew to the billiard room to smoke, play cards or chat. Dickens himself went to bed at midnight, leaving one of his sons in charge to look after the guests and to **see the gas out all right.**

There are many accounts of Gad's Hill hospitality. Not always did Dickens take centre stage. One visitor was the great violinist, Joseph Joachim, who played Tartini's *Devil's Sonata*. Dickens was overwhelmed by it.

Dickens was a genial and considerate host, and even turned tragedy into theatre. One of his dogs, an Irish mastiff called Sultan, was ferocious and usually had to be chained and muzzled. On one occasion a troop of soldiers was passing along the road. Sultan broke free of his chain and caused havoc in the ranks. He also killed and possibly ate a kitten. And he nearly swallowed Mrs Bouncer, a white Pomeranian dog belonging to Mamie. When he injured and terrified a little girl, his doom was sealed. George Dolby tells the story, quoting Dickens, how *Sultan was sentenced to death and a procession was formed, consisting of some six or seven men and boys from the stables and garden, a wheelbarrow and a gun. The dog evidently thought, in the bloodthirstiness of his nature, of being let loose to join in the procession, that they were going to kill some one or something else; and it was only when he had gone half-way across the large field at the back of the house, that his eye rested on the wheelbarrow with a gun in it. It seemed to strike him there was something wrong, and he at once became depressed, looking steadfastly at the gardener, and walked to his place of execution with his head down.*

Arrived at the corner of the field farthest from the house, one of the boys threw a large stone to induce the dog to go after it, or to lead him to believe there was something in the hedge where it stuck. When Sultan's attention was thus diverted, two barrels were discharged into his heart, and he died without a struggle or a cry, deeply regretted by his loving master, who, be it said, was the only friend he had.

Another pet had a long posthumous existence at Gad's Hill. In the 1840s when he lived in Devonshire Terrace, Dickens had owned a pet raven, called Grip (the name also of Barnaby Rudge's bird). Grip poisoned himself with white lead, uttering as his dying words, *Halloa, old girl!* Dickens had the bird stuffed and took him to his home in Tavistock Square and brought him to Gad's Hill Place. He was auctioned off with other effects after Dickens's death.

After the formal separation in the summer of 1858, Dickens's oldest son, Charley, chose to stay with his mother. Frank, Alfred and Sydney were, after the summer, sent to a boarding school in Boulogne. They did not come home for Christmas. It was no jolly family Christmas for the Dickens family.

It was clear that his second daughter, Katey, sided with her mother. She took the first opportunity to escape the household by marrying in 1860. She was wooed by Charles, artist brother of Wilkie Collins. Dickens was not happy about the marriage. Katey did not seem enthusiastic and there were suspicions that Charles was homosexual. The marriage took place, however, in July 1860 at Higham church, two miles from Gad's Hill Place. The best man was the painter Holman Hunt. Dickens wrote afterwards that **we had tried to keep it quiet here, but the church was filled with people, and the energetic blacksmith of the village had erected a triumphal arch in the court, and fired guns all night beforehand.** There were emotional strains, for the bride's mother was not invited – Dickens's hospitality did not extend to her – and Katey was in tears when the couple were seen off at Higham station, heading for Dover and a continental honeymoon. Later that evening, Dickens's other daughter, Mamie, found her father sobbing into Katey's bridal dress. **But for me,** he said, **Katey would not have left home.**

Two months later, in a further break with the past, Dickens organised a huge bonfire in the meadow at the back. Onto it he threw all the letters he had received. They included the letters from Catherine as well as from family friends and countless public figures and fans. Catherine kept the letters he had written to her as evidence *that he loved me once.* After the archival holocaust, his sons roasted onions in the ashes as Dickens sighed, **Would to God every letter I have ever written was on that pile.** Happily for posterity they were not, but were kept by their recipients and have been collected in 12 vast volumes, demonstrating what a stylish and brilliant correspondent he was.

The following year, 1861, Charley married a daughter of the publisher Frederick Evans. Charles Dickens had fallen out with Evans, disapproved of the marriage and did not attend the wedding ceremony. The quarrel with his son did not last and when a granddaughter was born, the family were regular visitors to Gad's Hill. The granddaughter, Mary Angela, called her grandfather Venerables or Wenerables.

In the years ahead the family was to become scattered. Walter, who had attended school at Wimbledon, took up a cadetship in an infantry division of the East India Company and set sail for India in the summer of 1861. Dickens was never to see him again, for he died in Calcutta in 1863. The third son, Frank, went out that autumn to join the Bengal Mounted Police and was savagely disappointed to arrive in Calcutta to learn of Walter's death. The fourth son, Sydney, left to join the navy. He incurred huge debts, which his father had to pay off, and Dickens was so cross that he refused to allow him to come to Gad's Hill. Another son, Alfred, also ran up debts. He failed to qualify to join the Royal Engineers, worked for a while in the City and then emigrated to Australia, where he was joined by the youngest son, Edward, known as Plorn. So Dickens never saw five of his seven sons after they took up their overseas careers.

Only the second youngest son, Henry, failed to disappoint

his father. He was hard-working and, after schooling first in Boulogne, then at Rochester Grammar and finally at Wimbledon, won a scholarship in 1869 to Trinity Hall, Cambridge. He was overjoyed and went to Higham station to meet his father off the train from London. *As he got out of the train*, recalled Henry over half a century later, *I told him the news. He said, "Capital! Capital!" – nothing more. Disappointed to find that he received the news apparently so lightly, I took my seat beside him in the pony carriage he was driving. Nothing more happened until we got half-way to Gad's Hill, when he broke down completely. Turning towards me with tears in his eyes and giving me a warm grip of the hand, he said, "God bless you, my boy, God bless you!"* Paradoxically, Henry succeeded in the one profession that his father had so consistently satirised – the law. There are as few good lawyers in Dickens's work as there are bad sailors. Henry went on to become a distinguished lawyer, a KC, a knight and the grandfather of the novelist Monica Dickens. He was the last of Dickens's children to die – in 1933.

At the time of Dickens's death only his sister-in-law Georgina and daughter Mamie were still at Gad's Hill Place. They were the keepers of Dickens's reputation and jointly edited the first collection of Dickens's letters. Georgina, the formidable Miss Hogarth, outlived her niece, Mamie, by over 20 years, dying in 1917 at the age of 90.

Dickens became a much-loved celebrity in his last years at Gad's Hill. He was an active benefactor of the village. The parish church was two miles from Gad's Hill and he was an occasional worshipper there. Between the railway station and Gad's Hill was Upper Higham, and a new church was built there in 1860. Dickens had a pew there in the chancel.

In May 1868 he returned to Gad's Hill after six months in the United States. He had been exhausted by the tour, and had been too unwell to travel to Chicago and the mid-West. But the return sea voyage had restored his vigour. It was expected that he would arrive at Higham Station. The villagers planned to meet him there and take the horse out of the carriage and drag him up the one and a quarter miles to his home. Mamie and Miss Hogarth heard about this, telegraphed Dickens and arranged for his carriage to meet him at Gravesend. The villagers, in the words of his readings manager, George Dolby, *turned out on foot, and in their market carts and gigs; and escorting Mr Dickens on the road, kept on giving him shouts of welcome, the houses along the road being decorated with flags. His own servants wanted to ring the alarm bell in the little belfry at the top of the house ...*

Dickens was not a well man in his last years. He was easily tired and was periodically lame. He rented a flat at Hyde Park Place for the sake of his unmarried daughter, Mamie, and also retained his bachelor pad off the Strand. He was also seeing Nelly Ternan at the house he acquired for her at Windsor Lodge, Peckham. He came down to Gad's Hill Place as often as he could, where he was working on *The Mystery of Edwin Drood*. The illustrator of this last novel was Luke Fildes, who would come to Gad's Hill to check on details. Dickens used to act out the scenes he wanted illustrated.

He had a final season of readings in the early months of 1870, ultimately bidding his audience at St James's Hall in London **a heartfelt, grateful, respectful, and affectionate farewell**. One day at Gad's Hill his son, Harry, heard the awful din of what seemed to be a very violent domestic row going on in the garden. At first he thought it was tramps. But the row went on with increased fury. He went outside and found his father rehearsing for "Sikes and Nancy", reading from *Oliver Twist*. By all accounts it was an intense act, emotionally and physically.

During his last month Dickens was also, typically, supervising the building of a new conservatory. This was the last of many improvements to the house. When Gad's Hill Place was sold after his death, it sold – partly because of the improvements, partly because of the association – at four times the price he had paid for it.

There were many claims on his time, social and professional, in London. He returned to Gad's Hill at the beginning of June 1870. On Sunday evening, 5 June, his daughter, Katey, sought his advice on a personal matter. Her artist husband was ailing and they were in need of money. She wanted to take up acting professionally. Sitting in the new conservatory he advised strongly against it. There were people in the theatre, he said, **who would make your hair stand on end.** (Well, he should know.) When she retired to bed – it was well after 11:00 – he called her back and talked of his plans, and his writing of *The Mystery of Edwin Drood*, **if, please God, I live to finish it. I say *if* because you know, my dear child, I have not been strong lately**. He went on to regret that he had not **been a better father – a better man**. It was 3:00 before they went to bed.

Next morning, Monday, Dickens was up early. He went to the chalet to work on the novel. Katey and Mamie were due to go to London. Unusually Katey went through the tunnel to say goodbye. *His head was bent low over his work,* she recalled, *and he turned an eager and rather flushed face towards me as I entered. On ordinary occasions he would just have raised his cheek for my kiss, saying a few words, perhaps in "the little language" that he had been accustomed to use when we were children; but on this morning, when he saw me, he pushed his chair from the writing-table, opened his arms, and took me into them.* She never saw him conscious again.

On the Monday afternoon he was fit enough to walk with his dogs into Rochester and back. The next day, Tuesday, he wrote more in the chalet and in the afternoon was driven with Georgina into Cobham, where he dismissed the carriage and walked the three or four miles back to Gad's Hill.

On Wednesday, 8 June, he was in good spirits, worked on the novel in the morning, crossed under the road for lunch, and after a cigar, returned, unusually to write more in the afternoon. He wrote several pages of *The Mystery of Edwin Drood*, including the beautiful loving lines on the city of

Rochester that are the introduction of the next section of this book. He returned to the house, and wrote a couple of letters. The only member of the family present, Georgina, noticed that he seemed changed and asked him if he was ill. **Yes, very ill**, he answered. **I have been very ill for the last hour.** He talked of going up to London after dinner and then had a seizure. Georgina urged him to lie down. **Yes**, he said, **on the ground**. These were his last words. He collapsed onto the floor. Georgina sent for Dr Steele, from Strood, who had regularly treated Dickens. Dickens was eased onto a couch, unconscious and wrapped up. Charley and the daughters were summoned back from London and his London doctor, Frank Beard, sent for. He and the daughters arrived and, with Georgina, held vigil through the night.

The following morning, Thursday 9 June, Charley arrived, and Dr Steele came up again from Rochester. Georgina arranged for Ellen Ternan to come. She reached Gad's Hill Place in the afternoon. Dickens never recovered consciousness. He died shortly after 6:00pm the same day in the drawing room, the ground floor room which is on the left as you face the front door. It was the fifth anniversary of the railway accident at Staplehurst when he and Nelly had nearly been killed together. He was 58.

In due course a death mask was made. The painter, John Millais, came to Gad's Hill and made a drawing of the face of the dead man. The body was placed in an oak coffin adorned with scarlet geraniums. In accordance with his instructions, his horse was shot. He had wanted to be buried locally, at Shorne Church perhaps, or at Rochester cathedral, but a national campaign called for burial in Westminster Abbey. Dickens hated the rituals of death and wanted no great funeral. So on Tuesday morning early the coffin was taken to Higham station, and on to Charing Cross. And then to Poet's Corner.

It has been argued that Dickens worked himself to death, dying prematurely. The readings, and especially the American tour of 1867–68, had exhausted him and ruined his health. His friend and first major biographer, John Forster, had advised against the readings and especially the American tour. But it could be that the readings actually kept him going.

His strenuous walking aside, Dickens was never a healthy man. He describes himself as having been **puny** as a child in Chatham, shunning hearty games. Throughout his life he suffered from streaming head colds; one such cold had prevented him from attending a theatre audition when he was 20. And although he was never the worse for it, he was a heavy drinker all his life and a smoker.

Dickens also did not come from a long-living family. His father died at 66 and his mother at 74, but of his siblings who survived infancy, three of his four brothers died in their thirties and one in his forties; only one sister, Letitia, lived into her seventies. There is a similar pattern with his own children. Nine (out of ten) survived infancy. Only four lived to a greater age than Dickens was when he died. Katey and Harry lived to the ages of 89 and 84 respectively, but two of the other children died in their twenties and one in his forties. The death of Charles Dickens at 58 was not an early death by the standards of his own family.

His eldest son, Charley, moved into Gad's Hill Place. He also inherited his father's role as editor/"conductor" of *All the Year Round*. Many of his father's effects were sold later in 1870. These included hundreds of bottles of wine, spirits and liqueurs. While Charley and his family lived in the house, Dickens's widow was often a visitor and used to come for Christmas. After Dickens's death, the family reunited around Mrs Dickens who, from being the novelist's discarded wife, became the widow of a national treasure, receiving a message of condolence from Queen Victoria.

Charley sold the house in 1879. It had several owners in the following decades. One of them had the offer from a potential American purchaser of £10,000 for the house, which he wanted to transfer – like London Bridge – to the United States. In 1924 the house became Gad's Hill School, a successful independent school. A great-great-grand-daughter of the novelist is a former pupil and a current member of the Board of Governors.

The Medway Towns

Rochester and Strood

A brilliant morning shines on the old city. Its antiquities and ruins are surprisingly beautiful, with the lusty ivy gleaming in the sun, and the rich trees waving in the balmy air. Changes of glorious light from moving boughs, songs of birds, scents from gardens, woods, and fields – or rather, from the one great garden of the whole cultivated island in its yielding time – penetrate into the Cathedral, subdue its earthy odour, and preach the Resurrection and the Life. The cold stone tombs of centuries ago grow warm, and flecks of brightness dart into the sternest marble corners of the building, fluttering there like wings.

These moving words were among the last that Charles Dickens wrote. They were penned in his chalet on Wednesday 8 June. He worked all day and was taken ill in the early evening and died the following afternoon. To the end there was no flagging of his literary power, as he conjured up with deftly crafted phrases his loving perception of the city of Rochester.

Rochester features in his first novel, *The Pickwick Papers*, and as Cloisterham in his last, *The Mystery of Edwin Drood*. It plays a major part in *Great Expectations* as the market town and there is a passing reference to it in *David Copperfield*. As Great Winglebury it features in *Sketches by Boz*. The Medway Towns – Rochester and Chatham primarily, but also the other towns of Strood, Gillingham and Brompton – were as important in Dickens's life and work as London. He had spent magical childhood years in Chatham, was stirred by the antiquities of the old cathedral city of Rochester and, after he moved to Gad's Hill in 1857, was fond of walking or riding the two miles or so into the city. He loved to show Rochester off to visitors. There he was a familiar figure, but not always correctly identified. One year before he died his American friend, James T Fields, was staying at Gad's Hill. Fields and Dickens were in Rochester together and the American was mistaken for the Englishman. Dickens encouraged the deception and handed over a parcel, saying loudly, **Here you are, Dickens, take charge of this for me.**

The two main Medway towns, Rochester and Chatham, have seen better days. Rochester was a Roman city and its cathedral and castle testify to its importance in early medieval times. At that time the first bridge over the Medway was built, making the city a major land transit stop between the capital, Canterbury and Dover, and the continent. Since the nineteenth century, however, there has been a steady decline. The main trans-Kent railway routes, both in the nineteenth and the twenty-first century, have bypassed the Medway towns, which have also been marginalised by the motorways.

An industrial zone on the Medway, south of the bridge at Rochester, produced many of the world's cement mixers and steam traction engines for much of the twentieth century. The towns became a major commuting region and benefited from tourism. Chatham in particular once prospered as a naval and military base, with a major shipyard and associated trades. But over the last century they have seen a gentle and dignified decline. Twenty-first century disparities of wealth are apparent in the contrast between the smart craft in the marinas and the rows of depressed terrace housing throughout the Medway towns.

Mr Micawber in *David Copperfield* contemplated a career in the Medway Coal Trade. **"My opinion of the coal trade on that river,"** declared Mrs Micawber, **"is, that it** may require talent, but that it certainly requires capital. Talent, Mr Micawber has; capital, Mr Micawber has not." The Kentish coalfields are well to the south and east of the Medway and so, despite his talent, even if Mr Micawber had been in possession of capital, it was unlikely that he would have prospered.

For Mr Pickwick, the **chief productions of these towns ... appear to be soldiers, sailors, Jews, chalk, shrimps, officers, and dockyard men. The commodities chiefly exposed for sale in the public streets are marine stores, hardbake, apples, flat-fish, and oysters.**

In the 1820s, the time of Mr Pickwick and when the young Charles Dickens was living locally, the Medway towns had a well-established Jewish community. It was mainly Sephardic and had commercial connections with the Low Countries and the Baltic. Often Jews acted as naval agents, drawing a profit from the prize money when ships captured during the wars were sold off. After the Napoleonic Wars many became chandlers or military tailors.

A few years earlier, Dickens wrote a thumbnail sketch of the town, disguised as Great Winglebury, in *Sketches by Boz*. The town, he wrote in Jinglesque prose, **has a long straggling quiet High Street, with a great black and white clock at a small red Town Hall, half way up – a market place – a cage – an assembly room – a church – a bridge – a chapel – a theatre – a library – an inn – a pump – and a post office.** He also places the town **exactly forty-two miles and three-quarters from Hyde Park Corner.** (Rochester is under 30 miles from the City of London – just over 30 from Hyde Park Corner.)

The mostly pedestrianised High Street that runs from Rochester Bridge to Star Hill is the spine of Dickensian Rochester. To the west of the bridge is the town of Strood. From there, the road to Gravesend climbs up to Gad's Hill. In the town on the right of the road was the old inn Crispin and Crispianus. This was severely damaged by fire in 2011 and is currently boarded up. There used to be a Dickens Room, commemorating the fact that this was a favourite watering hole for Dickens on his walks into the Medway Towns. He used to drop in for a glass of sixpenny ale, or some cold brandy and water. It was noted that he rarely spoke to anyone but seemed to survey the scene, taking everything in. He had his favourite seat in a corner near the fireplace. The landlady recalled one occasion when Dickens called in during a thunderstorm. He saw a lady with a baby in the rain outside and asked the landlady to call her in and give her some brandy. She drank the brandy and Dickens gave her a shilling, telling the landlady, **Now she will go on her way rejoicing.**

Today there are actually four parallel bridges over the River Medway – two carrying lanes of the A2 road, one carrying the railway and one carrying service pipes and cables. Until 1856 a medieval bridge was in use. This was the bridge on which Mr Pickwick strolled, **contemplating nature, and waiting for breakfast ... On either side the banks of the Medway, covered with cornfields and pastures, stretched away as far as the eye could see, presenting a rich and varied landscape, rendered more beautiful by the changing shadows which passed swiftly across it, as the thin and half-formed clouds skimmed away in the light of the morning sun.** No cornfields or pastures flank the river today. Nor do we see a rich and varied landscape: all is built over. On another occasion Mr Pickwick was on the bridge and shunned a **dismal** man, whom he thought might tip himself – taking Mr Pickwick with him – into the river. This was the bridge David Copperfield would have crossed over as a boy, **as evening closes in ... footsore and tired.** It was also the bridge across which Pip, in his prosperity, was pursued with taunts by Trabb's boy, in *Great Expectations*.

The medieval bridge was demolished by the Royal Engineers in 1856. Parts of the balustrade were recycled and placed on the esplanade to the south, and one part of the bridge was presented to Dickens, who had just bought Gad's Hill Place. He used it as the base of a sundial. A new road bridge was constructed and a year later a railway bridge built. The second road bridge was built in 1970.

The castle dominates the eastern side of the city of Rochester today, as it did in the time of Mr Pickwick:

"Magnificent ruin," said Mr Snodgrass with all the poetic fervour that distinguished him ...

"What a sight for the antiquarian," were the words which fell from Mr Pickwick's mouth, as he applied his telescope to his eye.

"Ah! Fine place," said the stranger [the plausible fraudster, Alfred Jingle], **"glorious pile, frowning walls – tottering arches ..."**

The castle is no more than a backdrop to Dickens's fiction, as to the events of *The Mystery of Edwin Drood*. The castle was in private hands until the nineteenth century, a crumbling ruin, or, as Dickens wrote in *The Pickwick Papers*, **Its towers roofless, and its massive walls crumbling away, but telling us proudly of its own might and strength, as when, seven hundred years ago, it rang with the clash of arms, or resounded with the noise of feasting and revelry.**

In the early years of the nineteenth century there were proposals for turning the castle into barracks. Access was forbidden. In 1842 Dickens, fresh from his American tour, brought Henry Wadsworth Longfellow and his future biographer, John Forster, to Rochester. Forster recalled how they confronted *one of those prohibitions which are the wonder of visitors and the shame of Englishmen.* [We] *overleapt gates and barriers, and setting at defiance repeated threats of all the terrors of the law coarsely expressed to us by the custodian of the place, explored minutely the castle ruins.*

The corporation of the City of Rochester acquired the freehold of the castle (for £6,572) in 1884. Today it is cared for by English Heritage.

The other great medieval building that has dominated the

geography and history of the city for nearly a millennium is the Cathedral Church of Christ and the Blessed Virgin Mary.

Old Cathedral too (Mr Jingle again), **earthy smell – pilgrims' feet worn away the old steps – little Saxon doors – confessionals like money-takers' boxes at theatres – queer customers those monks – Popes, and Lord Treasurers, and all sorts of old fellows, with great red faces, and broken noses, turning up every day – buff jerkins too – matchlocks – sarcophagus – fine place – old legends too – strange stories: capital.**

The cathedral, or **Kinfreederel** as the stone-throwing urchin, Deputy, calls it in *The Mystery of Edwin Drood*, is the background for that novel.

The outer buildings of the cathedral precincts also feature in much of the novel. When the London lawyer comes to Rochester, he too is impressed. **"Dear me," said Mr Grewgious,** who otherwise presents himself as an **Angular** man without imagination or poetry, **peeping in** [the cathedral]. **"It's like looking down the throat of Old Time."**

Inside the cathedral Dickens is commemorated by a brass tablet on the wall of the south transept *to connect his memory with the scenes in which his earliest and his latest years were passed and with the associations of Rochester Cathedral and its neighbourhood which extended over all his life.* Nearby, another tablet from an earlier century commemorates Richard Watts, founder of the charitable house for the relief of poor travellers.

Dickens's description of the architecture of the cathedral in *The Mystery of Edwin Drood* is literal. Beyond describing the picturesque and sometimes giving buildings human or animal characteristics, we do not go to Dickens for great architectural insights. He wrote of **the low arched Cathedral door** at the west front, **the massive grey square tower** and **the rugged steps** leading down to the crypt, with its **groined windows, bare of glass** and **heavy pillars which** support the roof **and engender masses of black shade.** He is far more eloquent when describing music and sounds associated with the building. In *Great Expectations* the only reference to Rochester Cathedral is when Pip reflects on how Estella has slipped out of his hands: **The best light of the day was gone when I passed along the quiet echoing courts behind the High Street. The nooks of ruin where the old monks had once had their refectories and gardens, and where the strong walls were now pressed into the humble sheds and stables, were almost as silent as their graves. The cathedral chimes had at once a sadder and a more remote sound to me, as I hurried on avoiding observation, than they had ever had before; so, the swell of the old organ was borne to my ears like funeral music; and the rooks, as they hovered about the grey tower and swung in the bare trees of the priory-garden, seemed to call to me that the place was changed, and that Estella was gone out of it for ever.**

To the south of the cathedral is Minor Canons Row, a terrace of eighteenth-century houses. Here in *The Mystery of Edwin Drood* lived the Reverend Mr Crisparkle and his mother. Dickens describes how **the houses had little porches over the doors, like sounding-boards over old pulpits.** They still do. By one of the doors is a plaque, not to the Crisparkles but to the actors, Sybil and Russell Thorndike, who spent some of their childhood in the tied cottage allotted to their father, who was a Canon of the Cathedral.

To the west of Minor Canon Row is the garden known as The Vines, called in *The Mystery of Edwin Drood* "the Monks' Vineyard". Edwin and his affianced Rosa Bud used to stroll in these gardens. These were the vineyards, just outside the walls of the city, of the medieval abbey connected to the cathedral. On the street to the west of the gardens is Restoration House, a massive construction which the perceptive observer will see was originally two houses. There is little architectural unity and no symmetry in the building, which was constructed in the sixteenth century but probably on medieval foundations. The two houses were joined up in the middle of the following century. In 1660 it was occupied by a disillusioned Cromwellian soldier, Colonel Gibbon, though owned by a Royalist, Francis Clerke. Gibbon hosted King Charles II on his return from 11 years' exile during the Commonwealth period. Hence the name of Restoration House. Another visitor to the house in the reign of King Charles II was the diarist, Samuel Pepys. He was visiting the Medway towns in his capacity as an official (like Dickens's own father) of the Royal Navy. He noted that the house was a pretty seat, with a cherry garden where he *met with a young, plain, silly shopkeeper and his wife, a pretty young woman, and I did kiss her*.

In 1986 the television comedian, Rod Hull, famous for his puppet, an aggressive emu, bought the house for £270,000. Hull was a local lad, having been born on the Isle of Sheppey. He spent half a million on the house but went bankrupt, and the house was repossessed.

Dickens made the house the model for Miss Havisham's house in *Great Expectations*: a house **of old brick, and dismal, and had a great many iron bars to it. Some of the windows had been walled up; of those that remained, all the lower were rustily barred. There was a courtyard in front, and that was barred; so, we had to wait, after ringing the bell, until some one should come to open it.**

On his last visit to Rochester, Dickens was seen leaning against the railings opposite Restoration House, gazing at the building. It is believed that if he had been able to continue writing *The Mystery of Edwin Drood*, the building may have made an appearance in that book.

In *Great Expectations* Miss Havisham's house is called Satis House. There is a Satis House on Boley Hill to the southeast of the Cathedral. It was the home of Richard Watts, sixteenth-century philanthropist and Member of Parliament for Rochester. Watts entertained his sovereign, Queen

Elizabeth I, in Rochester. She declared her *satis*faction with his hospitality and the name reflects the Queen's content.

Restoration House is today privately owned, but the house and gardens are open to the public some days during the summer.

Let us return to Rochester Bridge and walk through the city, along the High Street.

Dickens first knew the street between the ages of seven and eleven when he lived at Chatham. In middle age he returned to live at Gad's Hill and wrote about the Medway towns in an essay, "Dullborough Town", published in *All the Year Round* in 1860. As he perceived it, during the intervening 36 years **the town had shrunk fearfully. I had entertained the impression that the High Street was at least as wide as Regent-street, London, or the Italian Boulevard at Paris. I found it little better than a lane.**

The silent High Street, Dickens wrote in his Christmas story "The Seven Poor Travellers", **is full of gables, with old beams and timbers carved into strange faces. It is oddly garnished with a queer old clock that projects over the pavement out of a grave red brick building, as if Time carried on business there, and hung out his sign.**

The projecting clock is on the Corn Exchange on the left (northern) side of the road. In his 1860 essay he recalled his childhood impressions of that clock, which he had **supposed to be the finest clock in the world: whereas it now turned out to be as inexpressive, moon-faced, and weak a clock as ever I saw. It belonged to a Town Hall, where I had seen an Indian (who I now suppose wasn't an Indian) swallow a sword (which I now suppose he didn't.) The edifice had appeared to me in those days so glorious a structure, that I had set it up in mind as the model on which the Genie of the Lamp built the palace for Aladdin.**

But before we reach the Corn Exchange there are two other major buildings of Dickensian interest. On the right is the Bull Inn, or more correctly, the Royal Victoria and Bull.

This historic inn is on a medieval site, though the present building dates from the late eighteenth century.

This was the Winglebury Arms in *Sketches by Boz* and the place where the Pickwickians stayed on their visit to Rochester. Mr Jingle stayed elsewhere but he did commend the Bull as a "**nice house – good beds**".

Today the Royal Victoria and Bull hotel is largely closed for refurbishment, but the premises flourishes as the Rochester Bar and the Swank! Bar, to the east and west respectively. The Rochester Bar provides drinks, snacks and a snooker table, as well as sports television. The Swank! Bar on the other side of the arched entrance to the old inn courtyard provides, in the words of its website, *a quality experience whether enjoying an innovative brasserie style business lunch with free wifi, or meeting friends for an evening drink.*

In *Sketches by Boz*, the inn had **a great, wide rambling staircase, three stairs and a landing – four stairs and another landing – one step and another landing – half-a-dozen stairs and another landing – and so on –** [that] **conducts to galleries of bedrooms, and labyrinths of sitting-rooms ...** The staircase is a rectangular spiral but there are further narrower staircases leading to galleries of rooms. The staircase is where Jingle coolly insulted Dr Slammer in *The Pickwick Papers*. Those who stay at the hotel will not have great difficulty in visualising the hotel that Mr Pickwick stayed at.

"**Devil of a mess on the staircase, waiter,**" said the stranger. "**Forms going up – carpenters going down – lamps, glasses, harps. What's going forward?**"

"**Ball, Sir,**" said the waiter.

Today on the staircase and on the landing are portraits and paintings of variable quality. The hotel's heyday is long past to judge from photographs of former patrons of the hotel hanging on the landing walls – they include Edward Heath and Ernest Marples.

To the left at the top of the stairs is the ballroom, the scene of the ball attended by Mr Jingle (in Mr Winkle's borrowed clothes) and Mr Tupman.

It was – and still is – a long room, with crimson-covered benches, and wax candles in glass chandeliers. The musicians were securely confined in an elevated den, and quadrilles were being systematically got through by two or three sets of dancers. Two card tables were made up in the adjoining card-room, and two pairs of old ladies, and a corresponding number of stout gentlemen, were executing whist therein. On my visit to the room I found it being used as a store but it was possible to envisage it as Dickens described it in *The Pickwick Papers* – including the **elevated den**, a small overhanging minstrels' gallery.

It is claimed that Mr Pickwick – and Charles Dickens himself – occupied room number 17.

The inn also served as The Blue Boar in *Great Expectations*. After Pip received the 25 guineas from Miss Havisham so he could be formally apprenticed to his brother-in-law Joe, Pip's sister insisted that **nothing would serve her but we must have a dinner out of that windfall at the Blue Boar.** This was held, presumably, at one of the sitting-rooms upstairs for rather **late in the evening Mr Wopsle gave us Collins's ode, and threw his blood-stain'd sword in thunder down, with such effect that a waiter came in and said, "The Commercials underneath send up their compliments, and it wasn't the Tumblers' Arms".**

The management of the Blue Boar treated Pip in accordance with his presumed fortunes. When he returned, knowing that Miss Havisham had not been his benefactor, **I found the Blue Boar in possession of the intelligence, and I found that it made a great change in the Boar's demeanour. Whereas the Boar had cultivated my good opinion with warm assiduity when I was coming into prosperity, the Boar was exceedingly cool on the subject now that I was going out of property.**

It was evening when I arrived, much fatigued by the

journey I had so often made so easily. The Boar could not put me in my usual bedroom, which was engaged (probably by some one who had expectations), and could only assign me a very indifferent chamber among the pigeons and post-chaises up the yard.

The second of the buildings of Dickensian interest is the Guildhall. It stands opposite the Royal Victoria and Bull and was built at the end of the seventeenth century as the headquarters of the city council, its courthouse and gaol. The principal room is still known as the Court Hall. Here, in *Great Expectations*, Pip was ceremoniously bound to Joe as his apprentice. The Hall was a queer place, I thought, with higher pews in it than a church – and with people hanging over the pews looking on – and with mighty Justices (one with a powdered head) leaning back in chairs, with folded arms, or taking snuff, or going to sleep, or writing, or reading the newspapers – and with some shining black portraits on the walls, which my unartistic eye regarded as a composition of hardbake and sticking-plaster. Here, in a corner, my indentures were duly signed and attested, and I was "bound". The high pews have gone, but much has not changed. The portraits include those of King William, Queen Anne and Sir Cloudesley Shovell – admiral and MP for Rochester. There was formerly a market under the arches below and the building was the seat for local government until 1974. Today it is an excellent (free) museum, with a couple of floors devoted to the prison hulks that were based in the Medway estuary until the middle of the nineteenth century.

Proceeding eastwards – past two second-hand bookshops – we pass the Corn Exchange with the clock described in "Dullborough Town" – though Dickens placed the clock on the **town hall**.

A little further on the right is a fifteenth-century gateway surmounted by an eighteenth-century upper storey. It led into the monastery attached to the cathedral. It is described in *The Mystery of Edwin Drood*:

They all three looked towards an old stone gatehouse crossing the Close, with an arched thoroughfare passing beneath it. Through its latticed window, a fire shines out upon the fast-darkening scene, involving in shadow the pendent masses of ivy and creeper covering the building's front.

John Jasper lived in the gatehouse – "my bachelor gatehouse" – then known as Chertsey's Gate but now better known as Jasper's Gate. Dickens describes the gateway as **a lighthouse on the margin of the tide of busy life**. Next door lived the cathedral verger, Mr Tope, whose wife looked after John Jasper; the two households were interconnected. Today a Topes' restaurant occupies the old house.

Continuing eastward, just past the Information Centre, we come to Richard Watts's Charity. His monument is in the cathedral but the plaque on the wall of this building indicates that it was an endowed resort for *six poor travellers* who could stay the night – one night only – and be given four pence when they left. Dickens visited the house in 1854 with Wilkie Collins. **I found it to be a clean white house, of a staid and venerable air, with the quaint old door ... choice little latticed windows, and a roof of three gables.** He used the experience of the visit for his Christmas story later that year, "The Seven Poor Travellers". Dickens himself was the seventh – Collins was overlooked.

I found the party to be thus composed. Firstly, myself. Secondly, a very decent man indeed, with his right arm in a sling, who had a certain clean, agreeable smell of wood about him, from which I judged him to have something to do with shipbuilding. Thirdly, a little sailor-boy, a mere child, with a profusion of rich dark brown hair, and deep womanly-looking eyes. Fourthly, a shabby-genteel personage in a threadbare black suit, and apparently in very bad circumstances, with a dry, suspicious look; the absent buttons on his waistcoat eked out with red tape; and a bundle of extraordinarily tattered papers sticking out of

an inner breast-pocket. Fifthly, a foreigner by birth, but an Englishman in speech, who carried his pipe in the band of his hat, and lost no time in telling me, in an easy, simple, engaging way, that he was a watchmaker from Geneva, and travelled all about the Continent, mostly on foot, working as a journeyman, and seeing new countries – possibly (I thought) also smuggling a watch or so, now and then. Sixthly, a little widow, who had been very pretty and was still very young, but whose beauty had been wrecked in some great misfortune, and whose manner was remarkably timid, scared, and solitary. Seventhly and lastly, A Traveller of a kind familiar to my boyhood, but now almost obsolete, – a Book-Peddler, who had a quantity of pamphlets and Numbers with him, and who presently boasted that he could repeat more verses in an evening than he could sell in a twelvemonth.

Dickens's visit and story recorded the last years of the charity that dated back to the sixteenth century. By the middle of the nineteenth century the charity had accumulated a lot of money. In the 1850s it was reorganised by the Trustees; the rest house for travellers continued with a master and matron, but £4,000 was put aside for the construction of almshouses on the Maidstone Road, built in a Jacobean style – they can still be seen. Public baths were built and apprenticeships provided for the deserving poor. Many of the functions of the charity have been taken over by the Welfare State but Watts's charitable work still continues with support for specific assistance in local hospitals and with apprenticeships and financial support for students.

Walking further east we pass the site of the Roman and medieval walls. A stretch and a corner bastion can be seen to the north. Once we are beyond the walled city, buildings that date back to the Middle Ages are larger and more expansive. To the left is Eastgate House. A massive Elizabethan building, it is currently used for exhibitions and weddings. It was the model for the Nuns' House in *The Mystery of Edwin*

Drood and was described as **a venerable brick edifice, whose present appellation is doubtless derived from the legend of its conventual uses.** Here Rosa Bud went to the school run by Miss Twinkleton (a name curiously like Miss Pinkerton, whose Academy is the scene of the first chapter of Thackeray's *Vanity Fair*.) Dickens probably used the building as the model for another girls' school, Westgate House in *The Pickwick Papers*. Here Mr Pickwick scaled the wall in his attempt to entrap Captain FitzMarshall, aka Mr Jingle.

In the garden of Eastgate House is the chalet that was given to Dickens by Charles Fechter, and originally erected in the shrubbery across the road from Gad's Hill Place. **In the summer,** he wrote to John Forster, (**supposing it not to be blown away in the spring) the upper room will make a charming study.** There are two rooms, one above the other, each about 16 feet square. There was an outside staircase, and Dickens had mirrors fitted into the upper room. He installed a small table and a sloping desktop, coach and chairs. It became his favourite place of work in summer months. He was cut off from the house. *I used to hear what sounded like someone making a speech*, one young gardener recalled years later. *I wondered what it was at first, and then I found out. It was Mr Dickens composing his writing out loud.*

It was here in the chalet that Dickens wrote the last chapter of *Edwin Drood*, just before his fatal stroke. After his death, the chalet was moved to Crystal Palace for a year, and then found a home in the terrace garden at the back of Cobham Hall. It stayed there until 1961 when it was restored and erected in the gardens of Eastgate House. At present it is in need of repair. Rotten wood needs to be replaced. It is hoped that with funding raised by the local Dickens Fellowship and support from the National Lottery, the chalet will be fully restored. Part of the £23,000 raised by the Fellowship was the result of a raffle, the prize for which was an authenticated strand of Dickens's hair.

Diagonally opposite Eastgate House is 150–154 High

Street. This was the home of Mr Sapsea in *The Mystery of Edwin Drood*. It is a shambling construction of three storeys, with shops on the ground floor. In the novel it is described as **irregularly modernised here and there, as steady deteriorating generations found, more and more, that they preferred air and light to Fever and Plague.** The house is also considered to be where Mr Pumblechook in *Great Expectations* had his corn seed shop and residence, where Pip spent the night before setting off for London for the first time. He was **sent straight to bed in an attic with a sloping roof, which was so low in the corner where the bedstead was, that I calculated the tiles as being within a foot of my eyebrows.**

The pedestrianised High Street ends at the junction with Star Hill. A few yards up Star Hill on the right are the Royal Function Rooms. They occupy a building constructed in the 1880s for the Conservative Club, as is clear from relief lettering beneath the gables. A plaque records that this was the site of the Rochester Theatre. Built in 1791, it was where Dickens, as a child, was taken to see the clown, Grimaldi, whose memoirs he was later to edit for publication. Here was born his passion for the theatre and **a strong veneration for Clowns.** The acting was often ham and the sets amateurish, but this theatre moulded his sense of history and nurtured his love of Shakespeare. **Richard the Third, in a very uncomfortable cloak, had first appeared to me there, and had made my heart leap with terror by backing up against the stage-box in which I was posted, while struggling for life against the virtuous Richmond. It was within these walls that I had learnt as from a page of English history, how that wicked King slept in war-time on a sofa much too short for him, and how fearfully his conscience troubled his boots.** One story he remembered for the rest of his life was about an actor who completely forgot his lines at this theatre. He could neither hear the prompter nor attract his attention. But he had resource and strode off the stage with the words, *I will return anon*; he left to refresh his memory from the script.

It was at the Rochester Theatre that Mr Jingle in *The Pickwick Papers* was engaged to play, co-starring with a **"rum fellow"**, as Jingle said, **"– does the heavy business – no actor – strange man – all sorts of miseries – dismal Jemmy, we call him on the circuit"**. One of Dr Slammer's companions recognised Jingle as having acted at the theatre, and as a strolling player he was not socially significant enough to be a partner in a duel.

Dickens returned to this theatre in 1860 but found it in **a bad and declining way. A dealer in wine and bottled beer had already squeezed his trade into the box-office, and the theatrical money was taken – when it came – in a kind of meat-safe in the passage.** The theatre also appears in *The Mystery of Edwin Drood*: **A new grand comic Christmas pantomime is to be produced at the Theatre: the latter heralded by the portrait of Signor Jacksonini the clown, saying, "How do you do to-morrow?"**

Another Dickensian theatrical connection with the Medway towns is in the history of the family of his mistress, Ellen (Nelly) Ternan. Nelly's parents met in Rochester. Her father, William, had been an actor in Rochester, and was also a trader. William met Frances (Fanny), also an actor, through the theatre in the town, and, although they toured as an acting family, Nelly herself was born in a small house on the Maidstone Road in March 1839 – in the same year as Dickens's second daughter, Katey. (Oddly enough, just as Nelly was born about three miles from where Dickens died, so she died in Southsea about three miles from where Dickens was born. Even more oddly, she is buried in Highland Road cemetery in Portsmouth, a hundred yards or so from the grave of Maria Beadnell, Dickens's first love. Such a coincidence would stretch credulity if it appeared in fiction.)

Chatham

... a mere dream of chalk, and drawbridges, and mastless ships in a muddy river, roofed like Noah's arks ...

These were David Copperfield's impressions of Chatham when he walked from London to Dover in search of his great-aunt Betsey Trotwood. He had walked 23 miles from Black-heath and had just been swindled into selling his remaining disposable clothes in order to buy some food.

Mr Jingle in *The Pickwick Papers* summarised the town in a similar pithy way:

... Queer place – Dock-yard people of upper rank don't know people of lower rank – Dock-yard people of lower rank don't know small gentry – small gentry don't know tradespeople – Commissioner don't know anybody.

Chatham was home to Charles Dickens for seven years from 1816, when he was four, until the summer of 1823. Positive impressions of the town remained with him for the rest of his life. It was, in the words of his friend and biographer, John Forster, *the birthplace of his fancy*. If he had any home town, it was Chatham. His father worked at the dockyard, dealing with pay for the Navy; the Naval Pay Office where he worked dates from 1808, and survives, a handsome Georgian building. A plaque records the fact that John Dickens worked here. Added to it is another plaque noting that a great grandson of Charles Dickens, Captain PGC Dickens, was Captain of the Dockyard in 1963. The town of Chatham, its sailors and the neighbourhood, all appear in his work. The young Dickens left the town by stagecoach and returned by train. **The coach that had carried me away, was melodiously called Timpson's Blue-Eyed Maid, and belonged to Timpson, at the coach-office up-street; the locomotive engine that had brought me back, was called severely No. 97, and belonged to S.E.R., and was spitting ashes and hot water over the blighted ground.**

The winding River Medway, secluded from the Thames but not too far from the capital, made Chatham an appropriate

Ordnance Terrace, Chatham

location for the naval base. It functioned as such from the sixteenth century to 1984 when dockyard and naval barracks both closed. In a naval equivalent to swords being turned into ploughshares, wharves for battleships have been transformed into marinas for pleasure craft. The town has been ravaged by developers and a sad atmosphere prevails with a tang of having seen better and more meaningful times. Much of the Georgian dockyard has survived and is now a museum. So has the elegant Command House, on Riverside Gardens, overlooking the site of the original Tudor dockyard. But other examples of the eighteenth century architectural heritage have been destroyed, either by enemy action or by insensitive "improvements".

Dickens's first home here was in Ordnance Terrace. It was fictionalised as Gordon Place in the story "Old Lady" in *Sketches by Boz*. In the same book there are other memories of Ordnance Terrace. The story "Our Parish" has an old lady based on a kindly neighbour, Mrs Newnham. In the same story, the Half Pay Captain was based on another resident of the Terrace. And James Steerforth in *David Copperfield* was possibly based on George Stroughill, another neighbour. The household had a maidservant called Mary Weller, whose surname was probably the inspiration for the name of Dickens's first great comic creation.

Overlooking the railway station, the Terrace still happily survives. In the late 1960s the whole terrace was threatened with demolition, on the pretext that it needed to be restored. It is an elegant late-eighteenth century group of houses, with a plaque on the house Dickens occupied. The windows of the upper floors command a view of the whole town of Chatham, and of the Medway.

In his 1860 piece "Dullborough Town", written for *All the Year Round*, he wrote: **I began to look about me; and the first discovery I made, was, that the Station had swallowed up the playing-field** [where as a lad], **in the hay-making time**, [he had] **been delivered from the dungeons of**

Seringapatam, an immense pile (of hollyhock), by my own countrymen, the victorious British (boy next door and his two cousins). And had been recognised with ecstasy by my affianced one (Miss Green), who had come all the way from England (second house in the terrace) to ransome me, and marry me.

Dickens was never nostalgic about a pre-industrial Britain. He welcomed scientific and technological innovations. Any nostalgia he had was for the vision of his childhood; that playing field had stirred his child's imagination and now it **was gone. The two beautiful hawthorn-trees, the hedge, the turf, and all those buttercups and daisies, had given place to the stoniest of jolting roads: while, beyond the Station, an ugly dark monster of a tunnel kept its jaws open, as if it had swallowed them and were ravenous for more destruction.**

Ordnance Terrace leads to some hilly parkland that looks down on New Road, now the main road from Rochester to Canterbury. This New Road was built at the end of the eighteenth century to bypass the centre of Chatham. The parkland used to be the grounds of Fort Pitt, built while Dickens was a boy in Chatham. The fort was turned into a military hospital and then became a girls' school. The grounds were later transformed into the park. It was at **sunset, in a lonely field beyond Fort Pitt** that Mr Winkle, in *The Pickwick Papers*, nearly fought his duel with Doctor Slammer of the 97th Regiment.

In 1821 the Dickens family moved to cheaper quarters – to 18 St Mary's Place. The house they lived in was next door to the Providence Baptist Church of the young Reverend William Giles. Dickens attended a school run by him until June 1823. He was head boy and Giles inspired him. When Dickens's parents left Chatham at the end of 1822, moving to London, Charles stayed on with the Giles family. When he left, Giles gave him a packet of books and later, after the success of *The Pickwick Papers*, Giles sent a snuff box, addressed to *The Inimitable Boz*. Dickens cherished this title for the rest of his life.

At St Mary's Place the Dickens family took in a lodger, Dr Matthew Lamert, who may have been the model for Dr Slammer in *The Pickwick Papers*. Dr Lamert married Mary Allen, the widowed sister of Charles's mother. Lamert's son from his previous marriage took young Charles to the theatre in Rochester. (A few years later he also introduced him to the work of the blacking factory at Hungerford Stairs.) There is today nothing to indicate young Charles Dickens's second Chatham home. The house suffered damage in the Second World War and was later pulled down. Today the Iceland car park occupies the site. The chapel next door became a Salvation Army drill hall and the building lasted until the 1990s. The area, the Brook, now a busy through road, was for many years the town's red light district, the clientele being sailors on leave. As late as the 1940s the navy used to issue leave-bound sailors contraceptives.

The Brook is crossed by the High Street. To the west it is pedestrianised. Most of the buildings are from the post-Dickens nineteenth and twentieth centuries. Many places associated with Dickens's childhood have gone. There was a public house, the Mitre, where the boy Dickens used to sing comic songs. In the nineteenth century it was called The Mitre Inn and Clarence Hotel – for the Duke of Clarence, later King William IV, stayed here. In a lesser-known Christmas story, "The Holly Tree Inn", written in 1855, the narrator recalls this inn and how **I loved the landlord's youngest daughter to distraction – but let that pass. It was in this Inn that I was cried over by my rosy little sister, because I had acquired a black-eye in a fight**. The site of the inn is now occupied by a Primark.

To the east of the Brook is the Gala Bingo Hall, which is on the site of the workhouse. When the Dickens family were at St Mary's Place they recruited a diminutive servant girl from the workhouse who became the model for the

Marchioness in *The Old Curiosity Shop*. This was probably the first workhouse that Dickens was aware of – presumably providing material for *Oliver Twist*. Incidentally Mudfog is a name applied both to the location of Oliver's workhouse and also to Chatham in the "Mudfog Papers", stories he wrote for *Bentley's Miscellany* in 1837. Oliver Twist's Mudfog is north of London, for Oliver walks to London via Barnet. But the other Mudfog is a maritime town: **Mudfog is a pleasant town – a remarkably pleasant town – situated in a charming hollow by the side of a river, from which river, Mudfog derives an agreeable scent of pitch, tar, coals, and rope yarn, a roving population in oil skin hats, a pretty steady influx of drunken bargemen, and a great many other maritime advantages. There is a good deal of water about Mudfog, and yet it is not exactly the sort of town for a watering place, either.**

Nearby is Institute Road, where in the middle of the nine-teenth century there was a Mechanics Institute, providing education for the working classes. Dickens was a great sup-porter of these Institutes and in 1861 helped to raise funds for this one, giving six readings in the Chatham Opera House, on the site of which there is now a shop at 205 High Street.

This part of Chatham lies in the shadow of the Lines, the open country to the east. A twentieth-century war memorial is the hub of a number of footpaths over this public park-land. The site of a large car park beyond the war memorial is where the Pickwickians, with Mr Wardle, witnessed the military review: **the whole population of Rochester and the adjoining towns rose from their beds at an early hour … in a state of the utmost bustle and excitement. A grand review was to take place upon the Lines. The manoeuvres of half-a-dozen regiments were to be inspected by the eagle eye of the commander-in-chief; temporary fortifications had been erected, the citadel was to be attacked and taken, and a mine was to be sprung.** It is windy up here, and was so when Mr Pickwick was there. The wind snatched away his hat and the poor man had to chase after it; the hat and Mr Pickwick were rescued by Mr Wardle, and this was the beginning of a beautiful friendship.

When Dickens moved back to Kent, to Gad's Hill Place, he often revisited the sites of his childhood. On one occasion he wandered up to the Lines. **I took a walk upon these Lines and mused among the fortifications, grassy and innocent enough on the surface at present, but tough subjects at the core.**

To the north is Fort Amherst, built in 1756 to guard the landward approach to the dockyard. In its vicinity David Copperfield spent a night. He **crept, at last, upon a sort of grass-grown battery overhanging a lane, where a sentry was walking to and fro. Here I lay down, near a cannon; and, happy in the society of the sentry's footsteps ... slept soundly until morning.**

Beyond is Chatham Dockyard itself. John Dickens used to go regularly to Sheerness to pay the employees of the dockyard there. Sometimes he would sail on a seventeenth-century yacht, taking the young Charles and his older sister, Frances (Fanny) with him.

Many years later Dickens became friends with an aristocratic lady, Mary Boyle, a forgotten novelist and a fellow amateur actor. He met her through her relations, Mr and Mrs Watsons of Rockingham Castle, the model for Chesney Wold in *Bleak House*. Dickens had met the Watsons on one of his European sojourns. At Rockingham he took part with his upper-class friends in amateur dramatics and played Sir Peter Teazle opposite Mary's Lady Teazle. It was an improbable friendship, but they had Sheerness in common. Mary was two years older than Dickens and her father had been Commissioner of Sheerness Docks. If they never met when they were children, they at least had North Kent in common.

The historic dockyard has been transformed in the last decade. There are museums and visitors' centres, shopping malls and cinemas. One of the most interesting additions to the old yard is Dickens World, a "themed attraction", which is roughly on the site of the ship fitters' workshop, where winches, windlasses and rudders were made for the big ships. It had been an idea for several decades but was made a reality, at a cost of £62 million, in 2007. Victorian-style buildings have been constructed around a central roofed courtyard. There is a Victorian school, damp corridors representing Marshalsea, Peggotty's house and Fagin's Den. The Dickens Fellowship was consulted in order to ensure authenticity. The complex includes a cinema, a theatre, and meeting rooms – one of which provides the venue for meetings of the Medway Towns branch of the Dickens Fellowship. You can eat at the Six Jolly Fellowship Porters restaurant and you can take a boat ride through darkest Victorian London. Actors are employed to stroll around the courtyard playing the parts of Dickens's characters. It has been used as a set for films and television productions and the rock/folk group the Hoosiers used it as a location for their video, *Cops and Robbers*. There are arrangements for school outings, and you can even get married there. It has something for the whole family. Dickens would have loved it.

Around the Medway Towns

The Marshes

Ours was the marsh country, down by the river, within, as the river wound, twenty miles of the sea … the dark flat wilderness beyond the churchyard, intersected with dykes and mounds and gates, with scattered cattle feeding on it, was the marshes; and … the low leaden line beyond, was the river …

In this way, the scene is set at the opening of *Great Expectations*, the novel published serially from 1860 to 1861 and the first work written after Dickens's return to Kent and his residence at Gad's Hill. Oddly enough he does not name places but much of the novel reflects Dickens's rediscovery of a part of the country he had known as a child 40 years earlier – the time of the setting of the novel. Rochester is not mentioned by name but it is clearly the novel's **market town.**

The marshes – or **th'meshes** as both Joe and Mrs Gargery call them – are recognisable from Dicken's description: the dykes, the mounds and the gates, the scattered cattle. Some things have changed however; there is now a sea wall along the Thames and the land is no longer subject to flooding at high tide. The castle at Cooling used to be a Thames-side fort when built in the fourteenth century but today the river is two or more miles away. There are no longer prison hulks but there is a sense of brooding menace and desolation about the place. This can best be captured in the winter. It was Christmas Eve when Magwitch surprised Pip in the first chapter of *Great Expectations*.

In January I walked east of Gravesend on the 'Saxon Shore Way'. On the edge of Gravesend is the Ship and Lobster Inn, claiming to be the first and last pub on the River Thames. It may have been The Ship in *Great Expectations*. I left before 8:00am. There was a seasonal mist and I could hear the fog-horns of ships as they made their way up or down the Thames, but I was unable to see them. For the whole day the Essex coast was out of sight. I walked about 15 miles along by the sea wall and met nobody. It was bitterly cold with occasional flakes of snow. I could not stop for more than ten minutes for fear of being frozen to immobility. I sympathised with Magwitch and Compeyson for the night they spent on these marshes. But people had passed by recently, to judge from the human detritus I came across. One mile from Gravesend I found two or three rusting supermarket trolleys. After that I came upon a recently inflated balloon. And then a football. How had each of these items ended up on this path?

On each side of the Thames are forts, part of the defences of outer London. The first to be seen outside Gravesend is Shornemead Fort, built in the 1790s but redeveloped in the middle of the following century. It is a ruin, neglected and decaying; unwanted. The path curves to the north to a larger fort, Cliffe Fort, built in the 1860s opposite Coalhouse Fort on the Essex coast. The engineer responsible for constructing these forts was General Charles Gordon, later killed in Khartoum. Either of these forts could have served as the Battery in the early chapters of *Great Expectations*. It was a place Joe and Pip escaped for larky chats away from the unlarky chidings of Mrs Joe.

The village of Cliffe is now a mile from the sea, but it was once a port. A cordite factory and cement works have not added to its charms, but it has had its moments of history. It used to be called Bishop's Cliffe and was the location of meetings of Saxon bishops in the province of Canterbury. It has been argued that this was the first parliamentary system in England.

East of Cliffe Fort there is little to distract the eye. But it is probable that there was a hut – a lime kiln – between the village of Cliffe and the river where Orlick lured Pip in his prosperity and nearly killed him. **The direction that I took, was not that in which my old home lay** ... Chalk was burnt in lime kilns and the ashes were used as fertiliser. Huts dotted the marshes near the chalky hills. **It was another half-hour before I drew near to the kiln. The lime was burning with a sluggish stifling smell, but the fires were made up and left, and no workmen were visible. Hard by was a small stone-quarry. It lay directly in my way, and had been worked that day, as I saw by the tools and barrows that were lying about.** As usual, Dickens was very specific in his descriptions and directions.

I turned inland at Egypt Bay, which was one of the mooring sites for the prison hulks. These were ships converted in the eighteenth and nineteenth centuries into prisons to hold convicts who had been sentenced to transportation before they were dispatched to the colonies. North America before independence was first used as a destination for transported criminals, then it was mainly Australia. The hulks were also used to hold prisoners of war during the Napoleonic wars – mainly French but also men from other European countries allied to the French. They were moored near the shore and when the tide was out a lucky and resourceful convict might escape to the sand and mud. He need not have had to swim ashore: at high tide this would have been impossible if he had been in irons. In the sands alongside the Medway estuary the bones and skeletons of prisoners have been found, prisoners who had been unsuccessful in their bid for freedom. The practice of using hulks for prisons in and around the Medway estuary lasted until the 1870s.

Life in the hulks was grim. Convicts were detailed to carry out the toughest of manual labour in the dockyards.

One prisoner in *Great Expectations* summed it all up: **A most beastly place. Mudbank, mist, swamp and work; work, swamp, mist and mudbank.** As I passed Egypt Bay, the tide was out and it was possible to visualise the possible escape of a convict and his coming ashore and making his way through the dykes and marshes to some churchyard where the land began to rise.

I wandered south, away from the Thames. Even the footpaths marked on the map were not clear and it was only after several false starts that I reached a house with the splendidly Dickensian name of Swigshole. From there I walked over the wooded Northward Hill and down to the row of houses by Cooling Church. The names of the houses included one called Magwitch and another known as Fezziwig Cottage (after the family in *A Christmas Carol*). The main concern for residents of Cooling today is the possibility of an estuary airport. Many gardens had a poster protesting against the proposal.

In the cemetery around the parish yard are the graves of ten small children under three-foot-long lozenge-shaped tombstones. The children all died in infancy; six are from the Comport family who lived at Cooling Castle, four others are from another branch of the same family. Does the name Comport suggest the name of Compeyson, Magwitch's fellow prisoner and bitter enemy? Inside the church there is a memorial tablet to the Comport family.

It is unquestionably these graves that inspired Dickens in his description of the graves of Pip's parents and five brothers who all died in infancy. Dickens in his Gad's Hill years liked to bring visitors here. Occasionally he would walk from his home to Cooling Church and back in the afternoon, but he had known Cooling from his childhood in Chatham. Once, in the 1860s, he brought Marcus Stone, the young illustrator of *Our Mutual Friend*, to Cooling. **You see that church?** Dickens said to Stone, **That is where I saw the pauper's funeral in Oliver Twist.** The churchyard is more celebrated for the infants' graves and this has led people to see Cooling as the unnamed village where Pip and the Gargerys lived. Indeed one of the cottages is called The Forge. It may indeed have been a forge but in *Great Expectations* Gargery's forge is not near the church. There are other points that work against Cooling's claim. When Magwitch turned Pip upside down **"I saw the steeple under my feet"**. Cooling Church has a conical addition to the tower. Hardly a steeple, and certainly not visible if you are turned upside down. (Try it, next time you are there.) The only church in the Hoo peninsula with a steeple is Higham Church, two miles down the road from Gad's Hill, one mile beyond Lower Higham. The church in *Great Expectations* is – like Higham but not Cooling Church – cut off from the village: **our village lay, on the flat inshore among the alder trees and the pollards, a mile or more from the church**. Moreover in the novel there is a **gate at the side of the churchyard** that leads on to the open marshes. Dickens was not a regular churchgoer when he was at Gad's Hill but went occasionally to Higham Church and cooperated with the vicar in charitable work. He knew the church, and the location of the churchyard where Pip first met Magwitch fits Higham but not Cooling.

Other factors suggest Lower Higham as the Gargerys' village. Their village had a saw-pit, a windmill, a little shop and a public house. In Higham there was a saw-pit close to the disused canal. In the essay "Tramps", written in 1860 for *All the Year Round* and reprinted in *The Uncommercial Traveller*, Dickens wrote – a mixture of fact and fiction – about one tramp **lying drunk ... in the wheelwright's saw-pit under the shed where the felled trees are, opposite the sign of the Three Jolly Hedgers**. This essay was written in 1860, when he was also working on *Great Expectations*. Three Jolly Hedgers is suggestive of Three Jolly Bargemen, the tavern in the Gargerys' village. The old inn in the village used to be The Chequers, but is now closed.

The forge that he may have had in mind was possibly the forge at Chalk, three miles from Gad's Hill just outside

Gravesend. **Joe's forge adjoined our house, which was a wooden house, as many of the dwellings ion our country were – most of them, at that time.** The forge at Chalk is a clap-board construction, a common feature of the buildings of coastal Kent.

Of course *Great Expectations* is fiction and not reportage. Dickens, as we have seen, often described a building or location with such precision that we can identify it. But not infrequently he shifted the buildings around to fit the narrative geography of his novels. It seems that he imagined a village with elements drawn from different places. In *Great Expectations* he teases us by not specifying the places. And why not?

Cobham

... this is one of the prettiest and most desirable places of residence I ever met with.

This is Mr Pickwick's opinion of the village of Cobham when he walked out there through the woods from Rochester. After he moved to Gad's Hill Place it became one of Charles Dickens's favourite walks.

Cobham is separated from the spreading urbanisation of the Medway Towns by two or three miles of woodland and parkland. **A delightful walk it was: for it was a pleasant afternoon in June, and their way lay through a deep and shady wood, cooled by the light wind which gently rustled the thick foliage, and enlivened by the songs of the birds that perched upon the boughs. The ivy and the moss crept in thick clusters over the old trees, and the soft green turf overspread the ground like a silken mat.** From outer Strood a footpath passes under the motorway and over the railway and then up into the woods, part of the estate belonging to Cobham Hall, ancestral home of the Darnleys. The woods and grounds were designed by Humphrey Repton. The earls of Darnley lived at Cobham Hall from the eighteenth to the twentieth century. They derived their income from property in Ireland but during the nineteenth and twentieth centuries life did not go their way. During the second half of the twentieth century they sold the Hall, which is now an independent girls' school, and the grounds, which are today in the care of the National Trust.

The sixth Earl of Darnley was a friend of Charles Dickens – Dickens's scorn for the aristocracy was ideological rather than personal and did not prevent him from having cordial relations with noble neighbours. He was invited to use the private grounds of the Darnley estate whenever he wished, and to bring along any friends.

At the top of the climb from Strood we find an octagonal mausoleum – a Grade 1 Listed Building – recently restored and originally designed by James Wyatt for the fourth earl. Nearby, behind some iron fencing, is what is known as the Toe Monument. The fifth Earl as a young man came here to show friends how to use an axe, and proceeded to chop off one of his own toes. The monument marks the mishap.

When one emerges from the woods Cobham Hall can be seen to the right. It was built primarily in the sixteenth and early seventeenth centuries – **the quaint and picturesque architecture of Elizabeth's time – with eighteenth century additions designed by William Chambers and James Wyatt. Long vistas of stately oaks and elm trees appeared on every side; large herds of deer were cropping the fresh grass; and occasionally a startled hare scoured along the ground, with the speed of the shadows thrown by the light clouds which swept across a sunny landscape like a passing breath of summer.** The Hall and the gardens are featured in Dickens's essay, "Tramps", in which the Hall is seen through the eyes of an itinerant clock-repairer.

The path becomes a lane and reaches the village of Cobham at a crossroads. Cobham has three thriving public houses. The furthest from the park is the Leather Bottle. Here Mr Pickwick, Mr Snodgrass and Mr Winkle tracked down the fugitive Mr Tupman. **Having been directed to the Leather Bottle, a clean and commodious village ale-house, the three travellers entered, and at once inquired for a gentleman of the name of Tupman.** They were ushered into the parlour, **a long, low-roofed room furnished with a large number of high-backed leather-cushioned chairs, of fantastic shapes, and embellished with a great variety of old portraits and roughly-coloured prints of some antiquity.** Mr Pickwick's room was in the front, overlooking the churchyard. Here he sat up all night reading an old clergyman's manuscript.

The inn is still commodious and a warm and friendly place serving good food. The pictures and prints are worth a careful study, for this is a Dickensian museum. Many framed prints are of characters in the novels – Micawber, Mrs Gamp, Pecksniff – by various artists. Luke Fildes did the illustrations for *The Mystery of Edwin Drood* and one print is his moving drawing of Dickens's study at Gad's Hill after his death – *The Empty Chair*. (Moving but slightly misleading. Dickens died in the summer and his last writing was completed, not in the study at Gad's Hill Place, but in the chalet over the road.) There are pictures presented to the inn by Dickens's publishers, Chapman and Hall, and by JM Dent, who published the Everyman edition of his works in the twentieth century. One frame has picture postcards of a dozen characters; another is of cigarette cards. As well as many portraits of Dickens, there is also a programme of the Pickwick Bicycle Club, dated 1888. There are no fewer than three copies of a drawing of Mr Jingle by J Robertson Frith.

Dickens probably came here during his honeymoon at Chalk in April 1836 – he was writing *The Pickwick Papers* at the time. Four years later he returned, bringing his friends; his biographer, John Forster, and the artist Daniel Maclise.

There are also personal relics. His favourite chair is in one room. In another, behind a glass case, is **the immense leather bag** that accompanied him on his reading tours. Framed nearby is a poster for one of his last readings in 1870 at St

James's Hall, Piccadilly. Tickets in the stalls were seven shillings and five shillings, in the balcony three shillings. This was above an admission charge of one shilling. Tickets were available through Keith Prowse and Messrs Chappell, the company that organised the reading tours; both companies a century and a half later are still selling tickets for artistic events.

The most personal, and the most recent exhibit is an authenticated lock of Dickens's hair, barely visible in a glass case. This was the prize in the Dickens fellowship raffle held in early 2013 to raise money for the restoration of the chalet at Eastgate House, Rochester. The winner was a regular at the Leather Bottle and presented the lock, valued at £500, to the inn.

Outside the inn is a stone with cryptic letters:

BILST

UM

PSHI

S.M.

ARK

This reminds us of the episode in *The Pickwick Papers* when Mr Pickwick and his friends puzzled over some identical lettering: **This is some very old inscription,** said Mr Pickwick, **existing perhaps long before the ancient alms-houses in this place. It must not be lost.**

The Pickwickians were upstaged in their hypotheses by **the presumptuous and ill-conditioned Blotton, who, with a mean desire to tarnish the lustre of the immortal name of Pickwick, actually undertook a journey to Cobham in person, and on his return, sarcastically observed in an oration at the club, that he had seen the man from whom the stone was purchased; that the man presumed the stone to be ancient, but solemnly denied the antiquity of the inscription – inasmuch as he represented it to have been rudely carved by himself in an idle mood, and to display letters intended to bear neither more nor less than the simple construction of – "BILL STUMPS, HIS MARK."**

Dickens is mocking the scholarly pretensions of his own creation, but also laughing at the new wave of amateur archaeologists who were recording inscriptions indiscriminately. For example, a few miles away the prehistoric cromlech, Kit's Coty House, between Aylesford and Blue Bell Hill, also had graffiti that had sparked scholarly analysis. Dickens's satirical take on this is an extraordinary piece of confident cheek on the part of a young man of 24.

The **ancient alms-houses** are behind the Church of St Mary Magdalene (which has some of the finest brass effigies in the country), across the road from the Leather Bottle. Worth a detour, they are called Cobham College and date from the fourteenth century. The architect was probably Henry Yevele, responsible for parts of Westminster Abbey. Originally founded for five priests, the college passed to the family of Lord Cobham after the Reformation and is now, with its modern extension of six flats added in 2012, fulfilling its medieval function as sheltered accommodation for senior citizens.

South of Rochester

I have discovered that the seven miles between Maidstone and Rochester is one of the most beautiful roads in England.

Actually, the distance between the two towns is, according to the milestones, eight miles. Today vehicles are persuaded to take the north-south road further to the east. The main road in Dickens's time was the one that now leaves Rochester High Street just outside the Roman and medieval walls and passes between the Vines and Restoration House before steadily climbing up past the nineteenth-century buildings of Watts's Almshouses, and then, after a mile or so, Rochester Airport. Two motorways cross the road in the course of the eight miles, an erosion of what was once pretty wooded Downland countryside. A ganglion of dual carriageways, slip roads and roundabouts impede the walker in search of the beauties as seen by Dickens. Blue Bell Hill, where Dickens was fond of taking guests, especially American friends, was once as attractive as its name. **We often take our lunch on a hillside there in the summer, and then I lie down on the grass – a splendid example of laziness.** The woods are tucked away to the west of the main road but now one cannot escape from the drone of the motorway traffic. Blue Bell Hill is today a soulless commuter village.

One of the sites to which Dickens took his guests was Kits Coty, a megalithic burial chamber. For those unfamiliar with the area, this is today hard to find. In the 1840s he wrote to Forster from Broadstairs, proposing a **walk from Maidstone to Rochester and a visit to the Druidical altar on the wayside** [which] **are charming.** To the west is the village of Aylesford, with a fourteenth-century ragstone bridge over the Medway. It was formerly a most attractive village, but its charms have been drained away by the inexorable demands of the car and the pressing need to get somewhere else as fast as possible.

In Aylesford churchyard is the tomb of William Spong of Cob Tree. Spong is seen as the probable model for the affable Mr Wardle of Dingley Dell in *The Pickwick Papers*. The chapters on the first visit to Dingley Dell were written about the time Dickens was on his honeymoon at Chalk. It is likely that Dickens met Spong and came to Cob Tree then, and this may have been the prototype of Manor Farm, Dingley Dell. Many of the places in *The Pickwick Papers* are identifiable and without disguise, but it may be that he wanted to spare Spong any embarrassment, or uninvited visitors. There is no lake where Mr Pickwick and friends would have skated on their second visit, but there is a Manor Farm with a lake at Frindsbury on the northern outskirts of Strood. It may be that Dickens again shifted that geographical feature to a site that better suited his story.

"Pleasant, pleasant country," sighed the enthusiastic gentleman, as he opened his lattice window. "Who could

live to gaze from day to day on bricks and slates, who had once felt the influence of a scene like this? Who could continue to exist, where there are no cows but the cows on the chimney pots; nothing redolent of Pan but pan-tiles; no stone but stone crop?"

Cobtree Manor Park is now wooded parkland, a sylvan oasis and retreat from the surrounding motorised environment. It used to be the site of Maidstone Zoo, and was presented to the people of Maidstone by Sir Garrard Tyrwhitt-Drake in 1951.

Maidstone itself, with the county headquarters and local gaol, has lost the quiet charm of earlier decades. It was probably Muggleton in *The Pickwick Papers*: **a corporate town, with a mayor, burgesses, and freemen ... an open square for the market-place, and in the centre a large inn.** There have been claims for West Malling nearby to have been Muggleton, but the incorporation seems to tip the matter in Maidstone's favour. It would have been strange if Dickens, even in his fiction, overlooked the county town with which he was familiar, if not intimate. In a story told at Dingley Dell, "The Convict's Return", Dickens has a swipe at those who campaigned for the abolition of slavery abroad and were, at the same time – like William Wilberforce – complaisant about the state of factory workers in the newly industrialised north of England. **Muggleton is an ancient and loyal borough, mingling a zealous advocacy of Christian principles with a devoted attachment to commercial rights; in demonstration whereof, the mayor, corporation, and other inhabitants, have presented at divers times, no fewer than one thousand four hundred and twenty petitions against the continuance of negro slavery abroad, and an equal number against any interference with the factory system at home.**

Towards Canterbury

Dickens was less familiar with the countryside between

the Medway towns and Canterbury. He travelled along them when he was resident at Gad's Hill Place. But the best description of the road is in *David Copperfield* when David walks to Dover to find his aunt. Having been fleeced at Chatham, footsore and weary, he sets off on Watling Street and limps seven miles before resting by a stream, sleeping under a haystack. He is in hop-country. Along the way he was intimidated by tramps. **Some of them were ferocious-looking ruffians, who stared at me as I went by; and stopped, perhaps, and called after me to come back, and speak to them; and when I took to my heels, stoned me.**

After having a handkerchief stolen by one tramp who then brutally mistreated his partner, he was so frightened that, whenever **I saw any of these people coming, I turned back until I could find a hiding-place, where I remained until they had gone out of sight; which happened so often, that I was very seriously delayed.** When Dickens wrote his article on tramps for *The Uncommercial Traveller*, ten years after writing *David Copperfield*, the alarm of his fictional creation was replaced by humane curiosity about the wayfarers and vagabonds that wandered the Kentish roads in search of a livelihood. They were among those who were at the margins of society, people who stirred his compassionate feelings. He observed the seasonal migration of hoppers, when **the whole country-side for miles and miles will swarm with hopping tramps. They come in families, men, women, and children, every family provided with a bundle of bedding, an iron pot, a number of babies, and too often with some poor sick creature quite unfit for the rough life, for whom they suppose the smell of the fresh hop to be a sovereign remedy.**

East Kent

Broadstairs

This is a little fishing-place; intensely quiet; built on a cliff, whereon, in the centre of a tiny semicircular bay, our house stands, the sea rolling and dashing under the windows ... Under the cliff are rare good sands, where all the children assemble every morning and throw up impossible fortifications, which the sea throws down again at high-water. Old gentlemen and ancient ladies flirt after their own manner in two reading-rooms and on a great many scattered seats in the open air. Other old gentlemen look all day through telescopes and never see anything. In a bay-window in a one-pair sits, from nine o'clock to one, a gentleman with rather long hair and no neckcloth, who writes and grins as if he thought he were very funny indeed. His name is Boz. At one he disappears, and presently emerges from a bathing-machine, and may be seen – a kind of salmon-coloured porpoise – splashing about in the ocean. After that he may be seen in another bay-window on the ground-floor eating a strong lunch; after that walking a dozen miles or so, or lying on his back in the sand reading a book. Nobody bothers him unless they know he is disposed to be talked to, and I am told he is very comfortable indeed. He's as brown as a berry, and they *do* say is a small fortune to the innkeeper, who sells beer and cold punch.

Dickens regularly sang the praises of the small town of Broadstairs, tucked away in a bay between its larger Thanet sisters, Margate and Ramsgate. The area of Thanet, on the north east coast of Kent, has always had a distinctive personality. The three towns have today merged into one conurbation. Each town centre clings around a pier and an old harbour. Each has a surviving Regency terrace or two. Then the townscape drifts into suburbia and commercial zones, the gaps between buildings being filled up with ... cabbage fields.

Broadstairs was emerging as a fashionable resort for sea bathing in the 1830s, *for families*, as a contemporary guidebook wrote, *who prefer quiet and retirement to the more noisy pleasures of Margate and Ramsgate.*

Ramsgate also expanded during the years after the French Wars (as they were called at the time). Terraced houses and smart hotels overlooked the harbour. Ramsgate was the destination of the newly rich Tuggs family in *Sketches by Boz*, in preference to Gravesend (**"low"**) and Margate (**"commercial"**). The family took an outing on donkey-back to Pegwell Bay to the south. Today Ramsgate is the largest of the three Thanet towns.

Margate had been a pioneer resort in the late eighteenth century. Benjamin Beale is credited as the first pioneer of the bathing machine, and a fashionable town grew up on the hill above the old fishing village. With one or two terraces, a smart square, Cecil Square, and a Theatre Royal dating from 1787 and still functioning – the visitor can still identify traces of a smarter Margate. The town was the birthplace of the painter, JMW Turner, in 1775 and of the artist Tracey Emin nearly 200 years later.

Dickens first came to Broadstairs in 1837, bringing his wife and infant son, Charley, and staying at 12 High Street, a modest cottage, long gone and replaced by a shop (number 31) over which, in March 2013, there was still a Christmas decoration. A plaque records Dickens's residence here. It was not overlooking the sea; although he had just become famous with the publication of *The Pickwick Papers*, he was not yet financially secure enough or confident enough to rent

accommodation nearer the sea. **I have seen ladies and gentlemen walking upon the earth in slippers of buff,** he observed
on that visit, **pickling themselves in the sea in complete suits
of the same ... I have found that our next door neighbour has
a wife and something else under the same roof with the rest
of the furniture – the wife deaf and blind, and the something
else given to drinking.** His rooms looked out on to urban, not
maritime views. **You would hardly guess which is the main
street of our watering-place, but you may know it by its
being always stopped up with donkey-chaises. Whenever
you come here, and see harnessed donkeys eating clover out
of barrows drawn completely across a narrow thoroughfare,
you may be quite sure you are in our High Street.**

Dickens made Broadstairs his home for a few months
every summer or autumn for the next ten years. It was already
a favourite resort of Dickens's actor friend, William Macready. In 1839 Dickens stayed at 40 Albion Street, nearer the
sea and now part of the Albion Hotel. It was not too comfortable. There was a bower **which is shaded for you in the
one-pair front, where no chair or table has four legs of the
same length, and where no drawers will open till you have
pulled the pegs off, and then they keep open and won't
shut again.** The proximity to the sea made him more sensitive to its moods. Last night, he wrote to John Forster, **there
was such a sea! I staggered down to the pier and, creep-
ing under the lee of a large boat which was high and dry,
watched it breaking for nearly an hour. Of course I came
back wet through.** *Nicholas Nickleby* was completed during
this summer. He dedicated the book to Macready.

The following year he took Lawn House, in a small square
off Harbour Street. This is now Archway House. At the time,
1840, he was writing *The Old Curiosity Shop* and *Barnaby
Rudge*.

Dickens's routines in writing were becoming fixed. He
rose early and spent four hours writing. In the afternoon he
went for energetic walks but often with friends and family

whom he invited to Broadstairs – they had to look after themselves during the morning. After his walking he was ready to be social. He would walk with his family to the beach and to the pier. **We have a pier – a queer old wooden pier, fortunately – without the slightest pretensions to architecture, and very picturesque in consequence. Boats are hauled upon it, ropes are coiled all over it; lobster-pots, nets, masts, oars, spars, sails, ballast, and rickety capstans, make a perfect labyrinth of it.** It was Broadstairs in 1840 that was the scene of his first serious flirtation. He met a young lady, Eleanor Picken (who at twenty, was eight years his junior) at a party where there was some dancing. Eleanor later became a writer herself and, after Dickens's death, recorded her encounter, which must have been initially thrilling, but subsequently alarming. Inviting her to dance, he adopted a mock-archaic language: *Wilt tread a measure with me, sweet lady? Fain would I thread the mazes of the saraband with thee.*

To which she replied, *Aye, fair Sir, that I will right gladly. In good sooth, I'll never say Nay.*

They met in the daytime, in a group walking by the sea. On the jetty they danced a quadrille. Dickens's wife, as well as his younger brother, Frederick, was with them. He whistled a tune and Charles accompanied him on a pocket comb. Suddenly Dickens swept Eleanor off to the end of the jetty, grabbed her, and threatened to cast himself and her into the sea. She was suddenly scared. Her silk dress was soaked up to her knees and she screamed: *Mrs Dickens, help me! Make Mr Dickens let me go.*

Whereupon Catherine Dickens chided her husband: *Charles, how can you be so silly? You will both be carried off by the tide, and you'll spoil the poor girl's dress.*

Talk not to me of dress! Eleanor reported Dickens as saying, *When the pall of Night is enshrouding me in Cimmerian darkness, when we already stand on the brink of the great mystery, shall our thoughts be of fleshly vanities?*

This scene aside, Dickens was able to relax in Broadstairs in a way that seemed to be impossible in London: **I am in an exquisitely lazy state, bathing, walking, reading, lying in the sun, doing everything but working**.

The walking would be intensive. He would be observing people and buildings, everything. Sometimes his wanderings took him inland, away from the sea. The old village of Broadstairs was a mile from the bay, and was built around the Church of St Peter's, which he saw as **a hideous temple of flint, like a petrified haystack**. In 1845 he stayed at the Albion Hotel. He wrote to a friend, telling him he had **walked 20 miles a day since I came down, and went to a circus at Ramsgate on Saturday night**.

The sea was often rough. It had inspired Turner, and also thrilled Dickens. Until the coming of the railway in 1846, the main way of reaching the Thanet towns from London was by boat. September 1842 was particularly stormy: **the sea is running so high that we have no choice but to return by land. No steamer can come out of Ramsgate, and the Margate boat lay out all night on Wednesday with all her passengers on board ... We cannot open a window, or a door; legs are no use on the terrace; and the Margate boats can only take people aboard at Herne Bay**. Dickens, nonetheless, was fascinated by storms. The impressions of the storms were stored in his mind and were brought out in his description in *David Copperfield* of the storm that destroyed James Steerforth's boat. That took place at Yarmouth, but it was a Thanet storm Dickens had observed and was describing. The death of Steerforth, written at Broadstairs, was one of his favourite passages in his readings.

In the last two years of the 1840s Dickens took a flat at Chandos Place, south of the pier near what is today called Viking Bay. The flat looked **out upon a dark, grey sea, with a keen north-east wind blowing it in shore**. The railway brought more trippers. Dickens's portrait by Maclise was reproduced in his books, and Dickens was becoming a recognisable celebrity – indeed, part of the attraction of the town.

At home, Dickens was able to impose silence on his household so he could work during the mornings, but he could not control distractions outside the home. In 1848 he was complaining about the noise. **Vagrant music is getting to that height here, and is so impossible to be escaped from, that I fear that Broadstairs and I must part company in time to come. Unless it pours with rain I cannot write half-an-hour without the most excruciating organs, fiddles, bells, or glee-singers. There is a violin of the most torturing kind under the window now (time, ten in the morning) and an Italian box of music on the steps – both in full blast.** The following year he went to Bonchurch on the Isle of Wight in pursuit of tranquillity. Perhaps there was too much quiet, for he returned to Broadstairs later in the year, putting up at the Albion Hotel. **It is a rough little place, but a very pleasant one**, he wrote to a friend.

He was drawn to the elemental maritime character of Broadstairs. He wrote to friends constantly, wanting them to share the place with him, if not in person, at least through the allure of his descriptions. **The ocean lies winking in the sunlight like a drowsy lion,** he wrote about the town at low tide. Its **glassy waters scarcely curve upon the shore; the fishing-boats in the tiny harbour are all stranded in the mud ... Rusty cables and chains, ropes and rings, undermost parts of posts and piles, and confused timber defences against the waves, lie strewn about in a brown litter of tangled seaweed and fallen cliff ... The time when this pretty little semicircular sweep of houses, tapering off at the end of the wooden pier into a point in the sea, was a gay place.** And then, by contrast, at high tide: **The tide has risen; the boats are dancing on the bubbling water; the colliers are afloat again; the white-bordered waves rush in ... The radiant sails are gliding past the shore and shining on the far horizon; all the sea is sparkling, heaving, swelling up with life and beauty this bright morning.**

Fort House, Broadstairs

He had always wanted to rent Fort House for the season. This was the house on the Kingsgate road on the hill overlooking the harbour, pier and bay, and insulated from the din of trippers. It had been built in a mock Gothic style in 1801 for the commander of a fort that was next to the house. In the middle of the nineteenth century it was separated from the sea by a cornfield. The house became available in 1850 and he rented it that year and in the following year. (**It is more delightful here than I can express,** he wrote in 1851. **Corn growing, larks singing, garden full of flowers, fresh air on the sea. – O it is wonderful!**) The building was popularly known as Bleak House before Dickens came to Broadstairs, although at that time it was formally listed as Fort House. After Dickens's time it was renamed Bleak House, even though not a word of that novel was written there and this Broadstairs house does not actually feature in the novel – Esther Summerson's visit to Deal, on the coast towards Dover, was the nearest reference to the town. The Bleak House of the novel was clearly located in Hertford-shire near St Albans, although it is possible that some of the features of Fort House were reproduced in the fictional house – as Dickens did with other places. The House is now a hotel and restaurant. Some of the rooms are named after novels, but the room most redolent of Dickens is the study. Dickens's desk is in a niche overlooking the sea, where he could have drawn inspiration from the view – still or stormy, always studded with boats. The study's walls display photo-graphs of the author – and one of Nelly Ternan – as well as prints of some of his fictional creations. Personal mementos include a pen-knife and a garden chair brought here from Gad's Hill Place. On the wall outside is a plaque, record-ing Dickens's connection. The relief portrait of him depicts the older bearded Dickens – an odd touch for it was only after he was a regular visitor to Broadstairs that he grew the beard.

Another transfer of a building from one place to an alterna-tive fictional location was Dickens's use of Betsey Trotwood's home. In *David Copperfield* her house is on a cliff near Dover. Much of that novel was written in Broadstairs. Over the years – especially when he had stayed at the Albion Hotel, he had got to know a forceful lady, Mary Pearson Strong, who lived in a house in Nuckle's Place, south of the hotel. Her house is now the Dickens Museum. In the 1840s her property extended to the cliff edge. Today Victoria Parade separates the garden of the cottage from the cliff. She was the model for Betsey Trotwood, both in her robust and kindly nature, and in her ferocity towards people who brought donkeys near the house. (**"Janet ... Donkeys!"**) Dickens's son, Charley, remembered her as a charming old lady who often fed him tea and cakes. The house was the model for Betsey's cottage which was transferred to the cliffs above Dover: **a very neat**

little cottage with cheerful bow windows; in front of it, a small square gravelled court or garden, full of flowers carefully tended, and smelling deliciously.

Her parlour, the first room on the right as you enter, was described as Betsey's parlour. The house became known as Dickens's House at the end of the nineteenth century and became a museum in the early 1970s. There are letters of Dickens's on display, as well as furniture that belonged to him. Framed collections of cigarette cards – of places associated with Dickens and of the characters in his novels – are reminders of a cultural world of 50 or 60 years ago when smoking promoted popular education. Posters, older pictures of the town, and some of the old serial numbers of the novels fill the museum, managed with enthusiasm and encyclopaedic expertise by Eddie and Lee Ault.

Dickens did not always bring his wife to Broadstairs. In 1850, Catherine Dickens gave birth in London to their third daughter, Dora, named after David Copperfield's first wife – who had herself been based on Dickens's first love, Maria Beadnell. Dickens was in London for the birth but came back to Broadstairs alone by an afternoon train. He explained to his wife, **I still have Dora to kill – I mean the Copperfield Dora**. Not a very gallant remark to his wife who suffered discomfort from her ten pregnancies. It appeared utterly callous in the light of the fact that this daughter Dora died two years later. Was this the beginning of the end for Dickens's marriage? He seemed to resent the fact that his wife was so frequently pregnant – as if he had had nothing to do with it. He had wanted her to have little girls – replacements for her sister, upon whom Charles Dickens had doted until she died in his arms at the age of 17. But his wife produced seven sons, and only two daughters who survived infancy.

At one point when he was writing *David Copperfield*, Dickens ran out of paper. There was a stationery shop in the High Street near the junction with Albion Road. It also sold magazines, and he went to buy some more paper. A lady was ahead of him and asking for the latest serial number of *David Copperfield*. She was handed a number.

I've already got that, she said. *I want the next number.*

That won't be out until the end of the month, she was told.

Listening to this, unrecognised, Dickens recalled, knowing the purpose for which I was there, and remembering that not one word of the number she was asking for was yet written, for the first and only time in my life, I felt – frightened.

1851 was the last year he spent time in Broadstairs. That year he wrote an affectionate account of the place in *Household Words* – "Our Watering Place". It was a valedictory essay, for he only came back once after that – in 1859, prior to a reading tour.

Although Broadstairs became identified with Dickens, it was only in the twentieth century that Dickens tourism took off. The 1892 *Murray's Guide to Kent* makes no reference to Dickens's sojourns in the town. But today we have several plaques as well as a Barnaby Rudge pub, a Trotwood Place, a Nickleby Take Away Café (Thai cuisine) and Bumble's Antiques, as well as the Dickens Museum and Bleak House.

Broadstairs has retained the character of the smallest and most elegant of the three major Thanet towns. When the nouveau riche Tuggs family in *Sketches by Boz* are wondering where to spend a season, Gravesend, as we have seen, is rejected as **low**. Margate was worse – **nobody there but tradespeople.** Broadstairs does not get a mention, but they finally opt for neighbouring Ramsgate, which they find sufficiently genteel.

Margate

Margate has always had a rough reputation. Dickens did visit the town – he went to the theatre there several times in the 1840s. The theatre still functions and has recently been refurbished. But there are hints that he was also familiar with the red light district of the town, for in 1841 he wrote to Daniel Maclise suggesting that he might like to visit the prostitutes of Margate – **I know where they live**, he told the artist archly. Dickens was always interested in the people at the margins of society and did heroic social work with Baroness Burdett-Coutts in providing a refuge in Shepherd's Bush for vulnerable and abused women. He was still a happily married man in 1841, but it is likely that he had walked around the seedier parts of the town. After the collapse of his marriage it is possible that he did find outlets for his sexual energies. In the summer of 1859 he wrote to his doctor about a **small malady** arising from his **bachelor state;** this is interpreted as a reference to some venereal disease he had contracted. It is reasonable to infer that Nelly Ternan did not become Dickens's mistress until some years after he first became infatuated with her.

Nelly was a remarkable and resourceful lady. Over the 12 years of her relationship with Dickens she had to be, in the word used in Claire Tomalin's biography of her, *invisible*. After Dickens died she spent time with family in Europe and then returned to England and stayed with her sister in Oxford. There she met a young Oxford graduate in holy orders, George Wharton Robinson, 12 years younger than her. Nelly took 14 years off her age, making her apparently a suitable two years younger than the unsuspecting George. They fell in love and married, and Nelly had two children. Husband and children knew there was some family friendship with Dickens but had no idea of her actual past. After all she had, they believed, been only 17 when Dickens had died.

In 1877 the Reverend and Mrs Robinson came to Margate, where he became head of Margate High School. The school occupied a spacious site near the centre of the town and close to the sea; the site is now occupied by a supermarket, though the name College Walk is an echo of the former establishment. Their house was on Hawley Street. Nelly was able to play the part of headmaster's wife and was involved in local amateur dramatics. One of the roles she took was that of Mrs

Jarley, the owner of the waxworks in *The Old Curiosity Shop*.

She may have kept her liaison with Dickens from her immediate family, but she did find a confidant in the vicar of St John's Church, Margate, the Reverend (later Canon) William Benham. He later disclosed her story to Thomas Wright who, in 1935, after Nelly, the Canon and all Charles Dickens's children were dead, made it public in a biography of Dickens. Since then more and more details of the extraordinary story of Dickens's relations with Nelly have seeped out.

Deal

Deal, equidistant between Ramsgate and Dover, has over the years been a garrison and naval town. Its castle was part of the nation's defences built by King Henry VIII. It was also home to a station of the Life Boat service, of which Dickens was a great admirer. **These are among the bravest and most skilful mariners that exist. Let a gale rise and swell into a storm, and let a sea run that might appall the stoutest heart that ever beat; let the light ships on the sands throw up a rocket in the darkness of the night; or let them hear through the angry roar the signal guns of a ship in distress, and these men spring up with activity so dauntless, so valiant and heroic, that the world cannot surpass it.**

Esther Summerson in *Bleak House* came to Deal where the feckless Richard Carstone was stationed. She **came into the narrow streets of Deal and very gloomy they were, upon a raw misty morning. The long flat beach with its little irregular houses, wooden and brick, and its litter of capstans, and great boats and sheds, and bare upright poles with tackle and blocks, and loose gravely waste places overgrown with grass and weeds, were as dull an appearance as any place I ever saw ... But when we got into a warm room in an excellent hotel ... Deal began to look more cheerful.**

Dickens walked to Deal from Dover in 1858, a visit that became an essay published the following year in *Household*

Words: **A walk of ten miles brought me to a seaside town without a cliff, which, like the town I had come from, was out of the season too. Half of the houses were shut up; half of the other half were to let; the town might have done as much business as it was doing then, if it had been at the bottom of the sea.** Dickens was only a little more positive about the place than William Cobbett, who came here in 1823 and found it *a most villainous place. It is full of filthy-looking people.*

Today Deal is a quiet town, easily overshadowed by its larger neighbours, but still with its pier, museums and castle.

Dover

After noise chased Dickens away from Broadstairs, he tried Dover, a town that had several functions. It was a fishing town, one of the main ports for travel to the European continent – the English Channel is at its narrowest here – and, in parallel with many other seaside towns in the south-east, a smart and fashionable resort. It has also been a major base for the defence of England – with a castle, fortifications and a military history that goes back two millennia.

Today the social geography of the town reflects these functions. Townwall Street brings traffic rushing to join the embarkation queues, slicing the smarter early-nineteenth century town from the older town nestling under the cliffs.

Dover had already appeared in *David Copperfield*. Betsey Trotwood lived at Dover, and, having walked from London, the weary David sat down, **on the step of an empty shop at a street corner, near the market place**. A coffee house, Dickens Corner, marks the place where David collapsed before a kindly driver told him where his aunt lived. A plaque records the fictional event. Betsey Trotwood's cottage was on the cliffs, but the house he described was the house in Broadstairs.

The little narrow, crooked town of Dover hid itself away

from the beach, and ran its head into the chalk cliffs, like a marine ostrich. The beach was a desert of heaps of sea and stones tumbling wildly about, and the sea did what it liked, and what it liked was destruction. It thundered at the town, and thundered at the cliffs, and brought the coast down, madly. The air among the houses was of so strong a piscatory flavour that one might have supposed sick fish went up to be dipped in it, as sick people went down to be dipped in the sea. A little fishing was done in the port, and a quantity of strolling about at night, and looking seaward ... Small tradesmen, who did no business whatever, sometimes unaccountably realised large fortunes, and it was remarkable that nobody in the neighbourhood could endure a lamplighter.

Dickens brought his family here in 1852. **It is not quite a place to my taste, being too bandy (I mean musical; no reference to its legs), and infinitely too genteel. But the sea is very fine, and the walks are quite remarkable.** They stayed at 10 Camden Crescent for three months, during which Dickens wrote parts of *Bleak House*. Number 10 has disappeared but outside number 17 a plaque records Dickens's one-time residence nearby.

To the west is Harbour House. This used to be the grand hotel of the town, the Lord Warden, built in the early 1850s. Dickens was an early guest, staying there in 1855 and again in 1861. On the former occasion he visited the theatre in Snargate Street, built at the end of the eighteenth century and long since destroyed. It was **a miserable spectacle – the pit is boarded over, and it is a drinking and smoking place.** On the latter visit he gave some readings, and thought that the audience had **the greatest sense of humour.**

Folkestone

... it was a little fishing town, and they do say that the time was when it was a little smuggling town ... The old little fishing and smuggling town remains ... **There are break-neck flights of ragged steps, connecting the principal streets by backways, which will cripple the visitor in half an hour ... Our situation is delightful, our air delicious, and our breezy hills and downs, carpeted with wild thyme, and decorated with millions of wild flowers, are, in the faith of the pedestrian, perfect.**

In March 2013 *The Times* wrote that Folkestone was the fifth coolest place in Britain. For a generation it was yet another declining seaside resort but the former owner of Saga, Roger de Haan, has invested money with the expectation of a regeneration. It has a promising future.

Dickens made several visits to the town. It was quieter than Dover, and he came here in 1855, when he was seeking somewhere to replace Broadstairs. He stayed with his family at 3 Albion Villas – **a very pleasant little house, overlooking the sea** – just before the publication of *Little Dorrit*. Today the house has a plaque and still looks down on the cliffs and beach. The great hotel of the town was the Royal Pavilion Hotel, built in 1843. It has been replaced by the Grand Burstin Hotel, which could be anywhere in the world. Dickens stayed at its predecessor and wrote about Folkestone in an article, "Out of Town", written in 1855 for *Household Words*. In the piece Folkestone is Pavilionstone, named after the hotel. The hotel was built about 100 yards from the railway terminus, Folkestone Harbour Station. The new hotel was a great improvement on existing conditions for travellers; previously they were accommodated in **a strange building which had just left off being a barn without having quite begun to be a house.** The hotel, by contrast, provided every comfort: **you walk into that establishment as if it were your club; and find ready for you, your news-room, dining-room, smoking-room, billiard-room, music-room, public breakfast, public dinner, twice a day (one plain, one gorgeous), hot baths and cold baths. If you want to be bored, there are plenty of bores always ready for you.**

Royal Pavilion Hotel, Folkestone

The Channel Tunnel has taken custom away from Folkestone as a port. Folkestone Harbour Station still exists, just about, neglected and falling into ruin. The line is still there – descending from the town on one of the steepest gradients of any railway line in the country. The new hotel incorporates some of the old Royal Pavilion. Some furniture survives and the kitchens in the basement are original. The hotel is a refuge for older people of Folkestone, with bars, restaurants, gaming saloons and non-stop television in one of the lounges.

Canterbury

The sunny street of Canterbury, dozing, as it were, in the hot light ... its old houses and gateways, and the stately gray cathedral, with the rooks sailing round the towers.

Canterbury features centrally in only one of Dickens's novels – *David Copperfield*. Dickens never lived in or close to it, so the descriptions lack the intimacy of those of the Medway towns or Thanet. He visited and got to know the city well, however, and was fond in his last years of taking friends here. He was not always a fan of medieval architecture but appreciated the picturesque, and historical associations. **The venerable cathedral towers and the old jackdaws and rooks, whose airy voices made them more retired than perfect silence would have done; the battered gateways, once stuck full with statues, long thrown down, and crumbled away, like the reverential pilgrims who had gazed upon them; the still nooks, where the ivied growth of centuries crept over gabled ends and ruined walls; the ancient houses; the pastoral landscape of field, orchard, and garden – everywhere, on everything, I felt the same serener air, the same calm, thoughtful, softening spirit.** Dickens also used to observe the rooks whirling over Rochester cathedral. There they were compared with the monks of the past.

When David Copperfield bade farewell to Canterbury he **sauntered through the dear and tranquil streets, and again mingled with the shadows of the venerable gateways and churches. The rooks were sailing about the cathedral towers; and the towers themselves, overlooking many a long unaltered mile of the rich country and its pleasant streams, were cutting the bright morning air, as if there were no such thing as change on earth.**

In Dickens's *A Child's History of England*, written just after he had completed *David Copperfield*, there is a sense of place in his account of the murder of Becket in 1170. He wrote how **there was a near way between [Becket's] Palace and the Cathedral, by some beautiful old cloisters which you may yet see.** He described the angular nature of the interior, where **there were so many hiding-places in the crypt below and in the narrow passages above, that Thomas à Becket might even at that pass have saved himself.**

The visitor to the cathedral today has to pay £9.50 for the privilege (£8.50 for concessions and £6.50 for those under eighteen.) Entry to the cathedral at Rochester – and also Durham – is free; visitors are instead invited to make a donation. It is unfortunate that the poor and those on benefits are not encouraged to go inside Canterbury Cathedral. My first visit was by myself when I was 12 years old. In my twenties I was passing through Canterbury and took a few minutes off to drop into the place, went into the Romanesque crypt and by chance heard an organ playing a Bach passacaglia and fugue: an intensely memorable experience. High entry charges deter the curious cash-strapped young from these intense aesthetic encounters. The ticket barrier has been set up at Christchurch Gate, next door to the Starbucks café. Today I do not go into the cathedral; I do however go into Rochester Cathedral and voluntarily pay the amount Canterbury would have charged me.

Much of the traffic has been banished from central Canterbury. This has made it a safe place to wander round. It was not always so. Betsey Trotwood used to come from Dover to the city in her pony and trap. As David Copperfield recorded, **My aunt had a great opportunity of insinuating the gray pony among carts, baskets, vegetables, and hucksters' goods. The hair-breadth turns and twists we made drew down upon us a variety of speeches from the people standing about, which were not always complimentary; but my aunt drove on with perfect indifference, and I dare say would have taken her own way with as much coolness through an enemy's country.**

Betsey Trotwood came to Canterbury to see David, whom she had placed in Dr Strong's school. This is possibly based on King's School, which was a **grave building in a courtyard, with a learned air about it that seemed well suited to the stray rooks and jackdaws who came down from the cathedral towers to walk with a clerkly bearing on the grass plot.** The main part of King's School is to the east of the city walls. Between here and the city walls is Lady Wootton's Green. Here, at number 1, was the home of the fictional school's lexicographer headmaster, Dr Strong. In the secluded garden **peaches were ripening on the sunny south wall**. The house is now used as offices of Christ Church University.

Betsey Trotwood's lawyer, Mr Wickfield, lived to the west

of the city walls, beyond West Gate, at 71 St Dunstan's Street. It was **a very old house bulging out over the road; a house with long low lattice-windows bulging out still further, and beams with carved heads on the ends bulging out too, so that I fancied the whole house was leaning forward, trying to see who was passing on the narrow pavement below. It was quite spotless in its cleanliness. The old-fashioned brass knocker on the low arched door, ornamented with carved garlands of fruit and flowers, twinkled like a star; the two stone steps descending to the door were as white as if they had been covered with fair linen; and all the angles and corners, and carvings and mouldings, and quaint little panes of glass, and quainter little windows, though as old as the hills, were as pure as any snow that ever fell upon the hills.** The house still fits Dickens's description and is called The House of Agnes, currently functioning as a hotel and restaurant. It is a seventeenth-century building but its history goes back to medieval times, having been a pilgrims' inn.

Not far away is North Lane, round the corner 100 yards or so, where Uriah Heep lived with his mother, and where David Copperfield came on a visit. The alleged house has been demolished.

On another occasion Uriah was wandering on the eastern side of the city, on the Ramsgate road, when he overtook David, and made an appealing and eloquent explanation of his creepy, oleaginous character ... **"how little you think of the rightful umbleness of a person in my station, Master Copperfield! Father and me was both brought up at a foundation school for boys; and mother, she was likewise brought up at a public, sort of charitable, establishment. They taught us all a deal of umbleness – not much else that I know of, from morning to night. We was to be umble to this person, and umble to that, and to pull off our caps here, and to make bows there, and always to know our place, and abase ourselves before our betters. And we had such a lot of betters! ... 'Be umble, Uriah,' says father to me, 'and you'll get on.'"**

Wilkins Micawber, who, with uncharacteristic assiduity, worked to unmask Heep as a scheming villain, stayed at the Sun Hotel in Sun Street, described as a **little inn**. The Micawbers economised and **occupied a little room ... partitioned off from the commercial room, and strongly flavoured with tobacco smoke. I think it was over the kitchen, because a warm, greasy smell appeared to come up through the chinks in the floor, and there was a flabby perspiration on the walls. I know it was near the bar, on account of the smell of spirits and jingling of glasses**. The hotel survives and flourishes as a hotel and restaurant, though it does not quote the description of the Micawbers' room in its promotional literature. It has been completely refurbished in the last few years, and offers four-poster beds, but no parking facilities. Mr Micawber had dreams of his son becoming a chorister at Canterbury Cathedral, but his son's career took him no further than singing comic songs in public houses.

Dickens came to Canterbury in 1861 to give a reading. He stayed at the Fountain Inn. This used to be one of the great historic hotels of the city, claiming a history going back to the eleventh century, but it was destroyed by enemy action during the Second World War.

On Dickens's final visit in 1869 he brought friends to the city. They entered the cathedral, where a service was just starting. It seemed to be conducted in a casual manner. *The seeming indifference of the officiating clergy*, recalled one of the party, *jarred most acutely on Dickens's feelings, for he, who did all things so thoroughly, could not conceive how (as he afterwards said) any persons accepting an office, or a trust so important as the proper rendering of our beautiful Cathedral Service, could go through their duties in this mechanical and slip-shod fashion.* Perhaps Dickens was in a testy mood, for a little later he became impatient with a *tedious verger* who was showing the party around, shook him off and conducted his guests himself around the place *in the most genial and learned style in the world.*

Staplehurst

N O IMAGINATION CAN CONCEIVE the ruin of the carriages, or the extraordinary weights under which the people were lying, or the complications into which they were twisted up among iron and wood, and mud and water.

By the middle of the 1860s, when he was not on tour giving his readings, Dickens was spending much of his time in France. He set up retreats for Nelly Ternan and himself, probably in Boulogne, Paris and Normandy – Dickens covered his tracks well and much is still conjecture.

On Friday morning, 9 June 1865, he travelled from France back to London. He boarded the ferry from Boulogne. An unsympathetic observer, the wife of an American press owner, spotted him *travelling with not his wife, nor his sister-in-law, yet he strutted about the deck with the air of a man bristling with self-importance, every line of his face and every gesture of his limbs seemed haughtily to say, "Look at me; make the most of your chance. I am the great, the* only *Charles Dickens; whatever I may choose to do is justified by that fact".*

He was actually travelling with Nelly Ternan and her mother. They caught the boat train, operated by the South Eastern Railway Company, heading for London, which left Folkestone at 14:38. It reached Headcorn at 15:11. The train times then varied according to the tide. (There is still a train that leaves Folkestone West at 14:38, but it takes five minutes longer to take get to Headcorn.)

Dickens, Nelly and Mrs Ternan were in a first-class

compartment, in the first of seven first-class coaches. They were immediately behind the engine and tender and one second-class coach. Behind the first-class coaches were two more second-class coaches and three luggage vans. The train was not crowded; there were 115 passengers altogether, 80 in first-class, 35 in second.

Between Headcorn and Staplehurst the line goes over the River Beult twice. There was – and is – a small viaduct over the river at the second crossing. In the early summer of 1865 some wooden baulks of the viaduct were being replaced. This required the temporary removal of the railway lines. The work was carried out in the periods when there was no train expected, the rails being put back in position for the passage of trains. The work was mostly completed, but on this Friday a gang was still at work. The gang foreman, Henry Benge, somehow thought it was Saturday, and was not expecting a train for another two hours. Nor did he have on him a watch. It was the job of a flagman to be 1000 yards from any obstruction, in the event of any train unexpectedly approaching. On this day he was only 500 yards from the work on the viaduct. The track here was a long and straight stretch, and as the train was not due not to stop until it reached Redhill, it was travelling at a full speed of between 40 and 50 miles an hour. The flagman saw the train and desperately flagged it down. The brakes were applied and the train was able to slow down to about 30 miles an hour. Five of the coaches also had brakes and these were applied. But a train travelling at 45 miles an hour would travel the 500 yards between where the first signal was received and the viaduct in 20 seconds. At 30 miles an hour it would take 30 seconds. There was not enough time or distance for the train to come to a complete stop before the viaduct.

The momentum of the moving train carried the engine over the first part of the viaduct before it ground to a halt. The tender and the front two carriages, one second-class and the first-class one carrying Dickens and the Ternans, came

The Staplehurst Railway Accident

to a stop at a giddy angle over the river. The next first-class carriage broke away and tumbled the ten feet onto the dry bed of the river, bottom up, bringing down the following carriages, which fell into mud and water, either on their sides or on top of each other. The last carriages, including the guard's van, remained coupled together on the Headcorn side of the viaduct.

Confusion and terror. Dickens and the Ternans were in a locked compartment. At the moment of the disaster, they were all thrown together as the compartment tilted alarmingly. *Let us join hands and die together*, Nelly is reported to have said. The train came to a halt. Dickens clambered out of the window and hailed two guards. With their help Dickens extricated the ladies from the compartment and got them away from the train. Nelly was slightly injured. In the panic to get out of the compartment she left her jewellery behind. The railway officials were able to look after Nelly and her mother. Meanwhile, Dickens climbed back into the compartment and brought out his brandy-flask and top hat. He was able to fill his top hat with water – where from? Was there a tap at the bridge? Or on the train? Or did he scoop up water from the stream? **I was in the terrific Staplehurst accident yesterday,** he wrote the next day to John Forster, **and worked for hours among the dying and dead. I was in the carriage that did not go over, but went off the line, and hung over the bridge in an inexplicable manner. No words can describe the scene**, he added, describing the scene.

Ten people were killed in the accident and many were seriously injured. Dickens and the Ternans were lucky to be relatively unscathed physically. For two hours Dickens moved among the dead and wounded providing succour. He helped to get one man out of **a most extraordinary heap of dark ruins in which he was jammed upside down**. Having helped a number, he clambered back into his still swaying compartment to retrieve the latest manuscript instalment of *Our Mutual Friend*. The instalment included the tale of Mr and Mrs Lammle, a couple, each of whom was penniless and married the other believing they were marrying money.

Railway officials and medical assistance were soon on the scene. Many people were reluctant to disclose their names, anxious not to spread alarm among friends and family. A relief train came and took passengers on to London.

Dickens returned to London and stayed for two nights at his bachelor flat in Wellington Street, before returning to the tranquillity of Gad's Hill Place. He was met at Higham Station by his son, Charley, who drove him up to Gad's Hill in the pony and trap. He was a nervous passenger, anxious even at the speed of the pony, **Go slower, Charley**, he constantly exhorted, until they were travelling at less than walking pace. He stayed at Gad's Hill Place for three months recovering, during which time he wrote to the station master at Charing Cross asking after the golden trinkets that Nelly had left behind in the compartment. One had *Ellen* engraved on it. Dickens had been badly shaken. **I cannot bear railway travelling yet. A perfect conviction, against the senses, that the carriage is down on one side (and generally that is the** left, and *not* the side on which the carriage in the accident really went over), comes upon me with anything like speed, and is inexpressibly distressing.

Dickens was most anxious to avoid the Ternans' names being disclosed. An official enquiry was held; Dickens declined to give evidence. An inquest on the ten dead passengers was held at the Railway Tavern, Staplehurst, and concluded that there was culpable negligence on the part of the gang leader, Henry Benge, and also a supervisor, Joseph Gallimore, who had, in recent months, carried out insufficient checks. They were both committed for trial. Gallimore was acquitted and Benge sentenced to nine months' hard labour. The death certificates recorded the cause of death as *feloniously killed by Joseph Gallimore and Henry Benge.*

The accident had a profound effect on Dickens for the rest of his life. Only his closest friends knew that he had been with Nelly. He had not only had a narrow escape from death, but also from scandal. He was able to travel by train, but not in express trains, which slowed down his travel as he resumed his reading tours. He was for evermore a nervous passenger. **My reading secretary and companion knows so well when one of these odd momentary seizures comes upon me in a railway carriage, that he instantly produces a dram of brandy, which rallies the blood to the heart and generally prevails.**

The accident occurred on a Friday, always seen by Dickens as an auspicious day – it had been the day of his birth. But the date would come to take on even greater significance, as 9 June was the day of his death, five years later.

There is not much to be seen today that can remind us of the accident. The bridge over the river – hardly a viaduct, as some reports said – is away from the road or any public footpath. Trains rush over the bridge four times an hour during the daytime. The most economic and effective way of seeing the site is to take a day return ticket between Headcorn and Staplehurst. The Railway Tavern is a very friendly pub, not far from Staplehurst station. Some of the regulars know about the accident, but not about the location of the inquest. Perhaps a plaque or two are due.

Afterword

D ICKENS TRAVELLED EXTENSIVELY in his lifetime. He also loved reading books about travel. It was exceptional for an Englishman in his position to make *two* trips to America, as he did. In his later years he seriously contemplated a reading tour of Australia. He was familiar with France, especially Normandy and Paris, spent lengthy periods resident in Lausanne and Genoa, and travelled through much of Switzerland and Italy. He wandered around the British Isles, first as a journalist, later as a tourist and in his last decade as a public reader of his own works. Suffolk in *David Copperfield* and *The Pickwick Papers* and Yorkshire in *Nicholas Nickleby* are portrayed vividly, but there is not the geographical detail and sense of place that London and Kent have in his work; here Dickens was most at home. But these two places, as we have seen, had contrasting resonances for him as an individual and as a novelist. These contrasts were intensified after the collapse of his marriage in 1857/58.

There is a huge volume of literature, academic and lay, on Dickens. His novels, his journalism and his letters are a constant source of instruction and enlightenment. They disclose so much about ourselves, about him and about nineteenth-century England. But to get to grips with the genius of the man there is nothing like reading and rereading the novels – and, in my view, tramping the ground on which he trod.

Bibliography

Dickens's works

I have used the Penguin Classics series. There have been several editions, with different editors; I have worked with the latest available. I have also used other editions of other works, such as *A Child's History of England*, *The Christmas Stories*, *Master Humphrey's Clock*, *Reprinted Pieces* and *The Uncommercial Traveller*. The Penguin Classics editions are as follows, in chronological order of composition, with the original date of publication in brackets after the title, followed by the name of the editor of that volume in the series.

Sketches by Boz (1839), Dennis Walder, 1995
The Pickwick Papers (1836–37), Mark Wormald, 2000
Oliver Twist (1837–38), Philip Horne, 2003
Nicholas Nickleby (1839), Mark Ford, 1999
The Old Curiosity Shop (1841), Norman Page, 2001
Barnaby Rudge (1841), John Bowen, 2003
A Christmas Carol and Other Christmas Writings (1835–54), Michael Slater, 2003
Martin Chuzzlewit (1843–44), Patricia Ingham, 1999
Dombey and Son (1848), Andrew Sanders, 2002
David Copperfield (1850), Jeremy Tambling, 2004
Bleak House (1853), Nicola Bradbury, 2003
Hard Times (1854), Kate Flint, 2003
Little Dorrit (1857), Stephen Wall, 1998, and Helen Small, 2003

A Tale of Two Cities (1859), Richard Maxwell, 2007
Great Expectations (1860–61), Charlotte Mitchell, 2003
Our Mutual Friend (1865), Adrian Poole, 1997
The Mystery of Edwin Drood (1870), David Paroissien, 2002
Selected Journalism 1850–1870, David Pascoe, 2006
Selected Short Fiction, Deborah A Thomas, 1976

I have also consulted the Pilgrim Edition of the *Letters of Charles Dickens*, edited by Madeline House, Graham Storey and Kathleen Tillotson, 12 volumes, Oxford University Press, 1965–2002, and the Dickens Fellowship's Journal, *The Dickensian* (1905–).

Other works

Ackroyd, Peter, *Dickens*, Sinclair-Stevenson, London, 1990
Ackroyd, Peter, *Thames, Sacred River*, Chatto and Windus, London, 2007
Ackroyd, Peter, *Wilkie Collins*, Chatto and Windus, London, 2012
Addison, William, *In the Steps of Charles Dickens*, Rich and Cowan, London, 1955
Adrian, Arthur A, *Georgina Hogarth and the Dickens Circle*, Oxford University Press, London, 1957
Allbut, Robert, *Rambles in Dickens-Land*, Chapman and Hall, London, nd, c 1902
Allen, Tudor, *Little Italy, The Story of London's Italian Quarter*, Camden Local Studies and Archive Centre, London, 2008
Aslet, Clive, *The Story of Greenwich*, Fourth Estate, London, 1999
Aylmer, Felix, *Dickens Incognito*, Rupert Hart-Davis, London, 1959
Aylmer, Felix, *The Drood Case*, Rupert Hart-Davis, London, 1964

Bacon, George, *Ordnance Atlas of London and Suburbs*, Harry Margary, London, 2003 (first published, 1888)

Barlow, Eleanor Poe, *The Master's Cat, The Story of Charles Dickens as Told by his Cat*, The Dickens House, London, 1998

Boast, Mary, *The Story of Bermondsey,* The London Borough of Southwark, London, 2004 (first published, 1978)

Bradley, Simon, and Nikolaus Pevsner, *The Buildings of England: London 6: Westminster*, Yale University Press, New Haven and London, 2005 (first published, 1998)

Burke, Thomas, *Travel in England*, BT Batsford, London, 1942

Carey, John, *The Violent Effigy, a Study of Dickens' Imagination*, Faber and Faber, London, 1973

Cawthorne, Bob, *The Isle of Thanet Compendium*, Scribble and Doodle Books, Broadstairs, 2007

Cherry, Bridget, and Nikolaus Pevsner, *The Buildings of England: London 4: North*, London, 1999 (first published, 1998)

Chesterton, GK, *Charles Dickens*, Methuen, London, 1928 (first published 1906)

Clark, Peter (ed), *The Lefties' Guide to Britain*, Politico's, London, 2005

Collins, Philip (ed), *Dickens, Interviews and Recollections* (2 vols), Macmillan, London, 1981

Cowper, Francis, *A Prospect of Gray's Inn* (second edition), Grays, London, 1985 (first published, 1951)

Daniell, Timothy, *Inns of Court*, Wildy and Sons, London, 1985 (first published, 1971)

Davies, James A, *John Forster: A Literary Life*, University Press, Leicester, 1983

Denford, Steven, and F Peter Woodford, *Streets of Camden Town*, Camden History Society, London, 2003

Dexter, Walter, *The Kent of Dickens*, Cecil Palmer, London, 1924

Dickens, Henry, *The Recollections of Sir Henry Dickens, KG*, William Heinemann, London, 1934

Dickens, Mamie, *My Father as I Recall Him*, The Roxburghe Press, Westminster, 1897

Dolby, George, *Charles Dickens as I Knew Him*, T Fisher Unwin, London, 1885

Edmondson, John (ed), *Dickens on France*, Signal Books, Oxford, 2006

Elsna, Hebe, *Unwanted Wife: a Defence of Mrs Charles Dickens*, Jarrolds, London, 1963

Fitzgerald, Percy, *Bozland, Dickens' Places and People*, Downey, London, 1895

Forster, John, *The Life of Charles Dickens* (2 Vols), J M Dent, London and Toronto, 1927 (first published 1872–74)

Gadd, W Laurence, *The Great Expectations Country*, Cecil Palmer, London, 1929

Handbook for Travellers in Kent, 5th edition, John Murray, London, 1892

Hardwick, Michael and Mollie, *The Charles Dickens Encyclopedia*, Futura Publications, London, 1976 (first published, 1973)

Hardwick, Michael and Mollie, *Dickens's England*, J M Dent, London, 1970

Heffernan, Hilary, *Hop Pickers of Kent and Sussex*, The History Press, Stroud, 2008

Herber, Mark, *Legal London, A Pictorial History*, Phillimore, Chichester, 2007 (first published, 1999)

Hibbert, Christopher, *The Making of Charles Dickens*, Book Club Associates, London, 1968 (first published, 1967)

Holdsworth, William S, *Charles Dickens as a Legal Historian*, Yale University Press, New Haven, 1928

House, Humphry, *The Dickens World*, Oxford University Press, London, 1041

Hughes, William R, *A Week's Tramp in Dickens-Land*, Chapman and Hall, London, 1891

Hyde, Ralph and John Rocque, *The A to Z of Georgian London*, London Topographical Society, London, 1982

Jackson, TA, *Charles Dickens: The Progress of a Radical*, Lawrence and Wishart, London, 1937

Jessup, Frank W, *Kent History Illustrated*, Kent County Council, Maidstone, 1966

Johnson, Edgar, *Charles Dickens, His Tragedy and Triumph* (2 vols), Victor Gollancz, London, 1953

Kent, William, *London for Dickens Lovers*, Methuen, London, 1935

Kitton, Frederic G, *Charles Dickens, His Life, Writings and Personality*, The Caxton Publishing Co, np, nd

Kitton, Frederic G, *The Dickens' Country*, Adam and Charles Black, London, 1911 (first published 1905)

Lane, Anthony, *Thames-side Kent Through Time*, Amberley Publishing, Stroud, 2011

Langton, Robert, *The Childhood and Youth of Charles Dickens*, published by the author, Manchester, 1883

Lazarus, Mary, *A Tale of Two Brothers, Charles Dickens's Sons in Australia*, Angus and Robertson, Sydney, 1973

Macaskill, Hilary, *Charles Dickens at Home*, Frances Lincoln, London, 2011

MacDougall, Philip, *Chatham Through Time*, Amberley Publishing, Stroud, 2011

Mace, Rodney, *Trafalgar Square, Emblem of Empire*, Lawrence and Wishart, London, 1976

Mankowitz, Wolf, *Dickens of London*, Macmillan, New York, 1977 (first published, 1976)

Margate Delineated, 10th edition, Margate, 1829

Matz, BW, *Dickensian Inns and Taverns*, Cecil Palmer, London, 1922 (first published, 1921)

Matz, BW, *The Inns and Taverns of 'Pickwick'*, Cecil Palmer, London, nd

Megarry, Robert, *An Introduction to Lincoln's Inn*, The Honourable Society of Lincoln's Inn, London, 2007

Nayder, Lillian, *The Other Dickens. A Life of Catherine Hogarth*, Cornell University Press, 2012

Newman, John, *The Buildings of England: North East and East Kent*, Penguin Books, Harmondsworth, 1976 (first published, 1969)

Newman, John, *The Buildings of England: West Kent and the Weald*, Penguin Books, Harmondsworth, 1969

Newton, Douglas, *London West of the Bars*, Robert Hale, London, 1951

Nicklin, JA and EW Haslehust, *Dickens-Land*, Blackie and Son, London and Glasgow, nd

Nisbet, Ada, *Dickens and Ellen Ternan*, University of California Press, Berkeley and Los Angeles, 1952

Paterson, Michael, *Inside Dickens' London*, David and Charles, Newton Abbot, 2011

Picard, Liza, *Victorian London: The Life of a City 1840–1870*, Phoenix, London, 2005

Prettejohns, Graham, Brenda Mann and Larry Ilott, *Charles Dickens and Southwark*, The London Borough of Southwark. London, 1994 (first published, 1974)

Richardson, Ruth, *Dickens and the Workhouse, Oliver Twist and the London Poor*, Oxford University Press, Oxford, 2012

Rimmer, Alfred, *About England with Dickens*, Chatto and Windus, London, 1883

Sanders, Andrew, *Charles Dickens's London*, Robert Hale, London, 2010

Slater, Michael, *Charles Dickens*, Yale University Press, New Haven and London, 2009

Slater, Michael, *The Great Charles Dickens Scandal,* Yale University Press, New Haven and London, 2012

Smith, Lynda, *The Place to Spend a Happy Day, A History of Rosherville Gardens*, The Gravesend Historical Society, Gravesend, 2006

Solnit, Rebecca, *Wanderlust, A History of Walking.* Viking, New York, 2000

Stone, Richard, *Gray's Inn, A Short History*, The Masters of the Bench, London, 1997

Storey, Gladys, *Dickens and Daughter*, Frederick Muller, London, 1939

Summerson, John, *Georgian London*, Penguin Books, Harmondsworth, 1962 (first published, 1945)

Tomalin, Claire, *Charles Dickens, A Life*, Viking, London, 2011

Tomalin, Claire, *The Invisible Woman, The Story of Nelly Ternan and Charles Dickens*, Penguin Books, 1991 (first published, 1990)

Ward, AW, *Dickens*, Macmillan, London, 1882

Watts, Alan S, *Dickens at Gad's Hill*, Elvendon Press, Goring-on-Thames, 1989

Weinreb, Ben et al, *The London Encyclopaedia*, Macmillan, London, 2010 (first published, 1983)

White, Jerry, *London in the Nineteenth Century*, Vintage Books, London, 2008 (first published, 2007)

Wright, Christopher, *Kent Through the Years*, BT Batsford, London, 1975

Acknowledgements

Eddie Ault; Lee Ault; Patricia Barbor; Peter Barbor; Andrew Bryant; Christoph Bull; Pamela Bunney; Kevin Christie; Pearl Cooper; Jeremy Goad; Phillida Goad; Ayaan Mahamdallie; Hassan Mahamdallie; Nicola Hilton; John Knott; Sean Magee; Jane Martin; Robin Martin; Steve Martin; Judith Newberry; John Peverley; Ian Porter; John Rushworth; Zoë Rutherford; Eve Smith; Les Stather; Charlotte Taylor; Andrew Thompson; Ionis Thompson; Kat Whone; and Fernando at the George and Vulture Inn, London.

Above all I wish to thank Theresa, who gave constructive comment on the text and accompanied me on several tours of Dickens sites in London and Kent.

The author and the publisher wish to thank the following sources for kind permission to reproduce the illustrative material: Graham Salter/Lebrecht Music & Arts p20, p42, p60, p84, p98, p160, p194; Lebrecht Authors p220; Mary Evans Picture Library p229; Illustrated London News p236.

Index